SHEFFIELD UNIVERSITY ENGLISH LANGUAGE

Dear Student

Welcome to the University of Sheffield English Language Teaching Centre (ELTC).

We hope that you find your time with us both instructive and enjoyable.

Our teachers have experience of working with international students in a wide range of locations and situations, both in the UK and overseas. Our teachers and office staff are all here to support you in your studies – please don't be afraid to ask questions if you don't understand anything or you need some help.

At the University of Sheffield you will have the chance to meet students from the UK and all over the world. We hope you will make many friends and will be able to learn about different cultures. Visit our award-winning Students' Union and join some of the fantastic activities they organise.

Most of all we hope that you improve your English during your study with us before you progress onto your academic course or return to your own country.

Richard Simpson

Director, ELTC

ENGLISH LANGUAGE LEARNING OPPORTUNITIES OUTSIDE CLASS

ELTC SOCIAL ACTIVITIES

We have lots of activities outside the class to learn English and make friends. Our full-time Social Organiser is there to help you make the most of your time. Look out for information on the website, posters and from your teachers.

EDUCATIONAL VISITS

During your course (Sept.-June) there are regular visits to places of interest. Learn about the history and culture of the country. Mix with other students and teachers to practise English and learn new vocabulary.

If you want to try something new, make some friends, learn new skills or visit different places, then 'give it a go' is a pretty good place to start. There are regular weekend coach trips to interesting cities too.

http://su.sheffield.ac.uk/get-involved/give-it-a-go

If you want to find out about the 250 societies and committees on offer, you can simply chat to the staff at the Activities Information Desk or check them all out online.

http://su.sheffield.ac.uk/get-involved

Volunteer – for just a few hours, a day or regularly - the best way to discover Sheffield, try something new, develop your skills & have loads of fun. All of our projects are designed with students in mind. With a range of over 200 projects, there are loads for you to choose from so get active and get involved today.

http://su.sheffield.ac.uk/sheffield-volunteering

With 51 sports clubs for you to choose from, Club Sport provides many opportunities for you to enjoy your favourite sports and meet new people. There is also a gym you can join with a swimming pool.

http://www.sport-sheffield.com/

LANGUAGES SHEFFIELD

Languages Sheffield runs a regular Language Exchange evening throughout the academic year. The event is designed for people who wish to share, learn and practise a language with others.

http://www.languages-sheffield.org.uk/about-us/news-events/language-exchange

NEW
Language LEADER
ELEMENTARY
COURSEBOOK

IAN LEBEAU | GARETH REES

CONTENTS

Unit	Grammar	Vocabulary	Reading
1 Cities (p6–13)	*To be* (1.1) *There is / there are* (+ *any*) (1.2)	Cities (1.1) Adjectives (1) (1.1) Places in a city (1.2) More places in a city (1.3) Adjectives (1.4) Linkers: *and* (1.4)	10 facts about my city (1.1) Understanding main points *Famous cities* (1.2) *City focus: Cambridge* (1.3) *City fact file: Toronto* (1.4)
2 Work and study (p14–21)	Present simple (2.1) Present simple questions (2.2)	Jobs and places of work (2.1) At university (2.2) At work (2.3)	People at work (2.1) Identifying speakers University website (2.2) Identifying an audience Job advert (2.4) CV (2.4)
3 Nature (p22–29)	Question words (3.1) Adverbs of frequency (3.2) Pronouns: *it* and *they* (3.4)	Verbs connected with water (3.1) Adjectives (2) (3.2) Classroom objects (3.4) Linkers (3.4)	*What do you know about water?* (3.1) Job advert and two job profiles (3.2) Information on three charities (3.3)
4 Leisure time (p30–37)	Articles (4.1) *Can, can't* (4.2)	Using visual clues Types of film (4.1) Leisure activities, sports (4.2) Holiday resorts (4.3) Large numbers (4.4) Fractions and percentages (4.4) Approximation (4.4)	*World Cinema* website (4.1) Scanning for information Health club leaflet (4.2) Using topic knowledge Charts showing statistics of participation in sports (4.4)
5 Transport (p38–45)	Comparative adjectives (5.1) Superlative adjectives (5.2)	Transport (5.1) Travel (5.2) Linkers: *but* (5.4)	Speed of transport (5.1) *Big, bigger, best: urban transport around the world* (5.2)
6 Food (p46–65)	Countable and uncountable nouns *Some* and *any* (6.1) *Much, many, a lot of* (6.2)	Food and drink (6.1)	*Super food: do you eat it?* (6.1) Understanding reference (6.1) *My great food adventure* (6.2)

Listening	Speaking / Pronunciation	Scenario	Study Skills / Writing	Video
Understanding context Conversation between a teacher and a student (1.1) TV programme: *I love my city* (1.2) Describing the centre of Cambridge (1.3)	Describe cities (1.1) Find out about different cities (1.2) Contractions (1.2) Schwa (1.3)	Key language: saying where places are Task: using a map Scenario: describing where places are in a town	Write about your city or town (1.2) Study skills: using your dictionary (1) Writing skills: a city description	Meet the expert: an interview with Adam Gadsby, an international publisher, about interesting cities (1.2)
Interview with a student about her life and habits (2.2) Information about a job (2.3)	Talk about yourself and your studies/job (2.1) Interview other students about their lives (2.2) Word stress (2.3)	Key language: asking for information (1) Task: describing jobs Scenario: finding out about different jobs	Write about students in a survey (2.2) Capital letters (2.4) Study skills: using your dictionary (2) Writing skills: a CV	Meet the expert: an interview with Chris Holt, a pilot, about his working and home lives (2.1)
Predicting TV interview about deserts (3.1) Discussion about organising a weekend of fund-raising events (3.3)	Find out facts about water (3.1) Ask about routines and habits (3.2) Showing interest (3.3) Classroom instructions (3.4) Asking about words (3.4)	Key language: making suggestions Task: making and responding to suggestions Scenario: organising fund-raising events	Write about someone's routines and habits (3.2) Study skills: classroom language Writing skills: a description of a process	Meet the expert: an interview with Dave Stevenson, a wildlife photographer, photographing animals (3.2)
Interviews with two members of a health club (4.2) Asking a travel agent for more information on a resort (4.3)	Discussing preferences (4.1) Interview about ability (4.2) Weak or strong vowel (4.2) Linked sounds (4.3)	Key language: asking for information (2), saying 'no' politely Task: describing places and facilities Scenario: at a travel agent's	Study skills: working with numbers Writing skills: a description of a table or bar chart	Meet the expert: interview with Lynda Myles, a film producer and lecturer, about Martin Scorsese (4.1)
Three people talking about how they get around their cities (5.2) Phone conversation booking a plane ticket (5.3)	Talking about getting around a town/city (5.2) Collaboration (5.1) Vowel sounds (5.1) Stress in compound nouns (5.3)	Key language: buying a ticket Task: booking a flight Scenario: at a ticket agency	Write a paragraph about transport and travelling around your town/city (5.2) Self-evaluation (5.4) Study skills: Planning your written work Writing skills: description (a transport system)	Meet the expert: interview with Chloe Couchman, an expert on London tourism, about getting around a famous city (5.2)
Interview about South African food culture (6.2) Phone order for conference catering (6.3)	Talking about food and drink (6.1) Long turn taking Talking about food culture (6.2) Intonation (6.3)	Key language: requests and offers Task: making an order Scenario: conference catering	Write about your country's food culture (6.2) Making mistakes (6.4) Spelling (6.4) Judging interest (6.4) Commas in lists (6.4) Study skills: correcting your writing Writing skills: a restaurant review	Meet the expert: interview with Nikita Gulham, an Indian food expert, about Indian food traditions (6.2)

CONTENTS

Unit	Grammar	Vocabulary	Reading
7 Shopping (p54–61)	Present continuous (1): affirmatives and negatives (7.1) Present continuous (2): questions (7.2)	Shops and shopping (1): verbs (7.1) Shops and shopping (2): nouns (7.2) Linkers: because and so (7.4)	*What kind of shopper are you?* (7.1) Assigning headings (7.1) *The changing face of stores* (7.2) Using visual clues (7.4)
8 History and culture (p62–69)	Past simple of *to be* (8.1) Could, couldn't (8.2) *it, this, these* (8.4)	Buildings (8.1) Verbs + prepositions (8.2) Past time phrases (8.1) Managing new vocabulary (8.4) Grouping words by meaning (8.4) Using word webs (8.4) Using pictures (8.4) Word building (8.4) Using opposites (8.4)	*Çatal Hüyük* (8.1) *All change!* (8.2) Making deductions (8.2)
9 Inventions (p70–77)	Past simple: regular and irregular verbs (9.1) Past simple: negative and question forms (9.2)	Medical science (9.2) Linkers: *at the same time* and *next* (9.4)	*Leonardo da Vinci: man of art, man of ideas, man of inventions* (9.1) Evaluating (9.1, 9.4) *Medical inventions* (9.2)
10 Money (p78–85)	*Should, shouldn't* (10.1) *Have to, don't have to* (10.2) Problem-solving (10.1)	Money (nouns) (10.1) Money (verb phrases) (10.2) Introducing extra information (10.4) Linkers: *that* (10.4)	Poster advertising a talk about money safety for students (10.1) FAQs on loan company website (10.2) Profile of entrepreneur who took out loan (10.2)
11 Homes (p86–93)	*Will, won't* (11.1) *Be going to* (11.2)	Compound nouns (11.1) Rooms and furniture (11.3) Directions (11.4) Linkers: *when* (11.4)	*Separate lives* (11.1) Exploring the topic (11.1) *A modern home, your dream home* (11.2)
12 Travel (p94–101)	Present perfect (12.1) Present perfect and past simple (12.2)	Using verbs as nouns (gerunds) (12.2) Adjectives (12.4)	Understanding reasons *Children of the wind* (12.1) *Discovering the world* (12.2)

Language reference (p102-125) | Meet the Expert (p126-130) | Communication Activities (p131-147)

Listening	Speaking / Pronunciation	Scenario	Study Skills / Writing	Video
Five short conversations in shopping situations (7.1) Discussion about online shopping (7.2)	Discussion about shopping (7.1) Interview someone about shopping (7.1) Considering trends (7.2) Stressed words (7.3) Choosing images (7.4) Avoiding mistakes (7.4) Making notes (7.4) Preparing a talk (7.4)	Key language: giving advantages and disadvantages Task: describing locations Scenario: opening a shop	Informal language (7.4) Study skills: giving a short, informal talk Writing skills: informal writing (a customer review)	Study skills video: a student presentation about Harrods
Presentation about technology and cultural changes (8.2) Six short conversations with museum visitors (8.3)	Vowel sounds (8.1) Finding out about ancient civilisations (8.1) Comparing current ways of life with previous generations (8.2) Linked sounds (8.3)	Key language: making polite requests Task: finding out important information Scenario: at a museum	Write about an ancient civilisation (8.1) Study skills: remembering new words Writing skills: describing objects	Meet the Expert: an interview with Mark Weeden, a lecturer in Ancient Near Eastern Studies, about ancient civilisation (8.1)
Radio interview about the MRI scanner (9.2) Researching the topic (9.2) Radio programme about favourite inventions (9.3)	Verb endings (9.1) Talking about last weekend (9.1) Talking about first experiences (9.2) Stressed words (9.3)	Key language: giving reasons Task: giving a short presentation Scenario: everyday inventions	Write a short text about a historical figure (9.1) Making notes (9.4) Study skills: making notes while reading Writing skills: a short biography	Meet the Expert: an interview with Odette Aguirre, an acupuncturist, about the benefits of acupuncture (9.2)
Talk about money safety for students (10.1) Bank survey about money (10.3	Giving advice (10.1) Evaluating: different business ideas (10.2) Stressed words (10.3)	Key language: asking for and giving opinions Task: doing an opinion survey Scenario: survey about money	Write a reply to a student's problem (10.1) Study skills: making notes during a talk Writing skills: formal writing (an online form)	Study skills video: a talk about bank accounts
Discussion about features of a smarthome (11.2) Phone call about renting a flat (11.3)	Contractions (11.1) Speculating Talking about your lives in the future (11.1) Describing your home (11.2) Contractions (11.2) Explaining decisions Designing your dream home (11.2) Stressed words (11.3)	Key language: checking understanding Task: asking for information about accommodation Scenario: finding a flat	Study skills: examination skills Writing skills: an informal email	Meet the Expert: an interview with Godson Egbo, an architect, about homes of the future (11.2)
Interview with a student about living abroad (12.1) Talk about a memorable building (12.3)	Asking about experiences (12.1) Talking about holidays abroad (12.2)	Key language: taking long turns Task: recounting experiences Scenario: around the world	Ways of practising English (12.4) Using technology to learn (12.4) Study skills: learning outside the classroom Writing skills: a travel blog	Study skills video: a talk about using technology to learn English

Audioscripts (p148-157) | Irregular Verb List (p158) | Phonetic Charts (p159)

1 Cities

1.1 BIG CITIES: CITY FACTS

IN THIS UNIT

GRAMMAR
- to be
- there is, there are (+ any)

VOCABULARY
- cities
- adjectives (1)
- places in a city

SCENARIO
- saying where places are
- using a map

STUDY SKILLS
- using your dictionary (1)

WRITING SKILLS
- a city description

A

'I'm a city person – I go on holiday and I'm bored.' Danny Boyle, 1956–, British film director

VOCABULARY
CITIES, ADJECTIVES (1)

1 Using existing knowledge Match the cities in the box with the photos (A–D). (There are four extra cities.)

| Istanbul | Jakarta | Lagos | London | Mexico City |
| New York | Shanghai | Tokyo | | |

2 Match the adjectives (1–8) with their opposites (a–h), then choose two or three words for each city in the photos.

1	good	a	hot
2	old	b	dry
3	big	c	quiet
4	cold	d	new
5	wet	e	expensive
6	noisy	f	ugly
7	beautiful	g	bad
8	cheap	h	small

Istanbul – big, …

READING

3a Read the text and choose the correct answer.

Jakarta is
1 big and noisy.
2 small and quiet.
3 cold and expensive.

10 FACTS ABOUT MY CITY

Jakarta, Indonesia

1 It's in the west of Indonesia.
2 It's on the sea.
3 It's a big city.
4 It isn't a quiet city. In fact, it's very noisy.
5 It's the capital of Indonesia.
6 The weather is hot all year. It's wet from October to March.
7 It's famous for food.
8 The restaurants are good.
9 The boats in the old port are big. They're beautiful, too.
10 The buses aren't expensive.

3b Are these sentences about Jakarta true or false?

1 It's in Indonesia.   *true*
2 It's in the west of the country.
3 The weather is dry in December.
4 It isn't the capital of Indonesia.
5 The restaurants are bad.
6 The boats in the old port aren't beautiful.

BIG CITIES: CITY FACTS   1.1

LISTENING

8a 🔊 1.1 **Understanding context** Listen to two conversations and choose the correct endings for these sentences.
1 The conversations are between
   a two students.
   b two teachers.
   c a teacher and a student.
2 The situation is
   a on the phone.
   b in a school/university.
   c in a café.

8b Listen again and complete these phrases.

Mexico City
1 big, noisy, __old__
2 the _____ of Mexico
3 _____ buses

Istanbul
4 big, _____, noisy
5 _____ mosques
6 _____ in winter

SPEAKING

9a Look at Audio script 1.1 on page 148. Practise the conversations with a partner.

9b Work with a partner to make similar conversations between a teacher and a student.

GRAMMAR
TO BE

4 Read the text again. Complete the table.

affirmative (+)	negative (–)	question (?)
I'm (I am)	I'm not (I am not)	am I?
he's (he is)	he isn't (he is not)	is he?
she's (she is)	she isn't (she is not)	is she?
¹ __it's__ (it is)	it ² _____ (it is not)	is it?
you're (you are)	you aren't (you are not)	are you?
we're (we are)	we aren't (we are not)	are we?
³ _____ (they are)	they ⁴ _____ (they are not)	are they?

➜ Language reference and extra practice, pages 102–103

5a Choose the correct word.
1 London *is / are* the capital of the UK.
   It's / He's an old city.
2 Istanbul *aren't / isn't* the capital of Turkey.
3 Beijing and Shanghai *am / are* in China.
4 New York and Tokyo *aren't / isn't* hot in December.

5b Write one or two sentences about your city or town.
My city is noisy.

> **GRAMMAR TIP**
>
> Notice the short answers.
> 'Is London cold?' 'Yes, **it is**.'

6 Look at the questions and choose the best answer.
1 Is your city beautiful?
   Yes, it is. / No, it isn't.
2 Are you a student?
   Yes, I am. / No, I'm not.
3 Are the restaurants in your city bad?
   Yes, they are. / No, they aren't.
4 Is your teacher from the UK?
   Yes, he/she is. / No, he/she isn't.

7 Put the words in the right order to make questions. Then ask and answer the questions with a partner.
1 good in your city / coffee / Is / ?
   Is coffee good in your city?
2 expensive in your city / the buses / Are / ?
3 Is / in Europe / New York / ?
4 a big / Tokyo / city / Is / ?
5 Are / you / in your city / happy / ?
6 famous / Are / in your city / you / ?

1.2 PLACES IN A CITY

VOCABULARY
PLACES IN A CITY

1a Match the words in the box with the corresponding photo(s) on pages 8 and 9. You will not need all the words.

an airport   a beach   a bridge   a canal   a church
a cinema   a concert hall   a fountain   a harbour
a mountain   a museum   a park   a temple

1b Make a list of more buildings and places in a city. Compare your list with a partner's.

READING

2 Understanding main points Read the article about famous cities from an in-flight magazine below. Put these words in the correct gaps.

~~music~~   beaches   films   water

3 Read the article again and choose the best answer (a, b or c).
1 Copacabana is a famous _beach_.
   a park   b cinema   c beach
2 Rio is a good place for _____.
   a films   b music   c museums
3 Mumbai is a _____ city.
   a small   b busy   c quiet
4 Bollywood films are from _____.
   a Los Angeles   b Mumbai   c Venice
5 Venice is a _____ city.
   a big   b noisy   c small
6 Venice isn't a good place for _____.
   a cars   b people   c boats

Famous cities

In all cities there are large buildings, parks, museums and schools, but a lot of cities are famous for other things.

Rio de Janeiro, city of [1] _music_ **and city of** [2] _____
Rio is in the south-east of Brazil. The population is over six million. In Rio, there are mountains and lovely beaches. Copacabana Beach is famous for beach football. There are a lot of bars and concert halls with samba and bossa-nova music. There is a famous carnival every year. Rio is a fun city!

Mumbai, city of [3] _____
Mumbai is in the west of India. It's a big city with over ten million people. It's a busy city with a lot of entertainment. There isn't a carnival, but the city is famous for music and films. In Los Angeles, there's Hollywood; in Mumbai, there's Bollywood. In Mumbai, there are a lot of cinemas – over 200! It's an exciting city.

Venice, city of [4] _____
Venice is in the north-east of Italy. It isn't a big city – the population is under 500,000. In Venice, there aren't any buses or cars. There are 150 canals and a lot of boats. It's a beautiful city.

GRAMMAR
THERE IS, THERE ARE

4a Complete the sentences from the article.
1 In Rio, _there is_ a famous carnival.
2 In Mumbai, _____ a lot of cinemas.
3 In Mumbai, _____ a carnival.
4 In Venice, _____ buses or cars.

4b *There is (There's)/There are* introduces a place or thing. It tells us what is in a city, building, room or place. Look at sentences 3 and 4 in Exercise 4a. When do we use *any* in a negative sentence?

5 Complete the table below with the correct words in the box.

is   is   are   are   any   not   isn't

	singular	plural
+	There's a cinema. (There ¹ _is_ a cinema.)	There ² _____ 200 cinemas.
−	There isn't a theatre. (There is ³ _____ a theatre.)	There aren't ⁴ _____ theatres. (There are not any theatres.)
?	⁵ _____ there a park? Yes, there is. No, there ⁷ _____ .	Are there any canals? Yes, there ⁶ _____ . No, there aren't.

→ Language reference and extra practice, pages 102–103

6 Choose the correct form of *to be*.
1 In London, there *is / are* an opera house.
2 There *is / are* two international airports in New York.
3 In Brighton, there *isn't / aren't* any canals.
4 There *isn't a / isn't any* harbour in Mexico City.
5 *Is / Are* there any temples in Paris?
6 Are there any museums in Nairobi? – Yes, there *are / is*.

GRAMMAR TIP
a lot of = a large number of
In Mumbai, there are *a lot of* cinemas.

1.2 PLACES IN A CITY

SPEAKING
7 Work with a partner to find out about different cities.
Student A: Look at the table on page 131 and ask questions.
Student B: Look at the table on page 132 and ask questions.

LISTENING
8a 1.2 *I Love My City* is a TV programme. Listen to the programme and match the people with the cities.
1 Yukako   a Cape Town
2 Pablo   b Lima
3 Stefan   c Kyoto
4 Peter   d Chicago

8b Listen again. Tick (✓) the correct sentences.
1 Kyoto
   a There are a lot of new buildings.
   b There are a lot of old buildings. ✓
2 Lima
   a There are a lot of cafés.
   b There are a lot of cars and buses.
3 Chicago
   a There are a lot of museums.
   b There are a lot of temples.
4 Cape Town
   a There's a beautiful fountain.
   b There's a beautiful mountain.

PRONUNCIATION
9a 1.3 Contractions Listen and tick (✓) the sentence you hear.
1 a I'm from Chicago. ✓
   b I am from Chicago.
2 a They are very quiet.
   b They're very quiet.
3 a There's a beautiful mountain.
   b There is a beautiful mountain.

9b Listen again and repeat.

WRITING
10 Write about your city or town.
My city is in the north/south-east of . . . The population of my city is . . . My city is famous for . . . In my city, there are . . .

▶ MEET THE EXPERT

Watch an interview with Adam Gadsby, an international publisher, about megacities.
Turn to page 126 for video activities.

1.3 SCENARIO
ON THE STREET

PREPARATION

1 Match the places in the box with the symbols (1–15).

bookshop   building site   bus station   car park
college   gardens   library   market   post office
public toilets   railway station   shopping centre
swimming pool   tourist information centre   zoo

1 *bookshop*   2   3   4   5

6   7   8   9   10

11   12   13   14   15

2 **1.4** Listen to six sounds from a city. Match them with places in Exercise 1.

1 – railway station

3 Complete the text below with the words in the box.

England   famous   gardens   language
population   students

City Focus
Cambridge

Cambridge is a famous university city in the UK. It's in the east of ¹ *England*, 80 kilometres north of London. It's a small city with a ² _____ of 124,000. Cambridge is a beautiful old city, and is very green, with many parks and ³ _____. There are 31 colleges in the University of Cambridge – King's and Trinity are two ⁴ _____ colleges. There are 18,000 ⁵ _____ at the university. There are also a lot of English ⁶ _____ schools in the city.

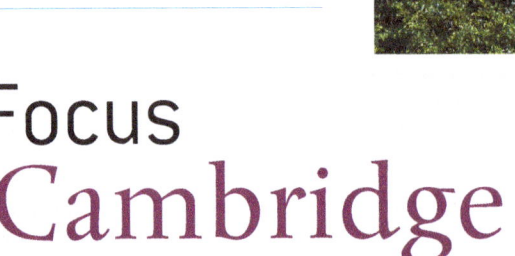
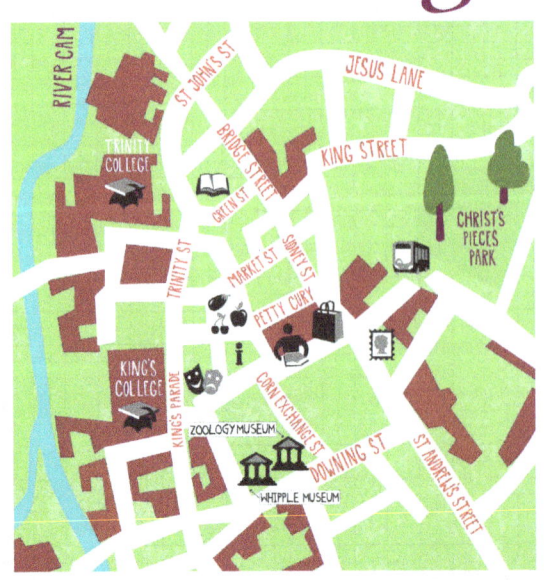

1.3 ON THE STREET

KEY LANGUAGE
SAYING WHERE PLACES ARE

4a 1.5 Look at the map of Cambridge and listen to a talk. Where are the people?
1. at a university
2. at an English language school
3. on a tour bus

4b Listen again and choose the best phrase (a, b or c) to complete the sentences.

1. The bookshop is
   a in Trinity College.
   b opposite Trinity College.
   c next to Trinity College.
2. The market is
   a next to Trinity College.
   b in the shopping centre.
   c between Trinity College and the main post office.
3. The bus station is
   a next to the park.
   b opposite the post office.
   c between the post office and the market.
4. The library is
   a opposite the bus station.
   b in the shopping centre.
   c between King's College and the tourist information centre.

5 Look at the map again and make sentences. Use the table to help you.

The post office		between	Trinity College.
The theatre		next to	the tourist information centre.
The library	is	in	King's College and the tourist information centre.
The market		opposite	the shopping centre.

The library is in the shopping centre.

PRONUNCIATION

6a 1.6 **Schwa** Work with a partner. Listen to these words. How do we say the underlined part? We call this sound the *schwa* /ə/. Practise saying the words.

stati<u>on</u>   opp<u>o</u>site   fam<u>ous</u>   Engl<u>a</u>nd

6b 1.7 Underline the parts of the words below with the schwa. Listen and check, then repeat the words. One word has two schwas.

canal   fountain   library   cinema
quiet   million

TASK
USING A MAP

7 Work with a partner to find places on a map. Use the language from Exercises 4b–5 and the Useful phrases to help.

Student A: Look at the information on page 131.
Student B: Look at the information on page 147.

USEFUL PHRASES
It's on the right/left of the map.
It's on the right/left of the library.
It's at the top/bottom of the map.

1.4 STUDY AND WRITING SKILLS

STUDY SKILLS
USING YOUR DICTIONARY (1)

1 [1.8] **The alphabet** What is the first letter of the English alphabet? What is the last letter? Listen and repeat the alphabet. Look at Audio script 1.8 on page 148.

2 [1.9] Complete groups 1–7 with these letters. Listen and check your answers.

~~C~~ E   J   K   L   N   O   P   T
U   X   Y

1 /eɪ/	A H __ __	
2 /iː/	B _C_ D __ G __ __ V	
3 /e/	F __ M __ S __ Z	
4 /aɪ/	I __	
5 /uː/	Q __ W	
6 /əʊ/	__	
7 /ɑː/	R	

3 Which letters are these? Practise saying the letters. Use the phonetic chart on page 159.

1	/siː/	_C_	5 /kjuː/	__
2	/dʒiː/	__	6 /juː/	__
3	/eɪtʃ/	__	7 /waɪ/	__
4	/dʒeɪ/	__	8 /zed/	__

4a Listen to your teacher spell some words. Write the words.

4b Work with a partner and spell words. Write your partner's words.
Student A: Look at page 132.
Student B: Look at page 131.

5 Number these words in alphabetical order. You have 30 seconds.

yes	☐	is	☐	
famous	☐	café	_1_	
market	☐	music	☐	
chair	☐	harbour	☐	
no	☐	cold	☐	
city	☐	park	☐	
mountain	☐	museum	☐	

6a Work with a partner and do a word race. Find these words in your dictionary. Write the next word from your dictionary. Who is first?

under	grass	map	head	sea
food	radio	thing	English	

6b Compare your words. Are they the same?

7 Listen to your teacher and write down the words you hear. Check your spelling in your dictionary.

8 A dictionary entry Look at the dictionary extracts below. Complete the labels (1–6) with the phrases in the box.

~~part of speech~~   definition   pronunciation   example
opposite meaning   different meanings of the word

P **po.ny** /ˈpəʊni $ ˈpoʊni/ *noun* (plural **ponies**) a small horse

po.ny.tail /ˈpəʊniˌteɪl $ ˈpoʊniˌteɪl/ *noun* long hair tied at the back of your head so that it hangs down: *Kim's hair was pulled back in a ponytail.* → see picture at HAIRSTYLE

pool¹ /puːl/ *noun* **1** a place that has been made for people to swim in SYNONYM swimming pool: *They have a pool in their back garden.* **2** a pool of water, blood, etc. is a small area of it somewhere: *There was **a pool of** oil under the motorbike.* **3** (no plural) a game in which you use a long stick to hit numbered balls into holes at the edge of a table. *You play or shoot pool.*

poor /pʊə $ pʊr/ *adjective* **1** someone who is poor has very little money and does not own many things ANTONYM **rich, wealthy**: *We were so poor we couldn't afford to heat the house properly.* • *He came from a poor background (= from a family that had very little money).* **2** something that is poor is not as good as it should be: *His schoolwork has been poor recently.* **3** (spoken) used to show that you feel sorry for someone: *Poor Ted had no idea what was happening.*

1 _____
2 _____
3 _____
4 _part of speech_
5 _____
6 _____

From the *Longman WordWise Dictionary*

9 Parts of speech The underlined words in sentences 1 and 2 are nouns. The underlined words in sentences 3 and 4 are adjectives.
1 There is a <u>harbour</u> in Sydney.
2 There is a <u>museum</u> in my city.
3 Mumbai is a <u>busy</u> city.
4 My city is <u>big</u>.

Which words below are nouns? Which words are adjectives? Use your dictionary. Write *n* or *adj* next to the words. (Dictionaries often use *n* for nouns and *adj* for adjectives.)

1	international *adj*	7	quiet
2	kilometre	8	shop
3	lovely	9	small
4	noisy	10	station
5	peaceful	11	university
6	port	12	zoo

STUDY AND WRITING SKILLS 1.4

WRITING SKILLS
A CITY DESCRIPTION

10 Look at the Toronto fact file for tourists. Complete sections 1–5 of the fact file with these headings.
- ~~General description~~
- Location
- Tourist attractions
- Size
- Climate

11a Adjectives Adjectives make descriptions interesting. Which of these words are adjectives, and which are nouns? Use your dictionary.

1 beautiful *adj*
2 busy
3 Chinese
4 modern
5 population
6 summer
7 view
8 warm
9 wonderful

11b Match adjectives from above with these descriptions. Use your dictionary to help you.

1 It isn't hot, it isn't cold. It's *warm*.
2 It's new. It's _____.
3 It's full of people, cars and noise. It's _____.
4 It isn't ugly. It's _____.
5 It's very good. It's _____.

12 Linkers We use *and* to join two sentences or ideas. Look at these examples, then join the pairs of sentences (1–6).

Toronto is a modern city. + ~~*Toronto is a busy city.*~~
= *Toronto is a modern and busy city.*

There is a restaurant at the top of the tower. + *There is a theatre* ~~*at the top of the tower*~~.
= *There is a restaurant and a theatre at the top of the tower.*

1 London is a big city. + London is an expensive city.
2 There are museums in the city. + There are theatres in the city.
3 Venice is a small city. + Venice is a beautiful city.
4 There are canals in the city. + There are a lot of churches in the city.
5 Sydney is a large city. + Sydney is a noisy city.
6 There is an opera house. + There is a beautiful harbour.

13 Write a fact file for your city or another city.
- Note information about the city.
- Put the information into sections, e.g. *Location, Climate* …
- Write sentences for each section. Use adjectives. Use *and*.

CITY FACT FILE ▶▶▶

Toronto

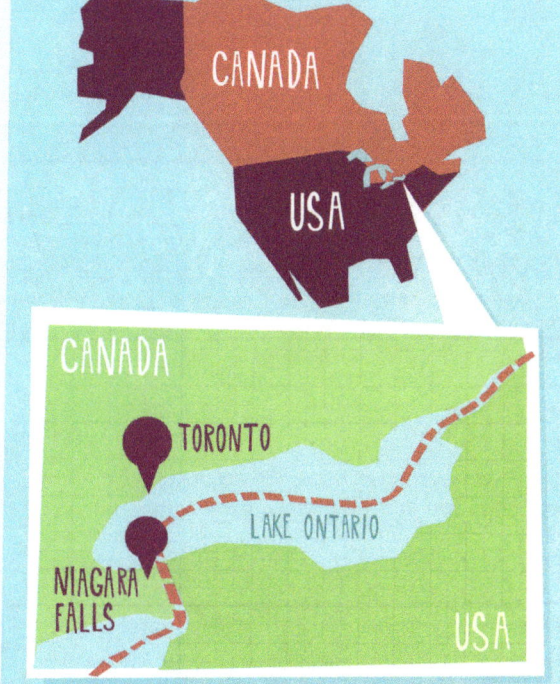

1 _____
Toronto is in the south-east of Canada, in Ontario. It is on Lake Ontario.

2 _____
In the summer, Toronto is warm (25°C) and in the winter, it is very cold (−10°C).

3 _____
Toronto is a big city. The population is 2.6 million.

4 *General description*
Toronto is a modern and busy city. There is a beautiful harbour. There are a lot of museums, theatres and restaurants.

5 _____
Chinatown – There are a lot of restaurants and Chinese shops here.
The CN Tower – There is a restaurant and a theatre at the top of the tower. The views are wonderful.
Niagara Falls – This beautiful tourist attraction is 160km from Toronto.

2 Work and study

2.1 WORKING LIFE

IN THIS UNIT

GRAMMAR
- present simple
- present simple questions

VOCABULARY
- jobs and places of work
- at university
- at work

SCENARIO
- asking for information (1)
- describing jobs

STUDY SKILLS
- using your dictionary (2)

WRITING SKILLS
- a CV

'In work, do what you enjoy.' Lao Tzu, 6th century BC, Chinese philosopher

VOCABULARY
JOBS AND PLACES OF WORK

1a Match the nouns in the box with the photos (A–G).

| an accountant | a businessperson | a doctor | a lawyer |
| a lecturer | a pilot | a web designer |

B – businessperson

1b Where do the people in photos A–G work? Choose from the words in the box.

| in a court | in a hospital | in an office | on a plane |
| in a shop | in a university |

A – in an office

2 Do you know anyone who does these jobs? What jobs do people in your family do?

I'm a businessperson.
My father is a lecturer.

READING

3 Read the article on the right, then correct the mistakes in these sentences.

1. Youna is 28. *Youna is 31.*
2. Youna works for a small clothes shop.
3. She doesn't meet any pilots.
4. Jos and Marco aren't from Amsterdam.
5. They fly to the USA.
6. They don't speak English.

People at work

We ask people around the world about their jobs.

Youna Kim

Youna is a businessperson. She's 31 and she lives in Seoul, in South Korea. She works for a big clothes shop. She says, 'I love my job. I go to a lot of countries and I buy clothes. But I don't wear them. They're for the shop – it sells the clothes.' Youna meets a lot of people in her job, but she doesn't meet any famous fashion designers!

Jos van der Linde and Marco van den Berg

Jos and Marco are pilots. Jos is 38 and Marco is 42. They live in Amsterdam, in Holland. They fly from Amsterdam to airports in Europe – for example, London, Rome and Frankfurt. They don't fly to the USA or to East Asia. Jos says, 'We like our jobs. We speak a lot of English and – in good weather – we see beautiful mountains, lakes and beaches.'

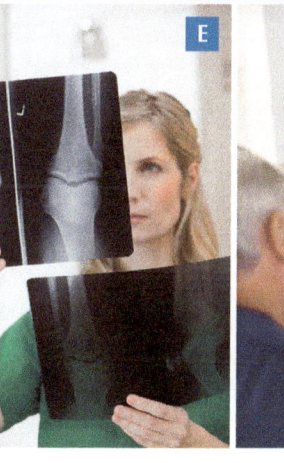
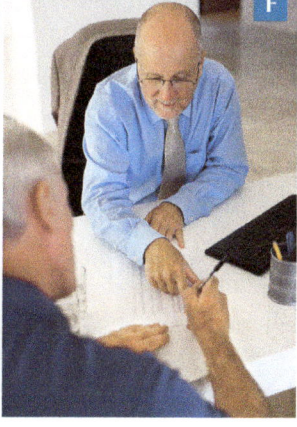

4 Identifying speakers Look at the article again. Who do you think says these things – Youna or Jos?

1 'The clothes aren't for me.' *Youna*
2 'I go to two or three countries in one day.'
3 'I don't live in Europe.'
4 'I see a lot of blue sky.'
5 'In good weather, my job is great.'

GRAMMAR
PRESENT SIMPLE

5 We use the present simple to talk about
a things that are generally/always true.
b things that happen again and again.

Match sentences 1–4 with a or b above.

1 I **go** to a lot of countries.
2 We **like** our jobs.
3 They **live** in Amsterdam.
4 Youna **meets** a lot of people.

6 Complete the sentences with verbs from the article.

1 Youna _works_ for a clothes shop.
2 She says, 'I _____ clothes.'
3 She _____ any famous fashion designers.
4 Jos and Marco _____ in Amsterdam.
5 They _____ to East Asia.
6 Jos says, 'We _____ beautiful mountains.'

7 Complete this table. Use the article on page 14 and verbs from Exercise 6 to help you.

affirmative (+)	negative (–)
I meet	I [1] _don't_ _meet_ (do not meet)
he/she/it [2]_____	he/she/it [3]_____ _____ (does not meet)
you meet	you don't meet (do not meet)
we [4]_____	we don't meet (do not meet)
they meet	they [5]_____ _____ (do not meet)

➥ Language reference and extra practice, pages 104–105

GRAMMAR TIP
Verbs ending in -y, for example *to fly* or *to study*, usually change to -ies in the present simple after *he/she/it*: She flies. He studies. (But She buys.)

8 Choose the correct verb.

1 Irina *live / lives* in Frankfurt.
2 Pilots *fly / flies* planes.
3 Luca *doesn't / don't* like doctors.
4 Accountants *doesn't / don't* work in a court.
5 A web designer *use / uses* a computer.
6 Lecturers and lawyers *don't / doesn't* work in a shop.

9 Make sentences about you, using the verbs in brackets.

1 I _____ in East Asia. (live)
2 I _____ a lot of coffee. (drink)
3 I _____ a lot of clothes. (buy)
4 My parents _____ Spanish. (speak)
5 My mother _____ in an office. (work)
6 My friends _____ to the beach in summer. (go)

SPEAKING

10a Write about you. Then give your notes to a partner.

My name is …   I live …   My job is …   I work/study …
I like / don't like …   I …

10b Tell the class about your partner.

Anna lives in Moscow. She's a student. She studies at Moscow University. She likes clothes and music, but she doesn't like opera. She …

▶ MEET THE EXPERT
Watch an interview with Chris Holt, a pilot, about his working and home lives.
Turn to page 126 for video activities.

2.2 STUDENT LIFE

VOCABULARY
AT UNIVERSITY

1a Put the words in the box into two groups: people and places.

campus   canteen   halls of residence
classroom   international students' office
lecture theatre   lecturer   librarian
library   professor   staff   student   tutor

1b Work with a partner. Make a list of more words about university life.

READING

2a *Identifying an audience* Look at part of a New Zealand university's website. Is it for lecturers, students from New Zealand or students from other countries?

2b Look at the blue boxes on the webpage. Find links to the information below.
1 The history of the university *About us*
2 The student football teams
3 Lecturers and professors
4 Flats and halls of residence

3 Match these questions with the gaps (1–8) on the webpage.
a Does the university have a foundation course?
b Does the university help with my visa application?
c What qualifications do I need?
d Do all the students live in halls of residence?
e Are there exams every year?
f Does the university give extra English language classes?
g Do students have part-time jobs?
h Do the halls of residence have kitchens?

4 Read the webpage again. Are these sentences true or false?
1 An IELTS score of 7.5 is good for this university. *true*
2 The university writes a letter for students for their visa.
3 Students do a one-year course before their main course.
4 The university gives classes to help you study.
5 There are exams every year.
6 Students live in different places.

CA CENTRAL AUCKLAND UNIVERSITY — *Education for life*

STUDENTS | ABOUT US | MAIN COURSES | STUDENTS | STAFF | CLUBS AND SOCIETIES | ACCOMMODATION

Summer schools
Student Services
Student Life
Application

International Students' Office

The top eight student questions

1 _____
You need an IELTS or PTEA qualification with the following minimum scores: IELTS 6.0; PTEA 51.

2 _____
Yes, it does. We give you an official letter to help you.

3 _____
No, it doesn't. We have short one-month courses, but we don't have one-year foundation courses.

4 _____
Yes, it does. These are available for all foreign students. We also have study-skills classes.

5 _____
Yes, there are. The exams are in June every year.

6 _____
No, they don't. Students live in the halls of residence on campus and in private flats off campus.

7 _____
Yes, they do. The kitchens have everything you need. Ten people share each kitchen.

8 _____
Yes, they do. Students work in cafés, bars and shops.

STUDENT LIFE 2.2

GRAMMAR
PRESENT SIMPLE QUESTIONS

5a Look at the questions in Exercise 3 and the answers on the webpage. Choose the correct word.
1. We form present simple questions with *do* or *is* / *does* + verb.
2. The verb is in the infinitive *with* / *without* the word *to*.
3. In short answers with *yes*, we use *do* or *does*; in short answers with *no*, we use *do* / *don't* or *doesn't*.
4. We *use* / *don't use* the verb *do* with *to be*.

5b Complete the table with the correct words. Use the verb *to teach*.

yes/*no* questions	
1 Do I/you/we/they _____ in a university?	
2 _____ he/she _____ in a university?	
Wh- questions	
3 What subject _____ I/you/we/they _____ ?	
4 What subject _____ he/she _____ ?	

➡ Language reference and extra practice, pages 104–105

6 Complete the questions with *do* or *does*. Then choose the correct answer for you.
1. A: _Do_ you like English?
   B: Yes, I do. / No, I don't.
2. A: _____ your brother go to university?
   B: Yes, he does. / No, he doesn't.
3. A: _____ your mother work?
   B: Yes, she does. / No, she doesn't.
4. A: _____ you have a lesson this afternoon?
   B: Yes, we do. / No, we don't.
5. A: _____ your parents speak English?
   B: Yes, they do. / No, they don't.
6. A: What languages _____ you study?
   B: English, Chinese, Arabic and Spanish.

7a Put the words in the right order to make questions.
Questions about work
1. do / What / you / job / have / ?
   What job do you have?
2. Do / work for / you / a small company / ?
3. in a normal day / do / do / What / you / ?
4. you / your / like / job / Do / ?

Questions about study
5. go to / school, / Do / college or university / you / ?
6. What / study / subjects / you / do / ?
7. course / you / Do / like / your / ?
8. live / Do / you / halls of residence / in / ?

7b Work with a partner. Does he/she work or study? Ask questions from Exercise 7a.

LISTENING

8a 2.1 A language school in the UK wants to know about the lives and habits of its students. Listen to an interview with Gina, a student, and complete the questions in the survey below.

Survey of English Language Students

Study habits	Yes or no?	More information
1 Do you _study_ English at the weekend?	yes	Sunday, for about an hour
2 Do you _bring_ a dictionary to class?		
3 Do you _____ a computer?		
4 Do you _____ the library and study centre?		
Work, travel and home life		
5 Do you also _____ a job?		
6 Do you _____ to school by train, bus or car?	–	
7 Do you _____ alone, with family or with friends?	–	
Free time		
8 Do you _____ your classmates outside school?		
9 Do you _____ sports?		
10 What other things do you _____ in your free time?	–	

8b Listen again. Complete the survey for Gina.

SPEAKING AND WRITING

9 Your college wants to find out about the lives of its students. Use the questions from Exercise 8a and interview other students. Make notes of their answers.

10 Write sentences about the students in your survey.
David studies English at the weekend. He doesn't bring a dictionary to class. He ...

17

2.3 SCENARIO
IN AN OFFICE

PREPARATION

1 What do people do in an office? Complete the phrases below with the verbs in the box.

answer   do   go to   organise   use   write

1 _write_ a letter, an email
2 _____ a letter, an email, the phone
3 _____ a computer, the internet, a photocopier
4 _____ a meeting, lunch, work
5 _____ the filing, the photocopying
6 _____ a meeting, an event

2a Match phrases 1–5 with phrases a–e.

1 communication skills   a write good letters
2 computer skills   b a degree in chemistry
3 qualifications   c Monday to Friday, from 9 to 5
4 salary   d $2,000 a month
5 working hours   e use a database program

2b Complete the questions with phrases 1–5 from Exercise 2a. Then work with a partner and ask and answer the questions.

1 Do you have good computer _skills_ ?
2 Do you have good _____ skills?
3 What is a good _____ in your country?
4 What school _____ do you have?
5 What are your working _____?

3 2.2 Petra wants a new job. She goes to an employment agency. Listen to the conversation and tick (✓) the information she gets. Does she want the job?

company address   holidays   location ✓   salary
work duties   working hours

4 Listen again and complete Petra's notes.

OFFICE ASSISTANT
Company name: DP Computer Export
Location: ¹_____ _____
Transport: good
Working hours: ²_____ a.m. to 5.30 p.m.,
   Monday to ³_____
Salary: ⁴_____ per month
WORK DUTIES
• ⁵_____ the phone
• do the ⁶_____ and the photocopying
• write and send ⁷_____ and ⁸_____
QUALIFICATIONS/SKILLS
school ⁹_____
basic ¹⁰_____
good computer and communication skills

2.3 IN AN OFFICE

KEY LANGUAGE
ASKING FOR INFORMATION (1)

5 [2.3] Complete these questions. Then listen and check.
1. What *information* do you want?
2. Where is _____?
3. Is it in the _____ centre?
4. What are the working hours and _____?
5. What does an _____ assistant do?
6. What are the work _____?
7. What _____ do I need?
8. What _____ do I need?

PRONUNCIATION

6a [2.4] **Word stress** There are three syllables in the word *internet*.
in – ter – net

Write the number of syllables in each word. Then listen and check.
1. internet *3*
2. duties
3. information
4. office
5. salary
6. qualification

6b [2.5] Listen to the pronunciation of *internet*. How do we pronounce it (a, b or c)?

a •internet   b in•ternet   c inter•net

6c Mark the word stress on the words in Exercise 6a. Then listen to Audio recording 2.4 again and check your answers. Work with a partner and practise saying the words.

7a Look at Audio script 2.2 on page 149. Listen again and underline the stress on the words in bold.

7b Work with a partner and practise saying the conversation.

TASK
DESCRIBING JOBS

8a Work with a partner to find out about different jobs.

Student A: Look at page 133. You work at an employment agency. Answer your partner's questions about the project manager job.

Student B: You want a job. Find out about the project manager job. Use the Key language in Exercise 5 to ask your partner for information.

8b Change roles. Do the role-play again.

Student A: Find out about the administration officer job.

Student B: Look at page 134. Answer your partner's questions about the administration officer job.

9 Choose a job for you (the office assistant job, the project manager job or the administration officer job). Tell your partner why you want that job.

I want the administration officer job. The hours are good and the salary isn't bad. There's good transport.

I don't want the office assistant job. The salary isn't good and I think it's boring.

19

2.4 STUDY AND WRITING SKILLS

STUDY SKILLS
USING YOUR DICTIONARY (2)

1 `2.6` **Word stress** Listen and choose the correct word stress.

1	a em•**ploy**•ment	b	**em**•ploy•ment
2	a **lec**•ture	b	lec•**ture**
3	a **or**•ganise	b	or•**ganise**
4	a pho•to•**cop**•y	b	**pho**•to•cop•y

2 Look at these dictionary entries. How do they show word stress? Is this the same as your dictionary?

E em•ploy•ment /ɪmˈplɔɪmənt/ *noun* (no plural) (formal) work that you do to earn money: *She had to leave school and find employment.*

L lec•ture¹ /ˈlektʃə $ ˈlektʃɚ/ *noun* a talk to a group of people that teaches them about a subject: *a lecture on Beethoven*
lec•ture² *verb* to teach a group of people about a subject: *Dr Marks lectures in biology.*

O or•gan•ise /ˈɔːɡənaɪz $ ˈɔːrɡəˌnaɪz/ *verb* to plan and arrange an event or activity: *The school has organised a trip to the sea.*

P pho•to•cop•y¹ /ˈfəʊtəʊˌkɒpi $ ˈfoʊtəˌkɑpi/ *noun* (plural **photocopies**) a copy of a document that you make using a photocopier: *Send a photocopy of your certificate to the college.*
pho•to•cop•y² *verb* (**photocopied, photocopies**) to make a copy of a document using a photocopier: *Could you photocopy this article, please?*

From the *Longman WordWise Dictionary*

3a What is the word stress of these words? Put them in the correct place in the table (A–D). Then check in your dictionary.

~~accountant~~ organise   company   visit   pilot
designer   location   email   design   complete

A • •	B • • •	C • • •	D • • •
			accountant

3b `2.7` Listen and repeat the words.

4 In the dictionary entries in Exercise 2, why are there numbers after the words *lecture* and *photocopy*?

5a Which words in Exercise 3a are verbs, nouns or both? Work with a partner to complete the table. Then check in your dictionary.
Student A: Check the words in columns A and B in Exercise 3a.
Student B: Check the words in columns C and D in Exercise 3a.

verb	noun	verb and noun

5b Complete these sentences with the correct form of a word in the table above.

1 An *accountant* manages a company's money.
2 I send about 50 _____ a day.
3 The office is in a good _____, near the station.
4 In his job, he _____ a lot of different countries.
5 The architect _____ a building, then the builders build it.
6 She works for a famous _____ – Nike.
7 Sarah is a _____. She works for British Airways.
8 _____ the form. Then send it to the company.
9 In his job, he _____ meetings for his boss.
10 The fashion _____ chooses the colours.

STUDY AND WRITING SKILLS 2.4

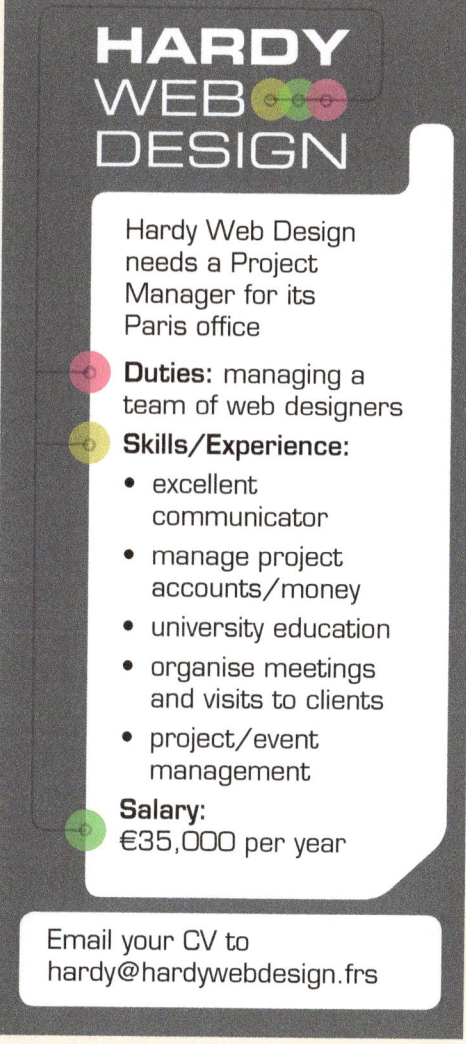

HARDY WEB DESIGN

Hardy Web Design needs a Project Manager for its Paris office

Duties: managing a team of web designers

Skills/Experience:
- excellent communicator
- manage project accounts/money
- university education
- organise meetings and visits to clients
- project/event management

Salary: €35,000 per year

Email your CV to hardy@hardywebdesign.frs

Curriculum Vitae – Sonia West

¹ Nationality : British

² _____ : 22/03/1987

³ _____ : 17 Park Road, Chelsea, London SWW3 2PS

⁴ _____ : (home) 0220 77808 6449 (mobile) 07924 5111637

⁵ _____ : soniwes@gdmail.com

⁶ _____

2010–present	Euro Business Design	Team manager
2008–2010	Cambridge Book Design	Project assistant
2004–2007	Blackstone's Booksellers	Sales assistant (part-time)

⁷ _____

2004–2007 Cambridge University
           BA (Hons) Maths and Computing
           First-class degree
1998–2004 Bristol School for Girls
           3 A levels: Maths (A); English (A); Economics (B)

⁸ _____

Computing skills: Word, Excel, PowerPoint
Languages: French (advanced), Chinese (intermediate)

⁹ _____

Sport: tennis and horse-riding
Travel: Europe, USA and East Asia
Cinema and theatre

WRITING SKILLS
A CV

6 Evaluating Read the job advertisement and Sonia West's CV above. Do you think she is a good person for the job? Why?/Why not?

7 Complete the gaps (1–9) in the CV with these headings.

~~Nationality~~   Email   Address   Interests
Date of birth   Education/Training
Other skills   Telephone   Employment

8 Are these sentences about Sonia true or false?
1. Sonia lives in the UK. *true*
2. Her degree result is not very good.
3. She is good at maths.
4. She has experience of work in a bookshop.
5. She has basic French.
6. She likes to stay at home.

9a Capital letters Look at the CV again. Which types of word have a capital letter at the beginning?

cities   people's names   languages   sports   companies
countries and continents   streets   school and university names
nationalities   levels of language (e.g. beginner)   school subjects

cities – London

9b Look at this information from another CV. Which words need capital letters? Correct the capitalisation.
1. stephen thorn *Stephen Thorn*
2. canadian
3. 19 hope street, toronto
4. toronto metropolitan university
5. ma (business and economics)
6. world computer company
7. spanish (elementary)
8. football
9. music: guitar and piano

10 Match items 2–9 in Exercise 9b with one of the headings from Exercise 7.

2 Nationality

11 Write your CV. Remember to put something in each section.

3 Nature

3.1 WET AND DRY

IN THIS UNIT

GRAMMAR
- question words
- adverbs of frequency

VOCABULARY
- verbs connected with water
- adjectives (2)

SCENARIO
- making and responding to suggestions

STUDY SKILLS
- classroom language

WRITING SKILLS
- a description of a process

A

'Let nature be your teacher.' William Wordsworth, 1770–1850, British poet

READING

1a Read the quiz on the right and answer the questions with a partner.

1b Check your answers on page 147.

VOCABULARY
VERBS CONNECTED WITH WATER

2a Which verbs from the box are connected with using water? Check new verbs in your dictionary.

| boil | change | cook | ~~drink~~ | find | freeze | make |
| sleep | stop | swim | wash | waste | | |

2b Complete these questions with verbs from the box. It is possible to use each verb more than once.

1. Do you _drink_ a lot of tea in the morning?
2. Do you _____ water to make coffee?
3. Do you _____ in the sea or in a swimming pool?
4. Do you _____ dinner in the evening?
5. Do you _____ your car every week?
6. Do you _____ two litres of water every day?

2c Ask and answer the questions with a partner.

A: *Do you drink a lot of tea in the morning?*
B: *No, I don't like tea.*

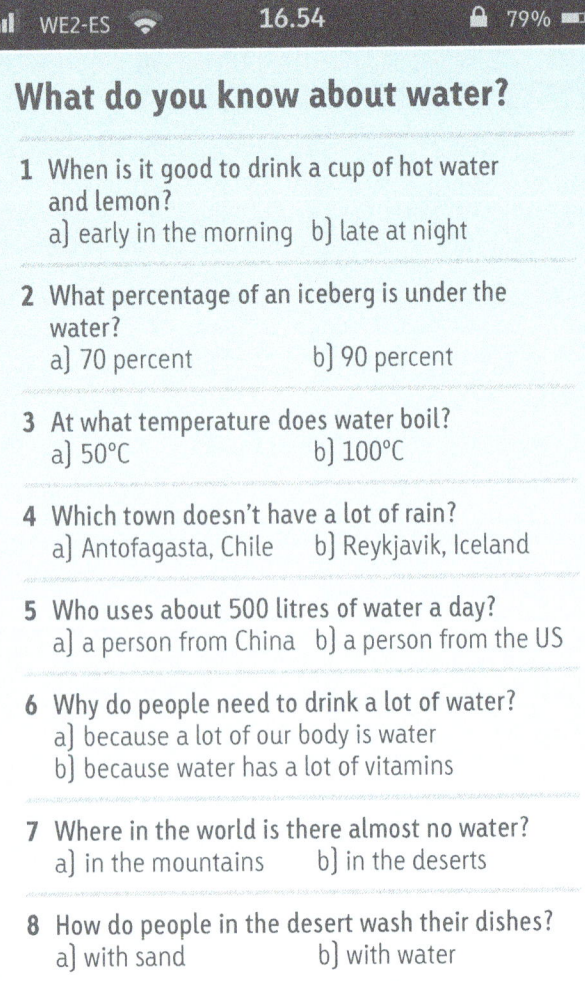

What do you know about water?

1. When is it good to drink a cup of hot water and lemon?
   a) early in the morning   b) late at night

2. What percentage of an iceberg is under the water?
   a) 70 percent   b) 90 percent

3. At what temperature does water boil?
   a) 50°C   b) 100°C

4. Which town doesn't have a lot of rain?
   a) Antofagasta, Chile   b) Reykjavik, Iceland

5. Who uses about 500 litres of water a day?
   a) a person from China   b) a person from the US

6. Why do people need to drink a lot of water?
   a) because a lot of our body is water
   b) because water has a lot of vitamins

7. Where in the world is there almost no water?
   a) in the mountains   b) in the deserts

8. How do people in the desert wash their dishes?
   a) with sand   b) with water

LISTENING

3a What do we call a place with almost no water? (Look at the quiz in Exercise 1.) Match photos A–E with the words in the box.

cactus   camel   plant   rock   sand

3b Do you know the names of any deserts? Where are they?

4a **Predicting** Dr Bader Al-Shammary is talking on a TV programme about deserts. Before you listen, tick (✓) the things you think he talks about.

animals   food   lemons   money   rain   the sea   temperature

4b 3.1 Listen to the interview and tick (✓) the ideas you hear.
1 Deserts are not all the same.
2 There's almost no water in deserts.
3 Life in deserts is difficult.
4 Dangerous animals live in deserts.
5 People don't live in deserts.
6 Desert people don't stay in one place.

4c 3.2 Listen to the first part of the interview again and complete the sentences with numbers.
1 In hot deserts, the temperature changes from _____ degrees in the day to _____ at night.
2 Only _____ percent of the world's deserts are sand.
3 Deserts have a maximum of _____ millimetres of rain a year.

4d 3.3 Listen to the second part of the interview again and complete these notes.
Life in the desert
- Animals: A lot of them sleep ¹ _in_ _the_ _day_. At night, they ² _____ _____ _____.
- Plants: The Saguaro cactus has five tonnes of ³ _____ _____ _____ _____.
- People: They move from ⁴ _____ _____ _____. In Australia, they eat ⁵ _____ _____ _____ _____.

WET AND DRY

3.1

GRAMMAR
QUESTION WORDS

5a Look at the quiz in Exercise 1 and Audio script 3.1 on page 149. Underline the question words (for example, *what*).

5b Complete the question words in the box. Then complete the sentences below.

wha*t*   whe_   whe__   wh_   wh_
h__   whi__

1 _What_ asks about a thing or an idea.
2 _____ asks about a person.
3 _____ asks about a place.
4 _____ asks about time.
5 _____ asks about the way we do something.
6 _____ asks about the reason for something.
7 _____ asks about a choice between two or more things.

GRAMMAR TIP

We sometimes use *What … ?* and *Which … ?* with a noun.
What percentage …?
Which languages …?

➡ Language reference and extra practice, pages 106–107

6 Choose the correct question word to complete these questions. Then ask and answer the questions with a partner.
1 *When / Who / Where* do you live?
2 *How / What / Who* do you study English?
3 *Which / Why / What* do you want to learn English?
4 *How / Who / Why* do you remember from your first school?
5 *Who / Where / What* do you meet your friends?
6 *Where / Which / How* hand do you write with, your left or your right?
7 *Why's / What's / When's* your favourite city?
8 *What / Who / When* do you drink coffee?

SPEAKING

7 Work with a partner to find out some more facts about water.

Student A: Look at the information on page 132.
Student B: Look at the information on page 131.

23

3.2 IN THE WILD

READING

1 Read the advert and answer these questions.
1. Who runs this competition?
2. What is the prize?
3. Is this competition open to everyone?
4. Do you think this is an interesting opportunity? Why?/Why not?

Tourism Australia

Best jobs in the world!

Enter the competition and win a great job for 6 months!

Two jobs available this year:
- Work in the rainforest – be a park ranger.
- Work with dolphins – be a wildlife officer.

Keep a blog to share your incredible experience with the world.

AU$100,000 salary

Accommodation included.

Are you interested in adventure?
Do you love nature and wildlife?
Are you a good communicator?
Aged 18–30?

If yes, send a video to apply.
To find out more about the jobs, **click here**

---

2 Find out more about the jobs.

Student A: Read about the wildlife officer on Kangaroo Island. How many work duties does she talk about?
Student B: Look at page 135. Read about the park ranger. How many work duties does she talk about?

3 Answer these questions about your wildlife worker.
1. Where does she work?
2. What work with people does she do?
3. What work with animals does she do?
4. What things does she like doing?

4a Tell your partner about your wildlife worker. Then listen and make notes about your partner's worker.

4b Read the other text to check the information.

A wildlife officer on Kangaroo Island

I always get up early, because every day I check for turtles on the beach and in the sea. This is one of my important duties and it's never boring. I'm always very happy when I swim with the turtles!

Then, in the afternoon, I sometimes take visitors on walking tours. They are popular because we often see koala bears. We see them about five times a week – and we always see kangaroos. That's not a surprise on Kangaroo Island!

On the other days, I help with the sea kayak tours – they're fun and we usually see beautiful animals like seals and dolphins. There are many of them here. We occasionally see large sharks. They come about once a month, but we never have any problems with them.

Working here is great!

VOCABULARY
ADJECTIVES (2)

5a Match adjectives in the wildlife officer text with meanings 1–6.
1. not interesting
2. the opposite of *sad*
3. many people like it
4. a nice thing to do; makes you smile
5. nice to look at
6. very good

5b What other adjectives can you find in the park ranger text and in the job advert?

6 Describing preferences Which job do you prefer? Why? Use adjectives from Exercises 5a and 5b.

IN THE WILD

3.2

8 Look again at the examples from the texts in Exercise 7c. Does the adverb of frequency go before or after *to be*? Does it go before or after other verbs?

9a Look at these expressions of frequency. Number them in order of frequency.

every day	[1]	once a month	☐
twice a year	☐	five times a week	☐
weekly	☐		

9b Find expressions of frequency in the texts. Where do we put them in a sentence?
1 after the verb and other words
2 after the subject, before the verb
3 before the subject

➥ Language reference and extra practice, pages 106–107

10 Put the words in the right order to make sentences.
1 I / feed / the / every day / kangaroos / .
2 I / take / visitors / on / usually / guided tours / .
3 A / once a year / visitor / gets lost / about / .
4 People / enjoy / the / always / mountain walks / .
5 There / are / every afternoon / sea kayak tours / .
6 I / get / never / bored / because / the natural world / always / is / incredible / .

11 Add an adverb or expression of frequency to the sentences to make them true for you.
1 I swim in the sea.
2 I watch wildlife shows on TV.
3 I go to national parks.
4 I travel by boat.
5 I use the internet.
6 I visit my grandmother.
7 I go to the cinema.
8 I play sport.
9 I read a newspaper.
10 I play computer games.

1 *I often swim in the sea.*

SPEAKING AND WRITING

12a Ask a partner about his/her routines and habits. Use the ideas in Exercise 11 and your own ideas. Use *How often … ?*

A: *How often do you watch wildlife shows on TV?*
B: *About once a month.*

12b Write sentences about the differences between you and your partner.

Irina watches wildlife shows on TV about once a month, but I never watch them.

▶ **MEET THE EXPERT**

Watch an interview with David Stevenson, a wildlife photographer, about photographing animals.
Turn to page 127 for video activities.

GRAMMAR
ADVERBS OF FREQUENCY

7a Match the sentence beginnings (1–2) with the sentence endings (a–b).
1 I always get up early
2 I never see koala bears
a because every day I check for turtles.
b because they don't live in rainforests.

7b Which word shows a frequency of 100 percent? Which word shows a frequency of 0 percent?

7c Find examples from the texts of the adverbs of frequency in the box. Then complete the table.

| always | sometimes | occasionally | often |
| usually | never | | |

adverb	examples (text and line)
always	*wildlife officer, line 1*
sometimes	_____
occasionally	_____
often	_____
usually	_____
never	_____

25

3.3 SCENARIO
SAVING NATURE

PREPARATION

1 Read about the three charities below. Which one is most interesting, do you think?

2 People do activities and hold events to raise money for charity. Look at these ideas. Do people do them in your country?
- a sponsored event (e.g. running, cycling, walking)
- a fund-raising performance (e.g. a music show, a singing competition)
- a fund-raising sale (e.g. art and photography, second-hand things, a bring-and-buy event)
- money collection on the streets

3a **3.4** At a university in the UK, the Student Committee is organising a weekend of fund-raising events for Pandas International. Listen to their discussion. What activities do they decide to have, and when?

3b What do these phrases describe? Listen again to check.
1 … are great fun.
2 … is not much fun.
3 I don't think … is a big problem.
4 There are many good …
5 … are always popular.
6 That's a nice idea.

Pandas INTERNATIONAL

There are only about 2,000 pandas alive in the wild, and we do not want to lose these wonderful animals. With your donations, we support the Woolong Panda Centre in China and plant forests of the pandas' favourite food – bamboo.

THE MARINE CONSERVATION SOCIETY

The seas and oceans face many problems from fishing, pollution and climate change. We create ocean parks to save the wildlife that lives in the sea. There is no fishing in these parks. We also work to stop pollution of the seas, with a focus on plastic pollution, which kills millions of sea animals every year.

SAVING NATURE

KEY LANGUAGE
MAKING SUGGESTIONS

4a 3.5 Complete these sentences from the conversation. Then listen and check.
1 _____ you got any ideas?
2 _____ have a sponsored cycling event.
3 _____ ideas for Saturday evening?
4 _____ don't we have a music event?
5 _____ about Saturday morning and afternoon?
6 _____ about a wildlife art and photography competition?

4b Which sentences in Exercise 4a ask for suggestions? Which ones make suggestions?

PRONUNCIATION

5a 3.6 **Showing interest** Listen to the end of the conversation again and answer these questions.
1 Does Jess think the art competition is a really good idea?
2 Does Andy think going for something to eat is a really good idea?
3 Does Chris think having a burger is a really good idea?

5b 3.7 Listen to two different ways to say *OK* (a and b). Which intonation shows strong interest or enthusiasm? Which shows weak interest or no enthusiasm?

6a 3.8 Listen to more phrases. Is the intonation strong interest (SI) or weak interest (WI)?
1 Great idea. _WI_   4 OK.   _____
2 Yes.   _____ 5 Fantastic. _____
3 Excellent.   _____ 6 Great.   _____

6b Work with a partner. Practise saying the phrases in Exercise 6a. Which intonation do you hear?

7 With your partner, make and respond to suggestions about this weekend. Use the language in Exercises 4a and 6a.

A: Let's go to the cinema.
B: Great idea!

TASK
MAKING AND RESPONDING TO SUGGESTIONS

8a You are on a Student Committee. You want to plan a weekend of fund-raising events for a charity from Exercise 1. Prepare ideas for fund-raising activities and events. Think about typical ideas and unusual ideas.

8b Work in pairs or groups thinking about the same charity. Agree what events to have, and when to have them. Make suggestions and reply to your partners' ideas. Use the language in Exercises 4a and 6a.

USEFUL PHRASES
That sounds fun/good.
That sounds interesting.
Good idea.
So, on Saturday, it's …
I don't want to do that.
I'm not sure.
That sounds boring.
In the evening, it's …

8c Describe your plan to other groups. Are your ideas the same? Do students with the other charities have different ideas?

Rainforest CONCERN
The rainforest is of great importance to the world, but it is disappearing. Every year, humans cut down trees in an area the size of England. The rainforest is home to many types of animals and plants, and the trees provide oxygen for the planet. We save the rainforest by buying large areas of it. This protects the trees from the big companies and gives hope to the animals.

3.4 STUDY AND WRITING SKILLS

STUDY SKILLS
CLASSROOM LANGUAGE

1 Classroom objects Work with a partner. Are these things in your classroom? Do you have them on your desk or in your bag?

a blackboard   a CD player   a chair
a computer   a coursebook   a DVD player
an English–English dictionary   a notebook
a pen   a pencil   a whiteboard

2a Classroom instructions Who usually says these sentences: the teacher, the student or both?

1 Open your books at page 28.
2 Work in pairs.
3 Do you understand?
4 Sorry, what do you mean?
5 Work on your own.
6 Check your ideas with your partner.
7 Can you repeat that, please?
8 What's the answer to number 1?
9 I don't know.
10 Close your books.

2b Match sentences a–e with five sentences from Exercise 2a with similar meanings.

a Sorry, I don't understand.
b I have no idea.
c Look at page 28.
d Can you say that again, please?
e Work with a partner.

3a Questions about a word The questions below are common in classrooms. Complete the questions with the words in the box.

~~What~~   How   Where   What   How   What   How

1 _What_ does 'evaporate' mean?
2 _____ part of speech is 'evaporate'?
3 _____ do you spell 'evaporate'?
4 _____ is the word stress in 'evaporate'?
5 _____ do you pronounce it?
6 _____ do you say 'evaporate' in Polish?
7 _____ is 'parować' in English?

3b 3.9 Match the questions from Exercise 3a with these answers. Then listen and check.

a E-V-A-P-O-R-A-T-E.
b It's on the second syllable.
c In English, it's 'evaporate'.
d When a liquid evaporates, it changes into steam or a gas.
e Parować.
f It's a verb.
g /ɪˈvæpəreɪt/

4 Asking about words Work with a partner. Ask for the English word, spelling and word stress for the things in some pictures.

Student A: Look at pictures A–D on page 133 and ask your questions. Answer your partner's questions about pictures E–H.
Student B: Look at pictures E–H on page 134 and ask your questions. Answer your partner's questions about pictures A–D.

STUDY AND WRITING SKILLS 3.4

WRITING SKILLS
A DESCRIPTION OF A PROCESS

5a Look at the picture and find the things in the box.

the sun   the ground   mountains   clouds   the sea
rivers   water vapour

5b Complete these sentences about parts 1–4 in the picture. Use the present simple form of these verbs.

evaporate   form   heat   move

1 The sun _____ the sea.
2 The water _____.
3 The water vapour _____ clouds.
4 The clouds _____ above the mountains.

6 Linkers Complete this description of the first part of the water cycle (parts 1–4). Use the phrases in the box. Some phrases can go in more than one gap. There is one phrase you do not need.

next,   finally,   then,   first of all,   after that,

¹_____ the sun heats the sea. ²_____ the water in the sea evaporates and it goes into the air. ³_____ the water vapour forms clouds. ⁴_____ the clouds move over the land and they move above the mountains.

7a Pronouns: *it* and *they* Look at these two sentences. What do *it* and *they* mean?
1 … the water in the sea evaporates and **it** goes into the air.
2 … the clouds move over the land and **they** move above the mountains.

7b We can use *and* with the pronouns *it* and *they* to join two sentences or ideas. Look at the examples in Exercise 7a, then join sentence pairs 1 and 2 below.
1 The water vapour goes into the air. + The water vapour forms clouds.
2 Animals go to the rivers. + Animals drink the water.

8 Look at the second part of the water cycle (parts 5–8). Put these sentences in the right order.
a The rain goes into the rivers. ☐
b The cycle begins again. ☐
c The rain falls to the ground. ☐
d The water vapour changes into rain. ☐
e The rivers carry the water to the sea. ☐

9 Now describe the second part of the water cycle (parts 5–8). Use the ideas in Exercise 8. Don't forget to use linkers and pronouns. Look at Exercise 6 to help you.

In the cold air, the water vapour …

The water cycle

4 Leisure time
4.1 SILVER SCREEN

IN THIS UNIT

GRAMMAR
- articles
- can, can't

VOCABULARY
- types of film
- leisure activities, sports
- holiday resorts

SCENARIO
- asking for information (2), saying 'no' politely
- describing places and facilities

STUDY SKILLS
- working with numbers

WRITING SKILLS
- a description of a table or bar chart

A

'All work and no play makes Jack a dull boy.' English proverb

VOCABULARY
TYPES OF FILM

1 Discuss these questions in small groups.
1. How often do you watch films?
2. Do you usually watch films at home or at the cinema? Which do you prefer? Why?
3. How often do you go to the cinema? Who do you go with?

2a Using visual clues Look at the four film posters (A–D). Decide which type of film from the box you think they are for.

an action/adventure film		a romantic comedy
an animation	a love story	a historical film
a horror film	a musical	a comedy	a war film
a western	a science-fiction film	a thriller

2b Answer these questions about the types of film in Exercise 2a.
1. Can you think of an example of each type of film?
   The Sound of Music is a musical. Man of Steel is an action/adventure film.
2. Which types of film do you like? Why?
   I like historical films because I learn a lot about the past.
3. What types of film are on at the cinema in your town/city now?

READING

3 Read the *World Cinema* website opposite and tick (✓) the correct answers.

On this website, there is information about
1. a film from Ireland.
2. films in Argentina.
3. the number of cinemas in Argentina.
4. a film about people in France.
5. Hollywood films.

4 Match words and phrases 1–5 with their meanings a–e.
1. actor   a. when people are busy doing things
2. director   b. It's normal, not different or unusual.
3. ordinary   c. These people are between 80 and 89 years old.
4. in their 80s   d. You see this person in films or plays.
5. active   e. This person gives instructions to actors in a film.

5 Read these sentences. Decide if they are true, false or the website doesn't say.
1. People in Argentina like Argentinian films. *doesn't say*
2. Argentinian directors make the same types of film.
3. Argentinian directors aren't interested in the history of their country.
4. *Amour* is easy to understand.
5. The actors in *Amour* are very good.
6. The director Michael Haneke speaks French.

30

SILVER SCREEN

4.1

GRAMMAR
ARTICLES

6 Articles are *a/an* and *the*. Look at these grammar rules. Match the rules to sentences 1–6.

a no article with plural nouns, to talk about people or things in general
   Argentinian films are popular.

b *a/an* with a singular noun, and to talk about a person's job
   an intelligent film

c *the* with singular or plural nouns, to talk about a known or specific person or thing
   the lives of ordinary people
   a French couple
   the couple

1 A film star is a famous actor. *b*
2 Thrillers are exciting.
3 Anne is a music teacher.
4 I like *Amour*. The actors are excellent.
5 Ian hates war films.
6 The musical *Grease* is still very popular.

GRAMMAR TIP

Use *an*, not *a*, when the noun begins with a vowel sound: *an actor, an idea*

➡ Language reference and extra practice, pages 108–109

7 Complete these sentences with *a/an*, *the* or no article (write Ø).

1 He's ___ actor.
2 Do you like ___ westerns?
3 Is there ___ cinema near your house?
4 What's the difference between ___ comedy and ___ romantic comedy?
5 *Tokyo Story*, by Yasujiro Ozu, is ___ number-one film of all time, people say.

SPEAKING

8a *Discussing preferences* Work with a partner. Ask and answer these questions. Give reasons for your answers.

1 What's your favourite film from your country?
2 What's your favourite film from another country?
3 Who's your favourite film star/actor?
4 Who's your favourite director?

8b Tell the class about your partner.

Julia's favourite director is Pedro Almodóvar because he makes very interesting films and …

MEET THE EXPERT

Watch an interview with Lynda Myles, a film producer and lecturer, about Martin Scorsese.
Turn to page 127 for video activities.

A DANNY BOYLE FILM
TRANCE B

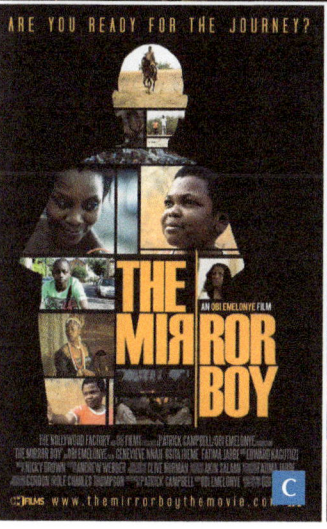
C

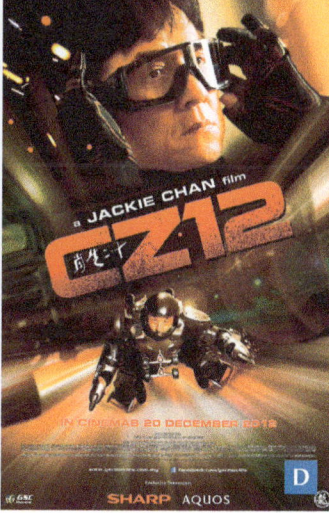
D

WORLDCINEMA.COM

Are you tired of Hollywood blockbusters? Then this is the website for you! We look at films from all over the world, from Ireland to Iraq, from Mali to Malaysia.

Country profile: Argentina by Lucia Polo

These days, Argentinian films are quite popular and we often see them in film festivals. The country has a lot of excellent film directors, for example Lucrecia Martel, Pablo Trapero and Juan José Campanella. They make different types of film: thrillers, comedies and even westerns – about the history of Argentina, the lives of ordinary people, and about life in the city or in the country. Argentinian actors are first class, too …

Read more >>

This week's film: *Amour*

The Austrian director Michael Haneke gives us an intelligent film about life and death, and about the power of love. The story is simple and there aren't any surprises. Anne and Georges (the excellent actors Emmanuelle Riva and Jean-Louis Trintignant) are a French couple in their 80s. The couple live in Paris, and are music teachers. They're happy and active. But then Anne becomes ill …

Read more >>

4.2 KEEP FIT

VOCABULARY
LEISURE ACTIVITIES, SPORTS

1a A lot of people do exercise in their free time. What do you do?

play basketball   play football   play tennis
go running   go swimming   go to a fitness club
dance   ride a bike   ski   do aerobics   do yoga
work out in a gym   do something different (what?)

1b Compare your answers with a partner. Use these questions.

Do you … ? How often do you … ? Where do you … ? When do you … ?

LISTENING

2a 4.1 Listen to interviews with two members of a health club. How many different sports or activities do they talk about?

2b Listen again and complete the questionnaire with Lisa's and Dan's answers.

excel health and fitness club

1 How often do you come to the club?
   Lisa _____   Dan _____

2 Do you use the running machines?
   Lisa _____   Dan _____

3 Do you work out in the gym?
   Lisa _____   Dan _____

4 Do you use the swimming pool?
   Lisa _____   Dan _____

GRAMMAR
CAN, CAN'T

3a 4.2 Complete these extracts from the interviews. Then listen and check your answers.

1 INT: What weight _____ you lift?
2 LISA: I _____ usually lift a lot, but I _____ lift 35 kilos.
3 LISA: Well, I _____ swim, so I _____ use it.
4 INT: Well, I'm sure our trainer _____ help you.
5 DAN: Oh, yes, I _____ . I can _____ that in about 30 minutes.
6 DAN: I _____ swim two kilometres, but I _____ swim five kilometres.
7 INT: _____ we test your fitness today?
8 DAN: Is that the time? I _____ stay, I'm afraid.

3b Underline the verbs in the present simple in Audio script 4.1 on pages 149–150. Circle the verbs with *can*. Complete these grammar points with *the present simple* or *can*.

1 We use _____ when we talk about regular actions or habits.
2 We use _____ when we talk about our abilities or what it is possible to do.

4a Look again at the sentences in Exercise 3a. Are statements 1–4 about *can* true or false?

1 In an affirmative sentence, we put *can* before a main verb.
2 In a question with *can*, we also use *do/does*.
3 In a negative sentence with *can*, we do <u>not</u> use *don't/doesn't*.
4 When we use *can* after *he/she/it*, we add *-s* to the main verb.

➤ Language reference and extra practice, pages 108–109

4b Tick (✓) the correct sentences and correct the mistakes in the others.

1 She can rides a horse.
2 They can to swim.
3 Can you ride a horse?
4 I can swim.
5 We don't can ski.
6 Lisa cans lift 35 kilos.
7 Do you can ride a bike?

PRONUNCIATION

5a 4.3 **Weak or strong vowel** Listen to six sentences. We can pronounce *can* with the schwa /ə/ or a strong vowel /æ/. Which sentence has the strong vowel? Practise saying the sentences.

5b 4.4 How do we pronounce the vowel sound in *can't*? Listen to four examples, then practise saying the interviews from Exercise 2a with a partner.

KEEP FIT 4.2

excel health and fitness club

Membership and opening hours
Full-time membership costs £100 per month.
Part-time membership costs £75 per month.

Opening hours
Full-time: Tues–Sun   06.30–22.30
Part-time: Tues–Sun   10.00–15.30, 19.30–22.30

FACILITIES AND SERVICES

Gym
The gym has modern equipment, including running, cycling and rowing machines. On your first visit, a trainer teaches you about the equipment and designs an exercise plan for you.

Swimming pool
Our pool is 20 metres long and 5 metres wide.

Café
You can buy sandwiches, fruit and drinks here. We show important sports events on the large-screen TV. There are computers and wi-fi. (Free internet and wi-fi connection for full-time members only. Small charge for part-time members.)

Classes
You can get a timetable for the classes from the reception desk. We offer the following classes: yoga, aerobics, spinning and dance.

Health and beauty centre
The health and beauty centre is for men and women. Our sunbeds are very popular. There is also a modern sauna. Part-time members cannot use the health and beauty centre.

READING

6a Scanning for information Read the health club leaflet above and find this information.

1 the day the club is closed
2 the three machines in the gym
3 the size of the swimming pool
4 the food they sell in the café
5 the classes the club offers

6b Read the leaflet again. Answer these questions.

1 How do you learn to use the running machines?
2 Where do you go for information about class times?
3 What are the four differences between full- and part-time membership?

7 Look at the leaflet and underline three sentences using *can* or *cannot (can't)*.

GRAMMAR TIP

The verb *can* also means something is possible.
You can buy sandwiches, fruit and drinks here.

8 Complete sentences 1–4 with the phrases in the box. More than one phrase can go in some gaps.

borrow books   find information   learn about the past
use a running machine

1 You can _____ from a library.
2 You can _____ in a fitness centre.
3 You can _____ on the internet.
4 You can _____ in a museum.

9 Choose a place from the box below. Think of three or four things you can/can't do in this place and tell a partner, but don't say the place. Can your partner guess it?

in the countryside   at home   in an internet café
in a library   in the mountains   in a park   at the seaside
at a sports centre   in my town

A: *You can read books. You can write. You can't buy books.*
B: *Is it a library?*

SPEAKING

10 What can your partner do? How often does he/she do those things? Use ideas in the box and interview your partner.

swim   run 10km   ride a bike   play tennis   ride a horse
speak another foreign language   sing   ski   drive a car
ice skate   play a musical instrument   cook   play chess

4.3 SCENARIO
AT A TRAVEL AGENT'S

PREPARATION

1a Complete the table with these holiday phrases.

a family room   a cottage   mountain biking
scuba diving   windsurfing   a sea view   a hiking trip
a painting class   a kids' club   a museum visit
play tennis and golf   go sightseeing   a dance show
a double room   a hotel

accommodation	sports and exercise	activities and entertainment
a family room		

1b Discuss with a partner.
1 Where do you often go for a holiday?
2 What kind of places do you stay in?
3 What kind of things do you do on holiday?

2 Many people go to all-inclusive resorts for their holiday. At these places, you have everything you need for a holiday. Look at the advert below and answer these questions.
1 Would you like to visit a Sarong Holiday Resort?
2 Do you like all-inclusive holidays? Why?/Why not?
3 Are there any all-inclusive resorts in your country?

SARONG
Holiday Resorts

THAILAND

All inclusive • All ages • All for fun
Great restaurants ... Water sports ...
Babysitters ... Evening entertainment ...

3a [4.5] Sarah wants to take her two children (aged 9 and 14) on holiday. She asks the travel agent for more information about the Sarong Resort. Listen and tick (✓) the things she asks about.

the bedrooms   food   evening entertainment   sports
the weather   local transport   children's activities

3b Listen again and answer these questions.
1 Do all the rooms have sea views?
2 Where do children sleep?
3 Can you eat breakfast in all the restaurants?
4 What sports can you do at the resort?
5 When does the babysitter work?

KEY LANGUAGE
ASKING FOR INFORMATION (2), SAYING 'NO' POLITELY

4 [4.6] Complete these sentences from the conversation. Then listen and check.
1 A: _____ you give me some information about the Sarong Holiday Resort?
   B: Yes, certainly. What would you _____ to know?
2 A: First of all, can you _____ me about the accommodation, please?
   B: Yes, of course. All the rooms are double rooms.
3 A: Are there any family rooms?
   B: No, I'm afraid _____.
4 A: _____ I play other sports – tennis, for example?
   B: I'm sorry. I'm afraid you _____.
5 A: _____ there a kids' club in the day?
   B: No, I'm afraid there _____.

PRONUNCIATION

5a [4.7] Linked sounds Listen to the pronunciation of *I'm afraid*. Notice the linking between *I'm* and *afraid*. In a short phrase, we often link the two sounds. For example, when the first word ends with a consonant sound and the second word begins with a vowel sound.

No, I'm afraid not.
I'm afraid you can't.
I'm afraid there isn't.

5b Listen again and repeat.

6 Find some more linked consonant–vowel sounds in Audio script 4.5 on page 150, then practise the conversation with a partner.

34

4.3 AT A TRAVEL AGENT'S

TASK
DESCRIBING PLACES AND FACILITIES

7 Look at the holiday resort adverts above. What do you know about the two countries? What do you think a holiday in each place is like? What do people probably do?

8a Read more about the two resorts.
Student A: Read the holiday brochure on page 136 and complete the 'Scottish Dream' column in the table.
Student B: Read the holiday brochure on page 138 and complete the 'Club Mexico' column in the table.

8b Work with a partner and role-play a dialogue between a customer and a travel agent. Use the Key language and the Useful phrases below.
Student A: You are the customer. You are interested in 'Club Mexico'. Ask the travel agent about it and complete your table on page 136.
Studen't B: You are the travel agent. Answer the customer's questions about 'Club Mexico'.

USEFUL PHRASES
Can I help you?
Can you give me some information about … ?
(the resort, the sports, the activities)
That sounds nice.
Finally, …
Thank you very much for …

8c Change roles. Do the role-play again.
Student A: Now you are the travel agent.
Student B: Now you are the customer. Ask the travel agent about 'Scottish Dream' and complete your table on page 138.

9 Which holiday do you prefer? Why?

10 Which holiday is good for Sarah and her family? Write a few sentences to say why each of the three holidays is good or bad for her.

I think … is a good place for her holiday, because she can … There is …
I don't think … is a good place for her holiday, because she can't … There isn't …

4.4 STUDY AND WRITING SKILLS

STUDY SKILLS
WORKING WITH NUMBERS

1 `4.8` **Large numbers** Match the numbers with the statistics, then listen and check.

| 195 | 6,900 | 3,200 | 21,700,000 | 63,200,000 |

1 This is the number of people in the UK.
2 This is the number of people in Australia.
3 This is the number of countries in the world.
4 This is the number of languages in the world.
5 This is the number of wild tigers in the world.

2a `4.9` Listen to these numbers. Tick (✓) the numbers that use the word *and*.

a 100
b 140
c 2,000
d 2,300
e 2,345
f 5,000,000
g 5,600,000
h 5,670,000

2b Listen again and repeat the numbers.

3 Work with a partner to practise numbers.

Student A: Look at page 142 and read the numbers to your partner. Then listen and write your partner's numbers.
Student B: Write the numbers your partner reads. Then look at page 140 and read the numbers to your partner.

4a **Fractions and percentages** Match the words (1–4) with the numbers (a–d).

1 a half   a ¼
2 a third   b ⅕
3 a quarter   c ½
4 a fifth   d ⅓

4b Now match the fractions in Exercise 4a with these percentages.

1 twenty percent (20%) =
2 fifty percent (50%) =
3 thirty-three point three percent (33.3%) =
4 twenty-five percent (25%) =

4c Write these numbers as percentages.

1 100 out of 1,000
2 50 out of 150
3 12 out of 24
4 50 out of 250
5 30 out of 200
6 75 out of 500

WRITING SKILLS
A DESCRIPTION OF A TABLE OR BAR CHART

5 Look at the table below (Figure 1) and complete these sentences.

1 Fifteen percent of _____ and _____ play sport eighteen days a month.
2 A quarter of _____ play sport two days a month.
3 A fifth of _____ play sport twelve days a month.
4 Fifteen _____ of women play sport twelve days a month.
5 A _____ of men play sport twenty-four days a month.
6 Thirty percent of women play sport _____ days a month.

Figure 1: People in Scotland: days of sport a month

	men	women
two days a month	20%	25%
six days a month	15%	20%
12 days a month	20%	15%
18 days a month	15%	15%
24 days a month	25%	30%

Adapted from: Scotland's People Annual Report: results from 2011 Scottish Household Survey

6 Now work with a partner to exchange information and complete another table.

Student A: Look at page 133. Tell your partner your information, then listen and complete the table.
Student B: Look at page 134. Listen and complete the table, then tell your partner your information.

7 **Approximation** What do these expressions mean? Choose the correct answer.

1 over 50%   a 49%   b 50%   c 51%
2 nearly 80%   a 78%   b 80%   c 85%
3 exactly 60%   a 59%   b 60%   c 61%
4 about 70%   a 70.4% b 70%   c 75%

STUDY AND WRITING SKILLS 4.4

8a Look at the bar chart (Figure 2) and complete these sentences. When you know the subject, you do not have to repeat *of men* or *of women*.

Men
1 Nearly _____% of men go swimming.
2 About _____% go cycling.

Women
3 Exactly _____% of women go swimming.
4 Over _____% go cycling.

8b Use the chart in Figure 2 to complete these sentences with the words in the box.

over (x2)   exactly (x1)   nearly (x2)   about (x1)

Men
1 _____ 20% do gym activities.
2 _____ 15% go tenpin bowling.
3 _____ 10% go jogging.

Women
4 _____ 20% do gym activities.
5 _____ 15% go tenpin bowling.
6 _____ 10% go jogging.

9a Using topic knowledge Figure 3 shows popular cultural events for adults in Scotland. Complete the table below with the percentage of people that go to each type of event, using the numbers in the box. Compare with a partner, then check on page 135.

31   21   17   6   27   28   54   5

Go to the cinema	____ %
Go to the theatre	____ %
Go to art exhibitions	____ %
Go to the opera and classical-music concerts	____ %
Go to museums	____ %
Go to dance events and ballet	____ %
Go to live pop and rock events	____ %
Go to historical places	____ %

9b Write sentences to describe the table above. Use language from Exercise 8.

Over half of people go to …

10a Ask ten different students about four or five of the leisure activities in Exercise 9a. Make a note of their answers.

Do you ever go to the cinema?
Do you ever go … ?

10b Write sentences to describe the information that you get.

Over 50% of the students go to the cinema.

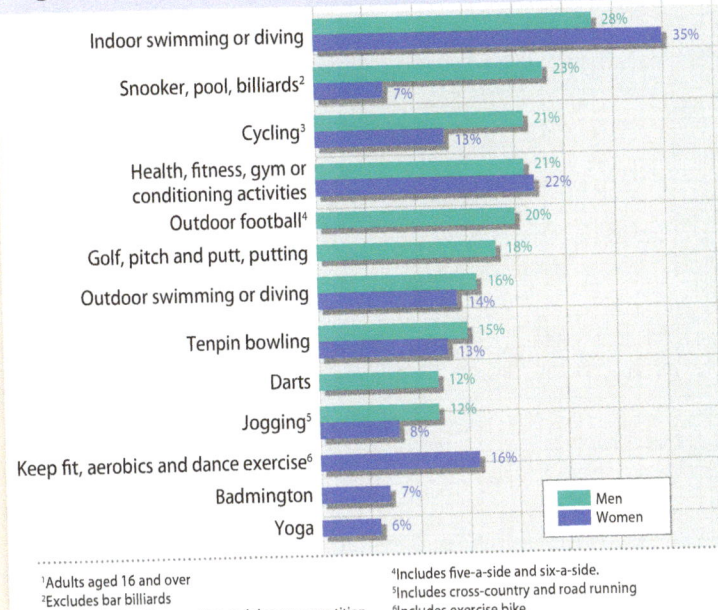

Figure 2: Adults in England: top active sports[1], 2007/08

[1] Adults aged 16 and over
[2] Excludes bar billiards
[3] Includes for health, recreation, training or competition
[4] Includes five-a-side and six-a-side.
[5] Includes cross-country and road running
[6] Includes exercise bike

Source: Taking Part: The National Survey of Culture, Leisure and Sport, Department for Culture, Media and Sport

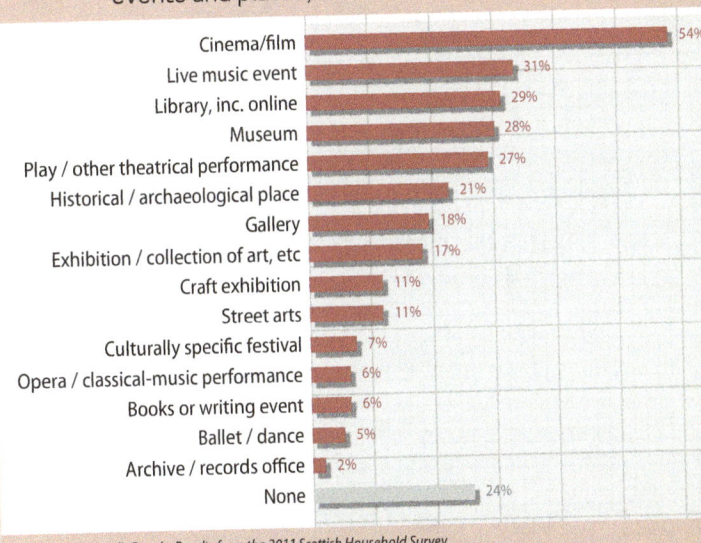

Figure 3: Adults in Scotland: popular cultural events and places, 2011

Source: Scotland's People: Results from the 2011 Scottish Household Survey

5 Transport

5.1 SPEED

IN THIS UNIT

GRAMMAR
- comparative adjectives
- superlative adjectives

VOCABULARY
- transport
- air travel

SCENARIO
- buying a ticket
- booking a flight

STUDY SKILLS
- planning your written work

WRITING SKILLS
- description (a transport system)

A

'O! for a horse with wings.' William Shakespeare, 1564–1616, British playwright

VOCABULARY
TRANSPORT

1a Match the means of transport in the box with the verbs (1–4) below.

| bike | boat | bus | car | lorry | motorbike | plane |
| ship | taxi | (underground/metro) | train | tram | ferry |

1 to travel/go by *bike, boat …*   3 to ride
2 to drive *a bus, a car …*   4 to fly

1b Which means of transport do you use? Which do you like/not like?

I usually travel by bus because buses are cheap.
I don't like motorbikes because they're noisy.

READING

2 Match the means of transport 1–5 with photos A–E.

1 high-speed train   4 passenger ship
2 sports car   5 private plane
3 passenger plane

3 Match the means of transport in Exercise 2 with these speeds. Then read the article and check.

a 56km/h *4*   d 486km/h
b 972km/h   e 903km/h
c 430km/h

📶 ONICO 🛜   09.22   76% 🔋

Question of the day

How fast can I travel? What are the top speeds I can go by sea, on land or in the sky?

Answer:

You're obviously in a hurry! Let's start with travelling on land. Modern cars can go very fast – the Bugatti Veyron Supersport has a top speed of about 430km/h, but there's a speed limit on the majority of motorways, so you can only drive at around 120km/h.

Trains are usually faster than cars. The Chinese high-speed train (CRH380A) can go at 486km/h, but it usually travels at a slower speed of 380km/h. You can take this train from Beijing to Shanghai – a journey of about five hours.

Of course, planes are faster than cars or trains. The Airbus A350 travels at about 900km/h – fast, but slower than the Cessna Citation X. This flies at 972km/h – but it's quite small and only carries a maximum of nine passengers.

But life isn't all about speed. Ships are a nice, easy way of travelling. They're slow – even a fast passenger ship reaches only 56km/h – but they're more comfortable and more relaxing than other means of transport. Isn't that sometimes important, too?

38

4 Tick (✓) the information you can find in the article.
1 We can't drive at 150km/h on the majority of motorways. ✓
2 The name of the Chinese high-speed train is the CRH380A.
3 The journey from Beijing to Shanghai takes about five hours.
4 The Airbus A350 can carry between 250 and 350 passengers.
5 Both the Airbus A350 and the Cessna Citation X can go at over 850km/h.
6 Travelling by sea is slow.

GRAMMAR
COMPARATIVE ADJECTIVES

5 We use comparative adjectives to compare one person or thing with another person or thing.

*Planes are **faster than** trains or cars.*

Complete the table with adjectives from the article.

adjective	comparative	
slow	¹ *slower*	
fast	² _____	
³ _____	nicer	
⁴ _____	easier	than
⁵ _____	more modern	
relaxing	⁶ _____	
comfortable	⁷ _____	

GRAMMAR TIP
A few common comparatives are irregular.
good → better; bad → worse
Note: for more spelling changes in comparative adjectives, see page 110.

➥ Language reference and extra practice, pages 110–111

6 Complete these sentences with the comparative form of the adjective in brackets.
1 Plane travel is _____ than car travel. (safe)
2 The Suez Canal is _____ than the Panama Canal. (long)
3 Buses are _____ in London than in São Paulo. (expensive)
4 Lorries are _____ in the USA than in the UK. (big)
5 Chicago O'Hare Airport is _____ than Paris Charles de Gaulle Airport. (busy)

PRONUNCIATION

7a 5.1 Vowel sounds Listen to the sentences in Exercise 6. What is the vowel sound in *than*?

7b Work with a partner. Make comparisons with these prompts. Be careful with the pronunciation of *than*.
1 trains / planes / cheap
2 planes / motorbikes / noisy
3 motorbikes / ships / exciting
4 bikes / cars / safe
5 trams / buses / common

SPEAKING

8 Collaboration Work with a partner. You want to buy a new car. Look at the information below and compare the cars. Use the adjectives in the box. Which car do you want?

| big | cheap | comfortable | expensive | fast |
| good | high | low | nice | safe | slow | small |

The Hyundai is faster than the Skoda.

Hyundai i10
Top speed 169km/h
Price £8,345
Size 3.6m x 1.6m
Comfort ★★★★
Safety ★★★★
CO_2 emissions 108g/km

Skoda Citigo
Top speed 159km/h
Price £7,720
Size 3.6m x 1.6m
Comfort ★★★★½
Safety ★★★★★
CO_2 emissions 105g/km

5.2 CITY TRANSPORT

READING

1 Read the article about urban transport in one minute. Match photos A–E with the cities in the article.

2 Read the article again. Which facts do these numbers refer to? Complete each sentence below with a word from the article.

| 3.6 million | 468 | 200 | 20 million | 2.4 billion |

1. the number of passengers a year on the Moscow _____ system
2. the length in kilometres of the St Petersburg _____ system
3. the number of stations on the New York City _____ system
4. the number of passengers a year on New York's Staten Island _____
5. the number of passengers a day at Shinjuku _____ station

3 Are these sentences true or false?
1. London is smaller than Moscow.
2. New York's metro system is smaller than some others.
3. People do not know about the buses in London.
4. London's underground trains are cheap.
5. There are many passengers in Tokyo's metro stations.

big bigger biggest

urban transport around the world

Great cities need good transport systems. Which cities have the best systems?

Moscow needs a good transport system because it is the largest city in Europe. The metro is the busiest system in Europe (2.4 billion passengers per year) and the stations are perhaps the most beautiful. Another Russian city, St Petersburg, is called a 'City of Trams' because it has Eastern Europe's longest tram system – over 200km long.

New York is a city that is famous for its size – the population is larger, the buildings are taller and the sandwiches are bigger than in many other cities. It has the world's biggest metro system (with 468 stations), the world's largest station (Grand Central with 44 platforms) and the busiest ferry in the world. The Staten Island ferry carries 20 million people past the Statue of Liberty every year.

London has perhaps the most famous buses in the world – the red double-deckers. It also has a good metro (or underground) system, and it is the oldest in the world. Unfortunately, it is also the most expensive in the world.

Many people think that public transport in Tokyo is the best in the world. It is certainly very busy and always crowded. In fact, the busiest train station in the world is Shinjuku Station, central Tokyo, with 3.6 million passengers a day.

CITY TRANSPORT

5.2

GRAMMAR
SUPERLATIVE ADJECTIVES

4a Match sentences 1–3 with a–c. Do we use superlative adjectives to compare one thing with another thing, or with several things in a group?
1 New York has the world's biggest station.
2 The London Underground is the oldest metro system in the world.
3 The London Underground is the most expensive metro system in the world.

a It's older than all the others.
b It's more expensive than all the others.
c It's larger than all the others.

4b Complete the table with superlatives from the article.

adjective	superlative
old	the [1] _____
large	the [2] _____
big	the [3] _____
busy	the [4] _____
famous	the [5] _____
beautiful	the [6] _____
good	the [7] _____
bad	the [8] *worst*

➔ Language reference and extra practice, pages 110–111

5a Use the table to complete the sentences about three metro systems.

metro system	New York	London	Tokyo
length (km)	337	402	195
ticket price ($)	2.42	7.34	2.46
age (first trains)	1904	1863	1927

Length (*long/short*)

The metro system in New York is [1] *longer* than the metro in Tokyo, but the London Underground is [2] _____ system of the three.

The metro system in New York is [3] _____ than the metro in London, but the Tokyo metro is [4] _____ system of the three.

5b Write pairs of sentences for the other information in the table.
- price (*expensive/cheap*)
- age (*old/modern*)

6 Work with a partner. Write the superlative form of the adjectives in the box. Then ask and answer questions about your country or city.

busy   comfortable   dangerous   exciting
fast   safe   slow

What's the fastest means of transport in Milan?

LISTENING

7a 5.2 Listen to three people talking about how they get around their cities. Choose the correct answers.

person	city	transport to college/work	journey to college/work
1 Mei	Beijing / Nanjing	motorbike / bus / metro / electric bike	30 minutes / 13 minutes
2 Fuad	Khartoum / Cairo	car / bus / metro	1 hour / 1 hour 30 minutes
3 Sandra	Amsterdam / Anderlecht	tram / boat / bike / motorbike	20 minutes / 12 minutes

7b Listen again. Which city/cities does each sentence describe? Check your answers with Audio script 5.2 on page 150.
1 The metro system is small.   *Beijing* and _____
2 The buses are busy.   _____ and _____
3 Bikes are popular.   _____ and _____
4 The metro is a nice way to travel. _____
5 Some people travel by boat.   _____

SPEAKING

8 Work in groups to answer these questions.
- How do you go to work, college or university?
- How long does your journey take?
- Can you use different means of transport?
- What's the best way to get around your town/city?

WRITING

9 Evaluation Write a paragraph about transport and travelling around your town/city. Use Audio script 5.2 on page 150 to help you.

The best way to get around Paris is the metro, because ...

▶ **MEET THE EXPERT**

Watch an interview with Chloe Couchman, an expert on London tourism, about getting around a famous city.
Turn to page 128 for video activities.

5.3 SCENARIO
AT A TICKET AGENCY

PREPARATION

1 Match sentences 1–4 with sentences a–d with a similar meaning.

1 The flight takes ten hours.
2 The plane departs at 17.00.
3 The arrival time is 17.00.
4 The price of the ticket is €500.

a The plane leaves at five o'clock.
b The ticket costs €500.
c The flight is ten hours long.
d The plane lands at 5 p.m.

2 **5.3** Complete the sentences below with the words in the box. Listen and check your answers.

| aisle | business | in-flight | return | standard | window |

1 I'd like a _return_ ticket to Rio, please.
2 I usually travel in _____ class, but sometimes my company pays and then I fly _____ class.
3 This airline has really good _____ service.
4 I always ask for a _____ seat. I love the view of the clouds.
5 I always ask for an _____ seat because I've got long legs!

PRONUNCIATION

3a **Stress in compound nouns** Listen again and underline the word with the strongest stress in each compound noun.

1 <u>return</u> ticket
2 standard class, business class
3 in-flight service
4 window seat
5 aisle seat

3b Practise saying the sentences with a partner. Check your partner's pronunciation.

4 Read the airline adverts and answer the questions.

1 Which airline is the cheapest?
2 Which airline has the best in-flight service?
3 Which airline has the most frequent flights?

TopAir
We give you more than other airlines

Full meal and drinks service
In-flight films and video games
In-flight head-massage service (extra charge)
Bigger seats and more leg room
We fly three times a week to all our destinations.

International Budget Air **IBA**

20% cheaper than other airlines.
How do we do it?
We have limited in-flight service:
• free snacks, extra charge for meals and drinks
• in-flight radio, extra charge for video films
We fly twice a week to each destination.

Low-cost airline of the year

Everything you want from an international airline

• Daily flights to all destinations
• Standard in-flight service
• Hot and cold meals
• Snacks
• Full drinks service
• In-flight films

OzAir

5 [5.4] Kasia wants to fly to New York from Australia. She phones a travel agent and asks for information about different flights. Listen and complete the table.

	Oz Air	Top Air
departs	8 a.m.	
arrives		5 p.m.
length	14 hours	
price		
in-flight service	good / very good / excellent	good / very good / excellent

6a [5.5] Which flight does Kasia decide to book, do you think? Listen to the rest of the conversation and check.

6b Listen again and complete this booking form.

```
Full name:     Kasia Kaplinska
From:  Sydney          To:  New York
Airline:       1_____
Departure date: 2_____   Return date: 3_____
Class:         4_____   Seat:         5_____
Payment method: 6_____
```

KEY LANGUAGE
BUYING A TICKET

7a [5.6] Complete these questions and write answers for the two airlines. Then listen and check.

1 When _____ it leave?
2 When _____ it arrive?
3 How _____ does it take?
4 How _____ does it cost?
5 _____ it a good airline?

7b Write the travel agent's questions for 1–6 on the booking form in Exercise 6b. Look at Audio script 5.5 on page 151 and check your ideas.

1 Which airline would you like to travel with?

8 Practise the conversation with a partner. Remember the pronunciation of compound nouns.

TASK
BOOKING A FLIGHT

9 Work with a partner and make a phone call between a business person and a travel agent.

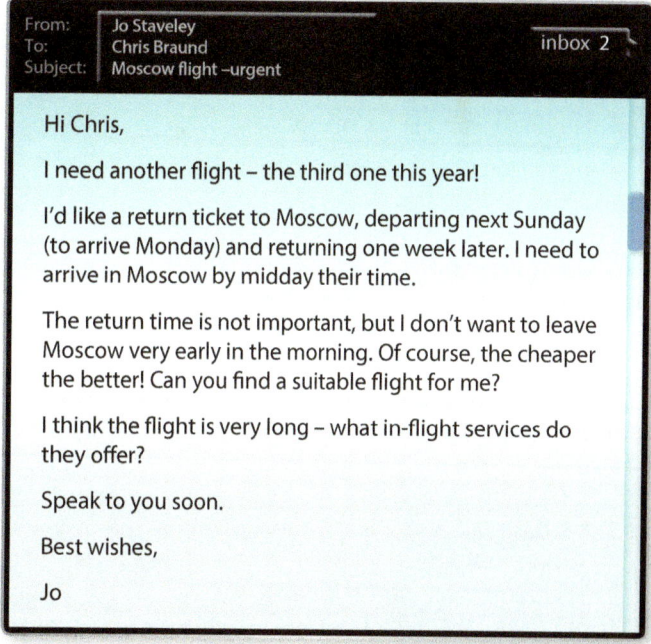

Student A: You are Jo, the business person. You live in Sydney, Australia. Read your email (below) to the travel agent and underline the important information. Then phone the travel agent and take notes of the information. Choose the best flight and make a booking.

Student B: You are Chris, the travel agent. Read the email below from a frequent customer. Look at the timetable and information on page 135 and follow the instructions.

```
From:    Jo Staveley
To:      Chris Braund                          inbox 2
Subject: Moscow flight – urgent

Hi Chris,

I need another flight – the third one this year!

I'd like a return ticket to Moscow, departing next Sunday
(to arrive Monday) and returning one week later. I need to
arrive in Moscow by midday their time.

The return time is not important, but I don't want to leave
Moscow very early in the morning. Of course, the cheaper
the better! Can you find a suitable flight for me?

I think the flight is very long – what in-flight services do
they offer?

Speak to you soon.

Best wishes,

Jo
```

USEFUL PHRASES

Customer	Travel agent
Can you tell me about … ?	Would you like … ?
How much does … ?	How would you like
When does … ?	to pay?
I'd like to …	
How long does … ?	

5.4 STUDY AND WRITING SKILLS

STUDY SKILLS
PLANNING YOUR WRITTEN WORK

1a Stages in writing Look at these stages in a piece of writing. Number them in the order you do them.

a Do a draft. ☐
b Join ideas together. ☐
c Read and understand the question or task. ☐
d Do a final copy. ☐
e Make changes and add new ideas to your draft. ☐
f Think of ideas and write them down. ☐
g Put ideas in the best order. ☐

1b Compare your order with a partner. Is it the same or different?

1c Self-evaluation Do you usually do these things when you write? Which things do you miss out? Why?

2 Organising information Look at these sentences about transport in Italy. Match them with the headings in the box.

| Air | General information | Rail |
| Road | Sea | |

1 People drive on the right.
2 Modern, comfortable trains run from one big city to another.
3 The speed limit is 50km/h in towns.
4 There are about eight important airports.
5 Italy has a very good transport system.
6 The Fréjus tunnel for cars and lorries runs for 13 kilometres under the Alps between France and Italy.
7 There are flights between most cities.
8 The longest underground railway, or metro, is in Milan.
9 Italy has about six major ports.
10 It has one of the best motorway systems in Europe.
11 Leonardo da Vinci is the name of an airport in Rome.
12 The biggest sea port is Genoa.
13 There are excellent links both within Italy and with other countries.

3 Word webs Use word webs to organise information in a visual way. This helps you remember the information. Use the word web below to record the information from Exercise 2.

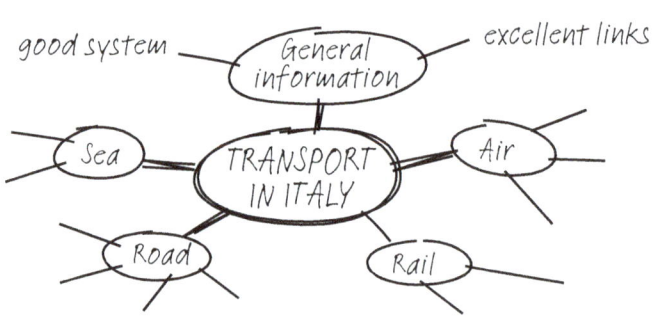

4a Work with a partner. Discuss the questions about transport in your area, your country or somewhere you both know well.
1 Is the transport system good?
2 What is the most popular way to travel?
3 How many big ports, airports or railway stations are there? Which is the biggest?
4 Which means of transport is the most expensive?
5 Are motorways free?
6 What is the speed limit on roads?

4b Now make a word web with the information from Exercise 4a.

STUDY AND WRITING SKILLS 5.4

WRITING SKILLS
DESCRIPTION (A TRANSPORT SYSTEM)

5 Paragraphs What is a paragraph? Look at these statements from students. Which are correct?
1 'You use paragraphs when you speak or write.'
2 'A paragraph is a group of sentences.'
3 'It's about one topic.'
4 'It's usually part of a long piece of writing.'
5 'It starts on a new line.'
6 'You use it when you jump from a plane.'

6 Read the text *Transport in India* quickly and match paragraphs 1–3 with these headings.
a Rail transport   b Road transport   c Introduction to the topic

7a Topic sentences The topic sentence of a paragraph tells us the topic of the paragraph. It is usually the first sentence in the paragraph. Underline the topic sentences in paragraphs 2 and 3 of the text.

7b Read this paragraph from the text, then choose the best topic sentence below (a–d).

> ⁴ There are a lot of boats and ships on the big rivers like the River Ganges. These boats carry people, animals, food and goods. Some people live on boats and catch fish to eat.

a Kanyakumari is in India.
b Indians make long journeys by boat.
c In some parts of India, river transport is important.
d Rivers in India are often dirty.

8 Ordering ideas Look at these sentences about air transport in India. Put them in the best order to make a paragraph.
a There are over 20 international airports.
b Indira Gandhi International Airport (Delhi) is the biggest international airport.
c Air transport is more important now than in the past.

9 Linkers We use *but* when we add different or surprising information to a sentence. Underline the examples of *but* in paragraph 2 of the text.

10 Each sentence below has too many *buts*. Correct the mistakes.
1 Flights in India are expensive but they're cheaper but at night.
2 On Italian motorways, but the speed limit is 130km/h but it's 50km/h in towns.
3 In Mexico, buses are cheap but long journeys can take but more than 24 hours.

11 Write three paragraphs about transport in your country or area. Use your notes from Exercise 4b and the text *Transport in India* to help you.

Transport in India

¹ India is a very large country with a population of over one billion people. There are very long distances between places. Different kinds of transport move people hundreds of kilometres every day.

² The most popular way to travel in India is by road, and there are over 4,200,000 kilometres of roads. India now has new roads, but there are still problems with road transport. The new roads aren't near a lot of the villages. Also, a lot of people are poor and cannot buy cars. Buses are very popular, but they are often very crowded.

³ The railway system carries more than 25 million people every day. The longest train journey is 4,286 kilometres and it goes from Dibrugarh in the north-east to Kanyakumari in the south. It takes 82 hours and there are 56 stops.

⁴ There are a lot of boats and ships on the big rivers like the River Ganges. These boats carry people, animals, food and goods. Some people live on boats and catch fish to eat.

6 Food

6.1 SUPER FOOD

IN THIS UNIT

GRAMMAR
- countable and uncountable nouns
- *some* and *any*
- *much, many, a lot of*

VOCABULARY
- food and drink

SCENARIO
- requests and offers
- making an order

STUDY SKILLS
- correcting your writing

WRITING SKILLS
- a restaurant review

'An empty belly is the best cook.' Estonian proverb

VOCABULARY
FOOD AND DRINK

1a Look at the photographs. Which things in the box can you see?

bananas   bread   broccoli   carrots
garlic   green tea   milk   noodles
nuts   olive oil   red peppers   oranges
rice   salmon   sardines   strawberries

1b Look again at the words above. Find the things below.
1 two things you can drink
2 two kinds of fish
3 four vegetables
4 three kinds of fruit
5 three things you often eat
6 two things you never (or almost never) eat or drink

READING

2 *Super food* is food that is very good for your health. Read the article. Which super food do you eat?

SUPER FOOD DO YOU EAT IT?

Eat the right food and you can be healthier. But what is the best food?

Berries, such as blueberries and <u>strawberries</u>, are the number-one fruit. **They**'re good for your heart and for your memory. They also fight <u>illnesses</u> such as cancer. For vitamin C, eat an <u>orange</u> every day.

Some vegetables are super food. Broccoli is a good example. It's high in vitamin C and it fights cancer.

<u>Carrots</u> are rich in vitamin A and **this** is good for your skin. Eat <u>garlic</u> often because **it**'s a natural medicine.

It's important to eat a lot of <u>nuts</u> because they're good for your memory. <u>Oily fish</u>, such as salmon and sardines, is very good for your heart. <u>Olive oil</u> is also good for **it**.

Lastly, are there any super drinks? Well, green tea is certainly **one**. A nice cup of green tea after your meal is good for your health and it can protect you from illnesses. Finally, don't forget to drink a lot of <u>water</u>. It doesn't have any <u>vitamins</u>, it doesn't give you any energy, but it's very important for you.

Next time you go shopping, check your basket for these types of food. Eat some super food and live longer.

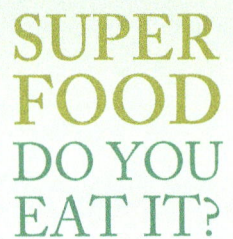

46

SUPER FOOD

6.1

3 Read the article again and complete these sentences with the correct food. You can use each kind of food more than once.
1. Oranges, _____ and _____ have a lot of vitamins.
2. Berries and _____ are good for your brain.
3. Berries, _____, _____ and _____ are good for your heart.
4. _____, _____, _____ and _____ fight illnesses.

4 Understanding reference Look at the article again and answer these questions.
1. In line 4, what does *They* mean? *berries*
2. In line 11, what does *this* mean? _____
3. In line 12, what does *it* mean? _____
4. In line 17, what does *it* mean? _____
5. In line 19, what does *one* mean? _____

GRAMMAR
COUNTABLE AND UNCOUNTABLE NOUNS; *SOME* AND *ANY*

5a Nouns can be countable or uncountable. Look at the example nouns in bold and write *countable* or *uncountable* above the grammar rules in the table.

Countable

Berries are the number-one fruit.

Some *vegetables* are super food.

Are there any super *drinks*?

A cup of green *tea* is good for your health.

Uncountable

Broccoli is high in vitamin C.

It doesn't give you any *energy*.

Eat some super *food* and live longer.

1_____ nouns …	2_____ nouns …
can have *a/an* in front of them.	do not have *a/an* in front of them.
have a plural form.	do not have a plural form.
can have *some* or *any* in front of the plural.	only use singular verbs.
	can have *some* or *any* in front of them.

→ Language reference and extra practice, pages 112–113

5b Read the examples in Exercise 5a again. Complete these grammar rules with *some* or *any*.
1. We use _____ in affirmative sentences.
2. We use _____ in negative sentences.
3. We (usually) use _____ in questions.

6 Look at the underlined words in the article. Which are countable and which are uncountable?

strawberries – countable

7 Complete these sentences with the correct form of the noun and the verb in brackets.
1. *Milk is* very important for babies. (milk + *to be*)
2. A _____ more vitamins than an orange. (red pepper + *to have*)
3. _____ good for your health. (fruit + *to be*)
4. Some _____ vitamin C. (vegetable + *to have*)
5. Some _____ bad for your health. (food + *to be*)
6. _____ any vitamins. (water + *not to have*)

GRAMMAR TIP
Some nouns can be countable and uncountable, with different meanings.

a tomato   some tomatoes   some tomato

SPEAKING

8 Work with a partner. Find differences in your pictures of food.

Student A: Look at the picture on page 137.
Student B: Look at the picture on page 139.

9 Work in groups and discuss the questions below. Use words from Exercise 1 and in the box.

cakes and biscuits	chicken	chocolate	coffee
crisps	fast food	ice cream	meat	pasta
pizza	potatoes			

1. What food do you usually/sometimes eat for breakfast? (lunch? dinner?)
2. What kinds of food and drink do you really like/dislike?
3. What healthy/unhealthy food do you eat?
4. Who has the healthiest diet?

47

6.2 FOOD CULTURE

READING

1 Look quickly at the blog extract. In which part (A–D) do you find information about these things?

1 fruit
2 a special occasion
3 the blogger's future plans
4 a drink

2 Read the blog again. Are these sentences true or false?

1 The blogger eats about twenty bananas a week.
2 The blogger likes cooked bananas.
3 Tea is not popular in Ethiopia.
4 Ethiopians like sweet coffee.
5 In Nigeria, the baby eats all the food at the ceremony.
6 Kola nuts mean the baby lives to an old age.

A My Great Food Adventure

Welcome to my blog. I am travelling to many different countries to find new food and dishes for a restaurant I want to open in London. At the moment I am in Africa.

B

Uganda Brilliant bananas

There are many types of banana in East Africa – over 200! I guess it's no surprise that people eat a lot of them here. In Britain, I don't eat many bananas, perhaps one or two a week. How many do they eat here? About twenty a week! In Uganda, they eat a lot of cooked bananas, and they're really tasty.

Read more >>

Ethiopia Coffee culture in the birthplace of coffee

Here, they don't drink much tea, but they do drink a lot of coffee. There's a special coffee ceremony and it takes a lot of time to make the coffee. How much time? Three hours! The ceremony starts with the washing of the green coffee beans and finishes with many cups of lovely, strong coffee. Not a lot of people add sugar to their coffee, but many people add salt!

Read more >>

D

Nigeria Baby-naming ceremony

At this ceremony, there's a lot of food, but it isn't all for the guests. They give seven types of food to the baby to bring it a good future. The baby doesn't eat much of this special food because the mother just touches the food to the baby's lips. Each type of food has a special meaning. Salt brings the baby a lot of happiness. Kola nuts give it a long life, and dried fish means …

Read more >>

FOOD CULTURE 6.2

GRAMMAR
MUCH, MANY, A LOT OF

3a Look at the blog and underline examples of *much*, *many* and *a lot of*.

3b Look at the words you underlined and complete these grammar rules.
1. We use _____ and _____ with countable nouns.
2. We use _____ and _____ with uncountable nouns.
3. We can use _____ and _____ in both affirmative and negative sentences. (But *many* is quite formal in affirmative sentences – we don't use it very often.)
4. We usually use _____ in negative sentences and questions, but not in affirmative sentences.

4 Complete these sentences with *much*, *many* or *a lot of*. Make two different sentences if you can.
1. Every week, Ugandans eat _____ fruit.
2. How _____ coffee does Ethiopia make?
3. In Uganda, they make _____ different dishes with bananas.
4. How _____ different things does the baby taste in the ceremony?
5. In the countryside, they don't eat _____ chocolate.
6. In the countryside, there aren't _____ modern cafés.

GRAMMAR TIP
We use *much*, *many* and *a lot of* in questions. But we do not use *a lot of* in questions with *how*.
How much money do you have?
How many people are there in the room?

➜ Language reference and extra practice, pages 112–113

5 Complete these questions. Sometimes you can make two questions. Then ask a partner the questions.
1. How _____ coffee do you drink?
2. How _____ bananas do you eat in a week?
3. Do you drink _____ water every day?
4. Do you eat _____ vegetables in a week?
5. Do you have _____ free time every day?
6. Have you got _____ things to do this weekend?

LISTENING

6 6.1 The blogger, Miranda, interviews a South African about his country's food culture. Listen to the interview. Tick (✓) the food that you hear.

beans   beef   chicken   corn   curry
desserts   kebabs   lamb   rice cakes
sausages   tomatoes   vegetables

7 Listen again and complete the notes.

What is traditional food in South Africa?
Food from different cultures: 1_____, Portugal, Holland, 2_____, Asia.
Biltong is dried 3_____.
Peri Peri is a spicy 4_____ dish.
5_____ comes from India.

Are there any traditional drinks?
Rooibos is a 6_____ tea.
It is 7_____ and popular.

Is food important in people's social lives?
Barbecue parties: every 8_____, friends and 9_____.

Is food important at festivals and ceremonies?
First-fruit ceremony: people eat 10_____.
Baby-naming ceremony: people eat 11_____ cakes.
National Barbecue Day: September 12_____

SPEAKING AND WRITING

8a **Long turn taking** Prepare to talk about the food culture in your country. Use Miranda's questions to help you prepare. Make notes.

8b With a partner, talk about the food culture in your country/countries.

9 Write about your country's food culture.

▶ **MEET THE EXPERT**
Watch an interview with Nikita Gulhane, an Indian food expert, about Indian food traditions.
Turn to page 128 for video activities.

6.3 SCENARIO
CONFERENCE CATERING

PREPARATION

1 Match the kinds of food (1–8) with the photos above (A–H). Then match them with the different countries (a–h).

1 sushi
2 pasta
3 noodles
4 curry
5 lamb kebab
6 couscous
7 caviar
8 chilli con carne

a Italy
b China
c India
d Russia
e Japan
f Morocco
g Turkey
h Mexico

2 Read the flyer below for an academic conference. Choose the best answers.

1 What is the subject of the conference?
  a The food industry
  b Food and culture
2 Who is the event for?
  a students and lecturers from Canada
  b students and lecturers from all over the world

FOOD – IDENTITY ON A PLATE
International Conference, City University, Toronto, Canada

- How does food make national identities?
- Is fast food the end of national food?
- What is international food?

100 places available

Speakers include:
Dr Mohammed Aziz (University of Cairo)
Prof. Jacques Rivette (The Sorbonne, Paris)

KEY LANGUAGE
REQUESTS AND OFFERS

3 6.2 Tariq is the conference organiser. He phones a catering company and orders the food for the conference. Listen and write his order in the 'Tariq' column on the order form on page 51.

4 Listen again and complete these sentences from the conversation.

1 Could we _____ fifty chicken salads, please?
2 _____ we have fifty cheese salads, then?
3 For dessert, we'd _____ a hundred ice creams and fifty apple pies.
4 Would you _____ some water or fruit juice?
5 _____ we have … some small bottles of apple juice?
6 _____ you like some coffee?

5 Look at the sentences in Exercise 4 and answer these questions.

1 Which sentences are requests, and which are offers?
2 Which is more polite, *could* or *can*?
3 Do we use *some* or *any* in offers and requests?

6 6.3 Put the words in the right order to make offers and requests. Then listen and check. Which are offers, and which are requests?

1 send / Could / some / me / coffee / you / ?
2 I'd / fifty / kebabs, / please / like / lamb / .
3 Can / water, / we / bottles / have / forty / please / of / ?
4 like / Would / you / bread / some / ?
5 chicken / like / salads, / please / We'd / some / .

6.3 CONFERENCE CATERING

PRONUNCIATION

7a 🔊 6.4 **Intonation** Listen to the two requests. Which one is more polite?
1. Could you send me some coffee?
2. Could you send me some tea?

7b It is very important to have polite intonation. Listen again to Audio recording 6.3 and repeat the offers and requests.

8 Which of these are replies to offers? Which are replies to requests?
1. That's no problem.
2. Yes, please.
3. Sure, no problem.
4. No, thank you.
5. No thanks.
6. Certainly.
7. I'm sorry, I'm afraid we haven't got any of those at the moment.

9a Work with a partner. Make the offers and requests from Exercise 6. Only reply when your partner is polite.

9b Look at Audio script 6.2 on page 151 and practise the conversation with your partner.

TASK
MAKING AN ORDER

10a You need to order the food for a conference lunch. There are a hundred people at the conference. Choose the food and complete the 'You' column on the order form.

10b Now work with a partner and role-play the conversation between the conference organiser and the supplier.

Student A: You are the conference organiser. Phone the supplier, Event Catering, and make your order.

Student B: You work for Event Catering, the supplier. Look at your supply list on page 137. Take the order from the conference organiser. Can you supply everything?

10c Change roles. Do the role-play again.

Student A: Now you work for Event Catering. Use your supply list on page 139 and take the order.

Student B: Now you are the conference organiser.

Event Catering Company
Best food, best service

Order form	Quantity	
	Tariq	You
First course		
Tomato and cheese salad Noodle soup Tomato soup		
Main course		
Cheese salad Chicken salad (Chinese-style with noodles) Beef curry (with rice) Lamb kebab (with rice and vegetables) Vegetarian curry (with rice) Vegetarian pizza (tomato, mushroom) Burger meal (chips, onion rings) Sushi meal (fish and vegetarian)		
Desserts		
Chocolate ice cream Apple pie Fruit salad		
Drinks		
Sparkling water Still water Lemonade Orange juice Apple juice		

6.4 STUDY AND WRITING SKILLS

STUDY SKILLS
CORRECTING YOUR WRITING

1a Making mistakes Read these statements. Do you agree with them? Write *yes*, *not sure* or *no*.
1 We all make mistakes when we learn a new language.
2 I don't like making mistakes in front of other students.
3 We can learn to correct our mistakes.
4 It's easier to correct mistakes in writing than in speaking.

1b Learners often make mistakes in grammar, vocabulary and spelling. Which kind do you make the most, do you think?

2 Grammar Correct the mistakes in the words in bold.
1 There **is** about ten eggs in the fridge.
2 Does he **likes** chocolate?
3 The **more** important thing in life is health.
4 They haven't got **many** money.

3 Vocabulary The words in bold below are incorrect. Replace them with the correct words from the box. You don't need all the words.

dish	fish	make	meat	to	two
vegetable	wear				

1 Broccoli and cabbage are kinds of **fruit**.
2 I eat one or **too** bananas every week.
3 We make this **plate** with chicken and beans.
4 Does he often **do** mistakes?

4 Spelling Choose the correct spelling. Then check in your dictionary.
1 I *ofen / often / oftan* eat a banana for lunch.
2 Olive oil is good for your *hart / heart / haert*.
3 Blueberries are good for your *brain / brane / brian*.
4 Are there any *glasses / glasess / glases* on the table?

5 Anh is a student from Vietnam. Her teacher uses a correction code for her work. Correct the mistakes in this piece of work.

Gr = grammar
WW = wrong word (vocabulary)
Sp = spelling

Food in Vietnam <u>are</u> healthy. It's important for food *(Gr)*
to look <u>beatiful</u>, too. We sit at a low <u>tabel</u> and eat *(Sp) (Sp)*
with chopsticks. Most people <u>eats</u> rice three or four *(Gr)*
times every day. Everywhere in Vietnam is near the
<u>see</u> or a river, so we eat a lot of fish. The fish markets *(Sp)*
<u>has</u> <u>difficult</u> kinds of fish. We often eat fish and *(Gr) (WW)*
meat together. We don't eat <u>many</u> cheese or milk. *(Gr)*

STUDY AND WRITING SKILLS 6.4

The Cedar Tree

OK, you like Lebanese food, but you're tired of the same old (and expensive) restaurants. The Cedar Tree can help. It's a new Lebanese restaurant in the city centre.

The place is clean and bright. There are interesting pictures on the red and white walls. The tables are big and the chairs are comfortable.

The meat and vegetable dishes are excellent, but don't forget the fish dishes – they're all fantastic. Finish your meal with a real Lebanese coffee.

The Cedar Tree is popular with local people, business people, students and tourists. After 8 p.m., it's always busy and noisy, but the service is fast and the waiters are friendly.

And the best thing? It's cheap! Two people can eat here for about £30. I think it's a fantastic new restaurant, so get down to The Cedar Tree now for a great Lebanese experience!

WRITING SKILLS
A RESTAURANT REVIEW

6 Discuss these questions with a partner.
1. How often do you go to restaurants?
2. What kinds of restaurant do you like?
3. What's your favourite restaurant?
4. Which restaurant on these pages would you like to go to? Why?

7 Read the review of the restaurant 'The Cedar Tree'. Is it positive or negative? Would you like to eat here? Why?/Why not?

8 The writer describes these things in the review. Number them in the order you read them.

a other customers ☐
b the food (good?/bad?) ☐
c the name of the restaurant 7
d the service/waiters ☐
e the kind of food (nationality?) ☐
f a description of the restaurant ☐
g the location ☐
h the writer's opinion ☐
i the price of the meal ☐

9 *Judging interest* A good review needs a good beginning. Look at these beginnings. Which are the most interesting?
1. There are eighteen French restaurants in the city. Well … nineteen now!
2. This review is about a new French restaurant in the city.
3. Can a new French restaurant be better than our old favourite 'Les Quatre Saisons'?
4. I love French food and I eat it every week.
5. Where's the best French restaurant in the world? In Paris? Or right here, in our city?

10 Look at this sentence from the review. How do we write things in a list?

'The Cedar Tree' is popular with local people, business people, students and tourists.

11 *Commas in lists* Put commas in the correct places in these sentences.
1. I love chips chocolate pizza and ice cream.
2. My favourite cities are Venice Kyoto Edinburgh and Sydney.
3. My favourite subjects are History French and English.
4. I like films ballet pop music and art exhibitions.
5. Our town needs a new shopping centre a bus station a car park a cinema and a swimming pool.

12 Write a review of a restaurant in your town/city. Check your work for grammar, vocabulary and spelling mistakes. Check another student's work, too!

53

7 Shopping
7.1 CONSUMER HABITS

IN THIS UNIT

GRAMMAR
- present continuous (1): affirmatives and negatives
- present continuous (2): questions

VOCABULARY
- shops and shopping: verbs and nouns

SCENARIO
- giving advantages and disadvantages
- describing locations

STUDY SKILLS
- giving a short, informal talk

WRITING SKILLS
- informal writing (a customer review)

'The main thing today is – shopping.' Arthur Miller, 1915–2005, US dramatist

SPEAKING

1 Work with a partner and discuss these questions.
1. Do you like shopping?
2. How often do you buy these things?

books   clothes   DVDs   food   shoes
furniture   make-up   stationery
electronic items (cameras, MP3 players, etc.)

3. What other things do you regularly buy?

READING

2a Assigning headings Read the magazine article and match each person in the photos on the right with a type of shopper.
- the window shopper
- the speed shopper
- the frequent shopper
- the internet shopper

2b Which type are you?

3 Read the article again. Are these sentences true or false?
1. José cannot buy the suit because it is expensive.
2. In her bags, Hiromi has got three things to wear.
3. Ulrike wants to buy a gift for someone.
4. Vince wants to buy a pair of trousers.

What kind of shopper are you?

There are many different types of shopper. These four people are shopping on Oxford Street, London – one of the busiest shopping areas in the world.

José The _____ shopper
Shopping habits: 'I really don't like shopping. I don't spend a lot of time in the shops and I choose things very fast.'
Today: 'At the moment, I'm looking for a new suit. There's a good dark-brown suit in this shop. It's expensive, but I can pay for it by credit card.'

 **Hiromi** The _____ shopper
Shopping habits: 'I go shopping every weekend. I usually buy clothes or things for my house. I love big department stores.'
Today: 'Right now, I'm carrying five new things – a coat, a shirt, a cookery book, a pair of shoes and a belt. Time to go home!'

54

CONSUMER HABITS 7.1

GRAMMAR
PRESENT CONTINUOUS (1)

4a Look at these sentences from the article and answer the questions below.
a Right now, I'm carrying five new things.
b I often shop online.
1 Which sentence describes things that happen again and again? What do we call this tense?
2 Which sentence describes an action that is happening now? What do we call this tense?

4b Find more examples of the present continuous in the article.

4c Complete the table.

subject	to be	verb + -ing
I	¹ _'m_ (am)	
you/we/they	're (² ____)	
he/she/it	's (³ ____)	looking at it.
I	⁴ ____ (am not)	
you/we/they	aren't (are not)	
⁵ ____ / ____ / ____	isn't (⁶ ____)	

→ Language reference and extra practice, pages 114–115

5 7.1 Complete these mobile-phone conversations. Use the present continuous form of the verbs in brackets. Listen and check your answers.
1 I can't talk now, I ____ some trainers. (try on)
2 Call me back later. I ____ . (drive)
3 Can you see me? I ____ at the corner, opposite the bank. (stand)
4 Can I call you back? The waiter ____ for me to order. (wait)
5 We ____ just ____ at the bus station. See you in five minutes. (arrive)
6 I'm in the car park, I ____ the food in the car. (put)

Ulrike The ____ shopper

Shopping habits: 'I often shop online because it saves both money and time. There are usually good bargains online and I don't need to travel to the city.'
Today: 'Tonight, I'm looking for a toy car for my brother's son. At the moment, I'm checking prices on a price comparison website to find a good bargain.'

Vince The ____ shopper
Shopping habits: 'I come to Oxford Street about once a month but I don't usually spend much money. I just like to look at the different things in the shops.'
Today: 'I'm not looking for anything special. Right now, I'm waiting for my friend. She's trying on a pair of jeans.'

6 Complete this paragraph with the correct form (present simple or present continuous) of the verbs in brackets.

Robert The sales shopper
I ¹ ____ (not go) shopping very often, but I always ² ____ (go) to the sales. I ³ ____ (spend) a lot of money in the sales, but I always ⁴ ____ (check) the prices to make sure I get a bargain! The shops ⁵ ____ (hold) their winter sales now, and today I ⁶ ____ (look) for a camera. I ⁷ ____ (think) about buying this one, but I'm not sure – the sales discount ⁸ ____ (be) only 15 percent.

7 7.2 Listen to five short conversations. Work with a partner and describe the situations. Use the phrases in the box.

in a bookshop   in a cinema   in a clothes shop
in a café   in a shoe shop   to ask for   to buy
to order   to try on   to look for

1 He _'s in a shoe shop. He's trying ..._
2 She ____
3 She ____
4 She ____
5 He ____

VOCABULARY
SHOPS AND SHOPPING (1): VERBS

8a Complete the phrases with the verbs in the box.

to buy   to check   to pay for   to go   to spend
to try on

1 ____ a new shirt by cash
2 ____ the prices in different shops
3 ____ clothes shopping
4 ____ £50 on DVDs
5 ____ a new computer on the internet
6 ____ a pair of jeans before you buy them

8b Complete the questions with a verb from Exercise 8a.
1 Do you often ____ clothes shopping?
2 Do you ____ the prices in different shops before you buy something?
3 Do you always ____ clothes before you buy them?
4 Do you often ____ things by credit card?
5 Do you ____ gifts for friends' birthdays?
6 Do you ____ a lot of money on music and movies?

SPEAKING

9 Ask a partner the questions from Exercise 8b. When you answer the questions, give extra information.
A: *Do you often go clothes shopping?*
B: *Yes, I do. I go about twice a month. I enjoy clothes shopping. I usually go to …*

55

7.2 SHOPPING TRENDS

VOCABULARY
SHOPS AND SHOPPING (2): NOUNS

1 Look at these words connected with shopping. Which ones have similar meanings?

customer   discount   products   internet shopping
price   service   (to) shop   goods   store
consumer   online shopping   supermarket

2 Discuss these questions with a partner.
1 Is shopping 'fun' for you? Do you think of it as a 'hobby'?
2 Which stores do you like/dislike? Why?
3 Is customer service important to you? Why?/Why not?

READING

3 Read the article quickly. What is it about?
1 online shopping
2 shopping in stores
3 hobbies
4 interesting experiences

THE CHANGING FACE OF STORES

A Online shopping is growing all the time, but real shops are still very important. In a real shop, you can touch, feel and try things. But these days, customers are also looking for an interesting or exciting experience in stores. For many people, shopping is like a hobby, and they want fun.

B How are stores giving them this experience? For a start, many stores do more than one thing. For example, some bookshops are also cafés. There are computer stores with spaces where you can work on your laptop or tablet.

C In some stores, you can learn how to use the products, and you can also learn new things, like how to cook or take good photos. Stores are also offering customers entertainment, with video and fashion shows. And customer service is improving. Stores are building a more personal relationship with the customer.

D All these things keep customers in the store for a longer time – so they buy more things, and want to visit the store again.

4a Are these statements true or false?
1 More people are shopping online than before.
2 Customers are looking for interesting shopping experiences online.
3 Some computer stores are also cafés.
4 In some stores, you can watch videos and fashion shows.
5 The relationship between customers and stores is more personal now.
6 People spend more time in a store if they have a good experience there.

4b Match the paragraphs (A–D) in the article with these topics.
1 examples of in-store experiences
2 the way that a lot of people think about shopping
3 the results of good in-store experiences
4 stores with two purposes

5a 7.3 Listen to these extracts from the article. Notice the pronunciation, rhythm and use of pauses.

5b Work with a partner.

Student A: Read paragraph B aloud to your partner. Think about the pronunciation, rhythm and use of pauses.
Student B: Listen to your partner. Then comment on the pronunciation, rhythm, etc.

Then change roles. Student B reads paragraph C.

GRAMMAR TIP

We can use the present continuous to talk about a changing situation.
Online shopping is growing all the time.

SHOPPING TRENDS 7.2

LISTENING

6 Discuss these questions with a partner.
1 How do you use the internet for shopping?
2 Do you read customer reviews/comments online before you buy something?
3 Do you use your phone for shopping? How?

7a 7.4 Listen to this discussion. Number the topics in the order you hear them.
a shopping using mobile devices ☐
b a new trend – 'in-line shopping' ☐
c what people are buying online ☐
d reading comments by other customers ☐
e where people are buying things (e.g. clothes) ☐

7b Listen again and complete these notes.

Internet shopping

1 Most popular online items: _____ _____
2 Research: experiences of other _____
3 'In-line shopping': a _____ of in-store and online shopping
4 Mobile devices — useful _____ (e.g. home, trains, offices)
5 More use of mobiles in-store — to look for _____

GRAMMAR
PRESENT CONTINUOUS (2)

8a Complete these questions, then check with Audio script 7.4 on page 152.
1 _____ are people buying?
2 Is _____ growing?
3 How are they _____ the internet?
4 _____ they doing that because it's cheaper?

8b Complete the grammar rules below about the word order in present continuous questions. Use the words in the box.

| after | question | subject | to be |

1 Questions can start with the verb _____ or with a _____ word.
2 The verb *to be* usually comes before the _____ of the question.
3 The main verb + *-ing* comes _____ *to be* and the subject.

➡ Language reference and extra practice, pages 114–115

9 Complete these questions with the words in brackets. Then ask and answer the questions with a partner.
1 _____ a lot these days? (you / travel)
   Yes, I am. I'm going to a lot of new places. / No, I'm not.
2 _____ a lot of English at the moment? (you / learn)
3 _____ much in the evenings? (you / go out)
4 What books _____ at the moment? (people / read)
5 What films _____ at the moment? (people / watch)

SPEAKING

10a Put the words in order to make questions about shopping in your country. Add two more questions if you can.
1 people's shopping habits / changing / are / How / ?
2 young people / What / buying / these days / are / ?
3 big / How much money / making / are / stores / ?
4 doing / What / to get / are stores / business / ?
5 in / What changes / town centres / happening / are / ?
6 the internet / people / How / using / are / ?

10b **Considering trends** Discuss the questions from Exercise 10a in pairs or small groups. Tell the class about your three most interesting ideas.

In my country, big supermarkets are becoming more popular. More people are using them, and small shops are closing down.

7.3 SCENARIO
OPENING A SHOP

PREPARATION

1 Charleston is a beautiful historic town in the south of the US. Match the shopping areas in the photos to these descriptions.

1. In this place, there are many stalls (open-air shops). You can buy fresh food and unusual things here.
2. This is the traditional place for shopping in the town. There are many small shops, cafés and restaurants here.
3. This place is not in the town centre. It has very large car parks and large, often famous, stores.
4. This kind of shopping area is outside the town. There are often motels, supermarkets and petrol stations here.

2 Brad and Zara want to start a small bookshop in Charleston. They want to sell books about film, TV and music. Read information 1–7 in Exercise 3a about downtown Charleston and answer these questions.

1. What are the advantages of this area for their shop?
2. What are the disadvantages?
3. Do you think it is a good place for the shop?

KEY LANGUAGE
GIVING ADVANTAGES AND DISADVANTAGES

3a **7.5** Listen to Brad and Zara talking about their plans for the shop. Tick (✓) the advantages and disadvantages of being downtown that they discuss.

1. It's a nice place. People like to come here.
2. There are interesting local shops: some cafés, an art shop, a music shop.
3. The area is safe – there's not much crime.
4. There aren't any bookshops in the area.
5. It's near the bus station.
6. The rent is high.
7. Many people go to the shopping mall outside the town.

3b Listen again and complete the sentences.

BRAD: So, what advantages does downtown ¹_____?
ZARA: Well, ²_____ of all, I ³_____ it's a nice place for people to visit …
BRAD: OK. Are there any ⁴_____ advantages?
ZARA: Yes, ⁵_____ advantage is that the area is safe.
BRAD: Right. What ⁶_____ the disadvantages?
ZARA: I think there are two ⁷_____ disadvantages.
ZARA: One ⁸_____ is that the rent is high …
ZARA: … and the ⁹_____ is that a lot of people go to the shopping mall outside the town.
ZARA: This ¹⁰_____ that sometimes there aren't very many customers downtown.

street market

downtown Charleston

7.3
OPENING A SHOP

3c Match the sentences in Exercise 3b with these descriptions.
1. asking about advantages/disadvantages
2. giving advantages/disadvantages
3. explaining why something is a disadvantage

PRONUNCIATION

4a [7.6] **Stressed words** In sentences, we stress some words more than others. Listen to Zara's sentences from Exercise 3b and notice the stressed words.
1. Well, first of all, I think it's a nice place for people to visit.
2. Yes, another advantage is that the area is safe.
3. I think there are two main disadvantages.
4. One disadvantage is that the rent is high …
5. … and the other is that a lot of people go to the shopping mall outside the town.
6. This means that sometimes there aren't very many customers downtown.

4b Listen again and repeat.

5 Look at Audio script 7.5 on page 152. Practise the conversation with a partner. Be careful with the stress.

TASK
DESCRIBING LOCATIONS

6a Work in groups of three. You are helping Brad and Zara with the bookshop plans. You are looking at information about different shopping areas.

Student A: Read about the market on page 140 and make notes in the table.
Student B: Read about the highway shopping area on page 142 and make notes in the table.
Student C: Read about the shopping mall on page 144 and make notes in the table.

shopping area	advantages	disadvantages
the market		
the highway shopping area		
the shopping mall		

6b Tell your group your information. Make notes about their information in the table.

7 Discuss the information in your group, using the Key language and the Useful phrases. Decide which is the best shopping area for the bookshop.

USEFUL PHRASES
There are two main advantages …
The first/second is …
The shopping mall is more expensive than the …
This means that …
I think the market is better because …

highway shopping area

shopping mall

7.4 STUDY AND WRITING SKILLS

STUDY SKILLS
GIVING A SHORT, INFORMAL TALK

1a A student is going to give a short talk about Harrods, a department store in London. Do you know anything about this store? Which other department stores do you know?

1b Choosing images The student chooses a background image for his talk. Look at the three images below. Which image do you think the student chooses, and why?

2a Avoiding mistakes These things can be problems when someone gives a talk. What other mistakes can a speaker make when he/she gives a talk?
- looking down at the floor
- looking at just one or two people
- speaking very fast
- wearing old or dirty clothes
- talking for too long

2b ▶ 7 Watch the talk. Check your answer to Exercise 1b. In which order do the other two images appear?

3 Watch the talk again. Tick (✓) the topics he talks about.
1 the building
2 the area
3 what you can buy
4 places to eat
5 store opening and closing times
6 internet shopping

4 Making notes Some people write down every word of their talk. Others make notes. Complete the notes for the talk with these words.

building   department   every   floors   food

HARRODS
- huge 1_____ store – London
- beautiful 2_____ (at night)
- open 3_____ day
- seven 4_____
- can find everything – give examples
- also 5_____ halls + cafés/restaurants (nearly 30) + bank

5 Complete these sentences from the talk. Then watch the talk again to check your answers.
1 In this short talk, I'd like to _____ _____ about my favourite store – Harrods …
2 It's _____ for its fantastic food halls …
3 One of the _____ _____ things is that there's even a bank …
4 To _____, Harrods says it's the best department store in the world.

6 Work with a partner and give a talk on Harrods. Use your notes from Exercise 4 and the phrases in bold in Exercise 5. Then listen to your partner's talk.

7a Preparing a talk Make a list of things we do when we prepare a talk. Match 1–6 with a–f.
1 Put your ideas
2 Check the pronunciation
3 Find out
4 Practise
5 Prepare some pictures or tables
6 Make some

a the talk.
b notes to help you remember things in the talk.
c to make your points clearer.
d in the best order.
e of difficult words.
f some interesting information.

7b Work with a partner and discuss the best order to do the six stages in Exercise 7a.

8 Prepare and give a short talk of about one minute on *My favourite shop* or *The best / worst / most unusual shop in my town/city*. Follow the stages in Exercise 7a.

STUDY AND WRITING SKILLS 7.4

WRITING SKILLS
INFORMAL WRITING (A CUSTOMER REVIEW)

9 Discuss these questions with a partner.
1. Do you ever shop for books? What kind of books do you buy?
2. Are they for you or presents for someone else?
3. Where do you buy them – in a bookshop, in a supermarket or on the internet?

10a Using visual clues Look at the book covers below. Do you know any of them? What do you think they are about?

10b Match the book covers with the customer reviews.

10c Would you like to read any of these books? Why?/Why not?

11 In a customer review of a book, we often read these things. Find examples of them in the reviews.
1. when and where the story happens
2. comments on the story
3. comments on the characters
4. something you can learn from the book
5. something the reader would (or would not) like to do now
6. the reader's general opinion of the book

12a Informal language Two features of informal writing are contractions (e.g. *it's*) and informal vocabulary (e.g. *great*). Find examples in the reviews.

12b Can you find any other features of informal writing in the reviews? Think about pronouns and punctuation.

13 Linkers The words *because* and *so* are linking words (they join two ideas). Find examples in the reviews, then complete these sentences with *because* or *so*.
1. Books are expensive in my country ___ I don't buy many.
2. I like *Matilda* by Roald Dahl ___ it's funny and clever.
3. I love long books ___ I read a lot of Russian novels.
4. I don't read many books ___ I haven't got much free time.

14 Write a customer review of one or two of your favourite books. Use the texts in Exercise 10b to help you. Use contractions and some informal vocabulary.

Soumia rated this book: ★★★★☆
I like this book because the story is beautiful and you learn about Egypt, both in the past and today. She writes in English, but I can hear the influence of her native Arabic. There's a lot of politics in the novel, so sometimes it's a bit difficult. Anyway, I'd love to visit Cairo now. I give this book 7 out of 10.

Andrea rated this book: ★★★★★
Some of his other novels are really strange, but this is different. The story is simple, beautiful and sad – it's about student life in Tokyo in the late '60s. The characters are real and I totally understand them. The ending is brilliant. I'm reading a lot of Japanese novels these days, so I know the good ones – this is one of the best!

Danny rated this book: ★★★★★
This is my favourite novel. It's about family life and love – around 100 years ago in Mexico. The story is interesting because it's a mixture of real life and magic. Food is very important in the book, and you can smell and taste the Mexican dishes! Find a copy and enjoy this great book – but don't read it when you're hungry!

8 History and culture
8.1 PAST TIMES

IN THIS UNIT

GRAMMAR
- past simple of *to be*
- *could, couldn't*

VOCABULARY
- buildings
- verbs + prepositions

SCENARIO
- making polite requests
- finding out important information

STUDY SKILLS
- remembering new words

WRITING SKILLS
- describing objects

'Every day of your life is a page of your history.' Arabic proverb

VOCABULARY
BUILDINGS

1a Work with a partner. Which of these things can you see in the picture of Çatal Hüyük page 63?

courtyard   door   entrance   furniture
garden   gate   ladder   painting
roof   room   wall   window

1b *Making comparisons* How are these buildings different from your home and street?

READING

2a Guess the answers to these questions. Then read paragraph A in the text about Çatal Hüyük and check.

1 This city is in modern-day
 a Iraq.   b Pakistan.   c Turkey.

2 The picture shows the place in about
 a 10,000 BC.   b 6000 BC.   c 2000 BC.

2b Read paragraphs B and C quickly. Which paragraph (A, B or C) has information about these things?

1 location   A
2 houses
3 size of population
4 people

Çatal Hüyük

A Çatal Hüyük (now in Anatolia, Turkey) was one of the world's first cities. In fact, many people think it is the oldest city. It was an important and busy place for 2,000 years, from about 7000 BC to 5000 BC. Compared with today's cities, it wasn't big; in 6250 BC, there were only about 6,000 people there.

B There weren't any streets in the city; most of the houses were around a central courtyard. There weren't any doors in the houses. There was an entrance to each house through a hole in the roof and down a ladder. Inside, there were paintings of animals and people on some of the walls.

C The people of Çatal Hüyük were, we believe, kind and peaceful. Many of them were farmers, but the city was also a centre of trade and ideas. Çatal Hüyük was rich and well organised, but life was very short: an average age of thirty-four years for men and twenty-nine for women. Women were important in this city: many were in high positions and there were a lot of special goddesses.

3 Use the words in the box to complete the summary of the text below.

farming   good   population   place   unusual

Çatal Hüyük was an important ¹_____ about 8,000 years ago, when the ²_____ was about 6,000. The city was one of the first ³_____ communities and also important for trade. People's homes were ⁴_____, but comfortable. Life was ⁵_____ for the people here, but it was also short.

PAST TIMES

8.1

GRAMMAR
PAST SIMPLE OF *TO BE*

4a We use the past simple to talk about events and situations that are finished. Look at these three sentences from the text, then underline more examples of the past simple of *to be* in the text.
1 Çatal Hüyük **was** rich and well organised.
2 The people **were** peaceful.
3 There **weren't** any streets in the city.

4b Complete the table with past simple forms of *to be*.

affirmative (+)	negative (–)	question (?)
I was	I wasn't	was I?
he/she/it ¹_____	he/she/it ⁴_____	was he/she/it?
you were	you weren't	⁸_____ you?
we were	we ⁵_____	were we?
they ²_____	they ⁶_____	were they?
there ³_____	there wasn't	⁹_____ there?
there were	there ⁷_____	were there?

GRAMMAR TIP
In more formal English, *wasn't* → *was not* and *weren't* → *were not*.

➤ Language reference and extra practice, pages 116–117

5 Complete these sentences with *was, wasn't, were* or *weren't*.
1 The people of Çatal Hüyük _____ peaceful.
2 Roman roads are famous – the Romans _____ very good at building them.
3 Who _____ Cleopatra?
4 _____ there any important cities in your country in AD 1000?
5 I _____ good at history at school – it was my worst subject!
6 There _____ a horrible history teacher at my school. Now, what _____ his name?
7 A: You _____ in the lecture on early cities. Where _____ you?
  B: We _____ in the café!

PRONUNCIATION

6a 8.1 Vowel sounds Listen to *was* and *were* in these sentences. What is the vowel sound?
1 The city was lovely.
2 There were gardens everywhere.

6b 8.2 Listen to seven sentences. Then listen again and repeat.

7a Look at these past time phrases. Put them in order, starting with the most recent.

1,000 years ago   last month   last week
last year   six weeks ago   yesterday
the day before yesterday   two hours ago

Two hours ago, …

7b Put these words in order to make questions. Then work with a partner and ask and answer the questions. Use time phrases.
1 last / school exam / your / was / When / ?
2 holiday / When / your / last / was / ?
3 When / your / visit to a museum / was / last / ?

SPEAKING AND WRITING

8a What do you know about the Mayan, Inca and Aztec civilisations?

8b Work with a partner to find out more about these civilisations.
Student A: Look at the information on page 138.
Student B: Look at the information on page 136.

9 Now choose one of the civilisations and write a few sentences about it.

The Mayan civilisation was in Mexico, Guatemala, Honduras and Belize. It was important …

▶ MEET THE EXPERT
Watch an interview with Mark Weeden, a lecturer in Ancient Near Eastern Studies, about an ancient civilisation. Turn to page 129 for video activities.

8.2 THEN AND NOW

READING

1 Which of these changes are true for your country? Can you think of any other changes?

1. Families are smaller now than they were fifty years ago.
2. People work shorter hours than in the past.
3. Nowadays, many people cook food from other countries.
4. Religion is more important now than in the past.
5. US culture (films, food, music) is popular.
6. These days, people usually go abroad on holiday.

2a Read the article about changes. Which countries or cultures does the reporter write about?

2b Complete the headings in the article with these words. There is one word that you do not need.

climate   economics   politics   technology

3 Read the article again. Who thinks the changes are positive and who thinks they are negative? Write P (positive) or N (negative).

1. Han Li
2. Bo Li
3. Evert Kask
4. Tootega

4 *Making deductions* Who says these things? Match the sentences with the names.

1. 'I'm looking forward to my holiday in London.'
2. 'Go to Toronto, son. There's no work here.'
3. 'I need to buy some petrol.'
4. 'On hot days, I just stay in the house.'
5. 'Why don't I drive over and see you in the Berlin office?'

a Tootega
b Bo Li
c Evert Kask
d Han Li

All *change!*

Countries and cultures change for many different reasons. Our reporter, Sarah Stephens, talks to people about changes in their countries.

Changes because of [1]_____

China is one of the fastest-growing economies in the world. Han Li's life is completely different from her grandparents' life. 'They couldn't travel to other countries, but I can. I can drive a car, but my grandfather could only ride a bicycle.' Bo Li, Han's grandfather, smiles and says, 'We can afford to buy an air conditioner. Before, we couldn't relax in the house during the hot summer.'

Changes because of [2]_____

Before 2004, Estonia was not part of the EU. Evert Kask, a businessman, says 'Business is better now we are in the EU. I can sell to other European countries and visit them for easy business trips. It was harder before. I could go, but it was expensive because of the visas. I can speak German and English now. I certainly couldn't do that before!'

Changes because of the [3]_____

The Inuits of Northern Canada are losing their old way of life because the environment is changing. 'The ice is disappearing now, so we can't get food in the old way,' says Tootega. 'When I was young, I could travel on the ice for days and find seals. Now, there is almost no ice. Our children can't learn the old skills and they are leaving our villages to find work in the cities. It makes me sad.'

THEN AND NOW 8.2

GRAMMAR
COULD, COULDN'T

5a Complete these sentences from the article with the correct verb. Which sentences are about the present and which are about the past?
1. I can _____ a car.
2. I could _____ on the ice for days.
3. They couldn't _____ to other countries.
4. Our children can't _____ the old skills.

5b Find more examples of *could* and *couldn't* in the article. Which form of the main verb do we use after *could/couldn't*?
a to + infinitive
b present simple
c infinitive without *to*

➡ Language reference and extra practice, pages 116–117

6 Complete these sentences with *can, can't, could* or *couldn't*.
1. He _____ find seals on the ice when he was young.
2. We _____ take photos at the museum yesterday – you can't take cameras with you.
3. We _____ fly to other countries today. Our grandparents _____ fly.
4. I _____ run far now, but I _____ run ten kilometres when I was younger.

7 Ask a partner what he/she could do at the ages of five, ten and fifteen. Use these ideas.

| cook | drive | ride a bicycle | speak a little English |
| swim | use a computer | write | |

A: *When you were five, could you ride a bicycle?*
B: *Yes, I could. / No, I couldn't.*

LISTENING

8 [8.3] Listen to a short presentation by two students about technology and cultural changes.
1. What is the title of their talk?
2. Which four inventions do they talk about?

9a [8.4] Listen to Marjorie's part of the talk. Tick (✓) the things she says.
1. People can travel longer distances.
2. People can live and work in different places.
3. Travelling is more comfortable.
4. Modern transport is not safe sometimes.
5. Modern transport is bad for the environment.

9b [8.5] Listen to Pedro's part of the talk and answer these questions.
1. What can we do because of the internet and smartphones?
2. What is the negative point about these things?
3. Do you agree with him?

VOCABULARY
VERBS + PREPOSITIONS

10a Listen to the whole presentation again (Audio recording 8.3) for these verbs, and choose the word you hear. Check your ideas with the script on page 153.
1. to focus on a *topic* / *technology* / *an idea*
2. to go on a *business trip* / *a tour* / *holiday*
3. to read about *places* / *subjects* / *people*
4. to move on to *the next point* / *another topic* / *the next type of technology*
5. to stay in *one place* / *our house* / *a group*
6. to chat to *friends* / *people* / *colleagues*
7. to talk to *strangers* / *someone* / *your teacher*

10b Complete the sentences with a verb and preposition from Exercise 10a.
1. This essay _____ religion and cultural changes.
2. I'm _____ the Mayan civilisation.
3. Before I _____ the next point, I want to say …
4. Do you _____ strangers on the internet?
5. We usually _____ holiday in August.
6. We _____ the garden all day in summer.
7. I _____ my friends on the phone every day.

SPEAKING

11 Work with a partner. Compare your way of life now with your grandparents' way of life when they were young. Think of four positive differences and four negative differences. Compare your ideas with another pair of students.

I can travel by plane to other countries, but my grandparents could only use trains.

8.3 SCENARIO
AT A MUSEUM

PREPARATION

1 Look at the photos. Work with a partner and answer these questions.
1 What country/city is this museum in?
2 What can you see inside, do you think?

2 Match sentences 1–8 with notices A–I. There is one notice you don't need.
1 You can't go in or out this way. D
2 You can leave your coats and bags here.
3 You can't make a lot of noise here.
4 You can't put your hand on this.
5 You can go through here in your wheelchair.
6 You can leave the museum through this door.
7 You can use this to go upstairs.
8 You can't use a camera here.

3 8.6 Harshil and Jessica work at a museum. Listen to six conversations with visitors to the museum. Match conversations 1–6 with topics a–f.
a how much something costs
b getting a map
c how old something is
d when something starts
e taking photographs
f where something is   1

4 Listen again and answer these questions.
1 Where is the cloakroom?
2 How much does the multimedia guide cost?
3 When does the film start?
4 How old is the statue?
5 How many maps does the Italian woman take?
6 Where do they take the photograph?

8.3 AT A MUSEUM

KEY LANGUAGE
MAKING POLITE REQUESTS

5 Put the lines of conversation 1 (below) in the right order. Check with Audio script 8.6 on page 153.

a Yes, madam. How can I help you? ☐
b You're welcome. ☐
c Could you tell me where the cloakroom is, please? ☐
d Oh yes. I see it. Thank you. ☐
e Certainly, madam. You see the main entrance over there? ☐
f Excuse me. ☐
g Yes. ☐
h Well, the cloakroom is just on the right. ☐

6a Complete this table with requests from the conversations in Exercise 3.

Could you	1 _____ me, please?
	2 _____ us a map of the museum, please?
	3 _____ a photo of us?
Could you tell me	4 _____ much they 5 _____?
	6 _where_ the cloakroom 7 _is_, please?
	8 _____ the film 9 _____?
	10 _____ old it 11 _____?

6b How can you respond to the requests in Exercise 6a? Look again at Audio script 8.6 on page 153.

Certainly, …

PRONUNCIATION

7 ▶ 8.7 **Linked sounds** Listen to three requests. How do we pronounce *could you*? What happens where the words join?

8 ▶ 8.8 Put the words in the right order to make requests. Listen and check.
1 Could / open / you / please / the / door, / ?
2 my coat, / you / Could / take / please / ?
3 me / Could / tell / you / when / finishes / the class / ?
4 Could / me / what / you / tell / 'wheelchair' / means, / please / ?
5 where / Could / tell / you / me / is / the / nearest shop / ?

9 Now make the requests and respond to them with a partner. Remember to use polite intonation.

TASK
FINDING OUT IMPORTANT INFORMATION

10 Work with a partner and make short conversations in a museum. Use the Useful phrases below.

Student A: Turn to page 143.
Student B: Turn to page 141.

USEFUL PHRASES

I'd like to do …	Sure, no problem.
Yes, sir/madam.	Let me see …
Please.	Not at all.
Certainly.	(Yes,) of course.
I'm interested in …	I'm afraid not.
That's no problem.	What would you like?
How can I help?	I'm afraid I can't do that.

8.4 STUDY AND WRITING SKILLS

STUDY SKILLS
REMEMBERING NEW WORDS

1 Managing new vocabulary How do you record and learn new vocabulary? Are these sentences true for you?
1 I have a special vocabulary notebook.
2 I make grammar and pronunciation notes about new words, e.g. *beautiful (adj)*.
3 I write translations for words.
4 I write English definitions for words, e.g. *wonderful – very good*.
5 I read my vocabulary notes every day.
6 I use online vocabulary trainers and apps to help me.
7 I learn ten new words every day.
8 I test my memory of new words every week.

2a Grouping words by meaning Put these words into two groups: materials and shapes. Then add more words to these two groups.

| circle | leather | metal | plastic |
| rectangle | square | wood | |

2b Using word webs Add more words to this word web. Can you add more than four?

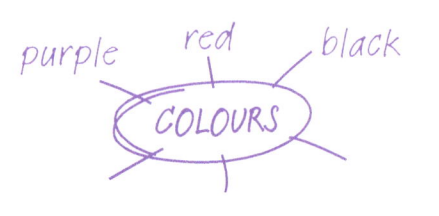

3a Using pictures Many dictionaries have pictures. Match these words with the things in the picture.

| door | garden | gate | house | roof |
| wall | window | | | |

3b Draw a simple picture for two or three words that you want to remember.

ladder

3c Thinking about the shape of a word can help you remember the spelling. Is the word long or short? Are there tall letters (e.g. *b* and *t*) or letters with a 'tail' (e.g. *p* and *q*)? Match these words with one of the shapes below.

vocabulary   plastic   beautiful

4a Word building Look at these dictionary extracts. *Circle* is the noun; what is the adjective?

> **cir·cle** /ˈsɜːkəl $ ˈsɚkəl/ *noun* **1** a round flat shape like the letter O, or a group of people or things arranged in this shape: *Draw a circle on a piece of paper.* • *We sat* **in a circle** *round the table.* → see picture at SHAPE
> **cir·cuit** /ˈsɜːkɪt $ ˈsɚkɪt/ *noun* **1** a track where people race cars, bicycles, etc.: *The racing cars go three times round the circuit.* **2** the complete circle that an electric current flows around: *an electrical circuit*
> **cir·cu·lar 1** /ˈsɜːkjələ $ ˈsɚkjələ/ *adjective* shaped like a circle SYNONYM **round**: *a circular table*

From the *Longman WordWise Dictionary*

4b Use your dictionary and find the adjectives for these nouns.
1 rectangle _____
2 square   _____
3 wood   _____

4c Complete the table with these words.

| long | widen | width | lengthen | weight |

noun	verb	adjective
1 ___	2 ___	wide
length	3 ___	4 ___
5 ___	weigh	

5 Using opposites Match the opposite pairs of the adjectives in the box.

| heavy | light | long | narrow | short | wide |

6 Practise new words Make sentences with five of the new words in this unit. Compare your sentences with a partner.

circular – A coin is circular.
plastic – I use plastic bags from the supermarket.

7 Which of these exercises do you like? Which do you think are useful for you?

STUDY AND WRITING SKILLS 8.4

WRITING SKILLS
DESCRIBING OBJECTS

8 Look at the photos below (A–D). These four objects are for sale on an internet auction site. Which sections can you find the objects in?
1. Antiques: Asia
2. Instruments: Europe
3. Instruments: North America
4. Collectables: North America

9a Match this description with one of the photos.
This item is very ¹_____. It is a ²_____ photograph album from Japan – when you turn the pages, you hear a beautiful song! It is about fifty years old. It is ³_____ (45cm long, 20cm wide) and it is in good condition. The album has got ten pages. These pages are now ⁴_____ with age. On the front of the album, there's a wonderful picture. It is of a ⁵_____ temple and Mount Fuji. Thanks for looking and good luck!

9b Complete the description above with these words.

musical   red   rectangular   unusual   yellow

10 *it, this, these* In the first sentence of the description, the words *This item* refer to the name of the item – a photograph album. What do the other highlighted words refer to? Compare your ideas with a partner.

11 Match the description below with one of the other photos. Then complete the description with the words in the box.

it (x5)   these   they   this (x2)

¹_____ item is unusual. ²_____ is a Shell® sign from the 1950s. The metal sign is shell-shaped and ³_____ is 30cm wide. ⁴_____ weighs one kilogram. ⁵_____ is yellow and ⁶_____ has the company name in red letters. ⁷_____ sign is in good condition, but there are some scratches on the side. ⁸_____ scratches are very small and ⁹_____ are not a problem. Hope you like it!

12a Complete the first sentences of these descriptions of the objects in photographs C and D. Use the information in the boxes below.

Native American Drum
¹_____ is a traditional drum from the ²_____. American Indians made it ³_____ years ago for me when I was on holiday there. Its total weight is ⁴_____ grammes.

Balalaika
¹_____ is a traditional instrument from ²_____. It makes a lovely sound and it is ³_____ years old. It ⁴_____ 500 grammes.

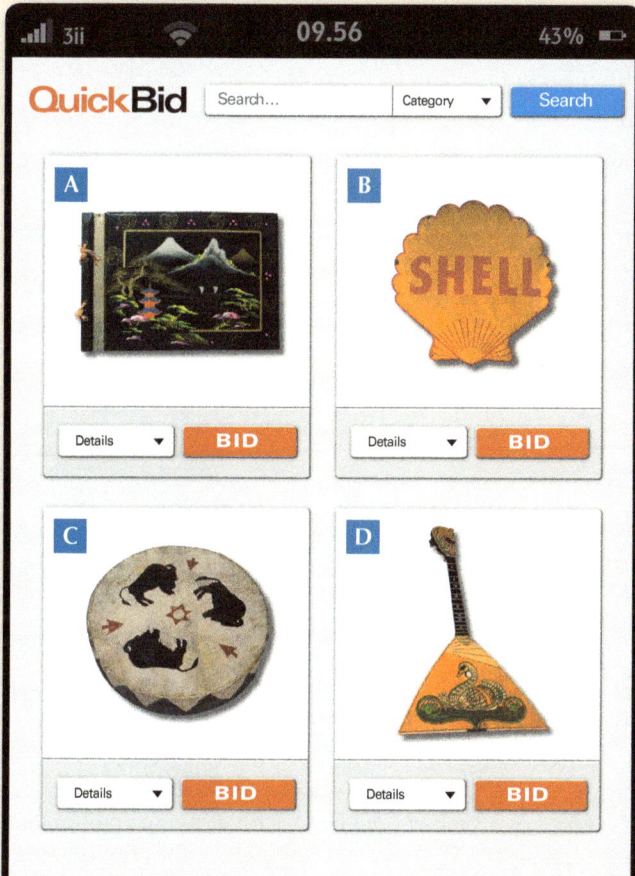

▼ Item: Native American Drum

Country: US
Age: 20 years
Total weight: 350g
Material: top – leather; body – wood
Shape: circular
Width: 30cm
Height: 8cm
Colours: white, black
Picture: animals (bison), arrows, star
Condition: very good (small scratch on the side)

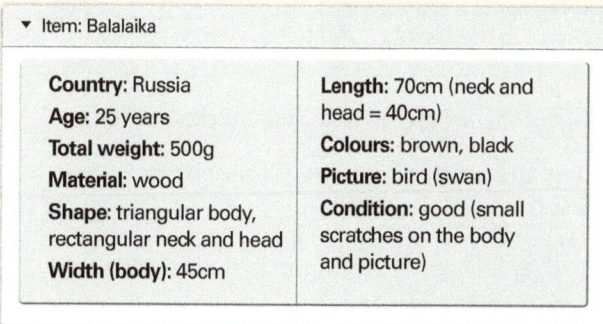

▼ Item: Balalaika

Country: Russia
Age: 25 years
Total weight: 500g
Material: wood
Shape: triangular body, rectangular neck and head
Width (body): 45cm
Length: 70cm (neck and head = 40cm)
Colours: brown, black
Picture: bird (swan)
Condition: good (small scratches on the body and picture)

12b Work with a partner. One of you writes a description of the drum. The other writes a description of the balalaika. Then read and check your partner's work.

13 What were the final prices of these objects, do you think? Match a price with each object. Would you like to buy any of these objects?

$150 $650 $75 $50

9 Inventions
9.1 MARVELLOUS MINDS

IN THIS UNIT

GRAMMAR
- past simple: regular and irregular verbs
- past simple: negative and question forms

VOCABULARY
- medical science

SCENARIO
- giving reasons
- giving a short presentation

STUDY SKILLS
- making notes while reading

WRITING SKILLS
- a short biography

Alfred Nobel

Levi Strauss

Leonardo da Vinci

'To invent, you need good imagination and a pile of junk.' Thomas A. Edison, 1847–1931, US inventor, scientist and businessman

READING

1 What do you know about the three people in the pictures? Discuss them with a partner.

2a Leonardo da Vinci was a famous inventor. Look at these inventions. Which are his ideas or inventions, do you think?

the bicycle	the car	the diving suit
the helicopter	high heels	the parachute
the radio	the robot	the telescope

2b Read the article quickly and check your ideas.

3 Read the article again. Are these sentences true or false?
1 When he was young, Leonardo was at a large school.
2 Leonardo was an engineering student.
3 A lot of modern inventions use his ideas.
4 The robot could only move its legs.
5 The car could only travel a short distance.
6 Leonardo's helicopter is the same as the modern ones.
7 Modern divers use Leonardo's diving glove.

4 *Evaluating* Put the inventions in the article in order of importance. Then compare your ideas with a partner.

GRAMMAR
PAST SIMPLE: REGULAR AND IRREGULAR VERBS

5a When we talk about finished events and times in the past, we use the past simple.

*In 1500, **he returned** to Florence.*

infinitive *return* → past simple *returned*

Read the first paragraph of the article again and find other examples of the past simple. Complete this table.

infinitive	past simple
return	*returned*

GRAMMAR TIP

We usually add *-ed* to the infinitive to form the past simple, but sometimes there are spelling changes.
study → *studied*   *travel* → *travelled*   *live* → *lived*

➡ Language reference and extra practice, pages 118–119

5b 9.1 Complete these sentences with your answers from Exercise 5a. Then listen and check.
1 Leonardo _____ his studies of art in 1468.
2 He _____ these studies in 1472.
3 He _____ money, so he started work as an engineer.
4 Leonardo _____ as an engineer for thirty-two years.
5 He _____ in Milan from 1472 to 1500.
6 He _____ to Florence after twenty-eight years in Milan.

Leonardo da Vinci

Man of art
Man of ideas
Man of inventions

HIS LIFE

Leonardo da Vinci (1452–1519) lived in a small town in Italy with his grandparents. He studied at home and enjoyed music, singing and mathematics. At the age of sixteen, he wanted to study art, so he moved to the city of Florence for art classes. He finished his studies after four years. He then worked in Milan as an engineer and he started his life as an inventor. In 1500, he returned to Florence, and in 1516 he travelled to France, where he stayed for the rest of his life.

HIS INVENTIONS

Leonardo da Vinci lived and worked before people used electricity and petrol for power, but he had the first ideas for many machines that we use today.

The robot
Leonardo built his robot in 1495. The robot stood up, sat down and held things in its arms.

The car
A single passenger drove the car. It travelled 40 metres at a time.

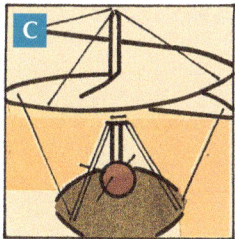

The helicopter
Leonardo designed the first helicopter, but he never made it. His design used a screw to lift the helicopter into the air. This is different from the modern design, but the general idea is similar.

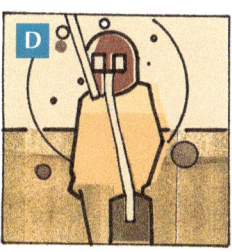 

The diving suit
Leonardo made the suit from leather and added long pipes to carry the air to the diver. He also invented special gloves for divers. Today, divers use them on their feet!

These are just some of Leonardo's hundreds of inventions. He also invented a parachute and even high heels!

MARVELLOUS MINDS
9.1

PRONUNCIATION

6a **9.2** **Verb endings** The past simple ending -ed has three possible pronunciations. Listen to these examples and repeat them.

- /d/ enjoyed
- /t/ helped
- /ɪd/ needed

6b Match the verbs from Exercise 5b to these sounds. Then listen to Audio recording 9.1 again and repeat the sentences.

- /d/
- /t/
- /ɪd/

> **GRAMMAR TIP**
>
> Some verbs in the past simple are irregular. We don't add -ed to the infinitive.
> He **had** the first ideas. (infinitive: have)
> He **built** his robot in 1495. (infinitive: build)

7 Read the article again and find the past simple forms of these verbs.

1. stand _____
2. sit _____
3. hold _____
4. drive _____
5. make _____

➤ Language reference and extra practice, pages 118–119

8 Complete these sentences with the past simple of the verbs in brackets. Is each verb regular or irregular? (See the irregular verb list on page 158.)

1. Last month, I _____ three films at the cinema. (see)
2. Last year, we _____ to Hawaii on holiday. (go)
3. He _____ Russia in 2006. (visit)
4. They _____ in a hotel by the sea last summer. (stay)
5. Yesterday, I _____ home at midnight. (get)
6. My father _____ mathematics at university. (study)
7. When I was a child, I _____ in a small town. (live)
8. I _____ to class by bus this morning. (come)

SPEAKING

9 Tell a partner about last weekend. What verbs do you need to use? Make a list.

Last weekend, I visited my grandparents on Saturday. I had lunch with them.

Last Sunday, I went skiing. I had a great time.

WRITING

10a Look at the information on page 144 about Alfred Nobel and Levi Strauss. Write a short text about each person.

10b **9.3** Listen and compare your texts.

71

9.2 MEDICAL INVENTIONS

VOCABULARY
MEDICAL SCIENCE

1 Choose the best word. Use your dictionary.
1 *Science* / *Medicine* is the study and *trial* / *treatment* of illnesses.
2 *Teeth* / *Skin* and *bones* / *the heart* are hard parts of the body.
3 A *scientist* / *doctor* usually works in a *laboratory* / *waiting room*.
4 A scientist uses *tools* / *equipment* to do *examinations* / *experiments*.

READING

2 Look at items A–D and match them with paragraphs 1–4 of the article on the right.

3 Complete the table with information from the article.

Medical inventions			
	date	country	other information
scalpel	3000 BC	1 _____	didn't change for 2 _____ years
acupuncture needles	3 _____	4 _____	still popular in 5 _____ and other countries
6 _____	700 BC	7 _____	didn't change until 8 _____
9 _____	10 _____	Holland	people didn't want to look at 11 _____ things then

GRAMMAR
PAST SIMPLE: NEGATIVE FORM

4 Underline the negative forms of the past simple in the article. Then complete this rule.

To make the negative of the past simple, we use: subject + _____ + _____ + infinitive without *to*.

Note: when we speak, and in informal writing, *did not* → *didn't*.

➜ Language reference and extra practice, pages 118–119

5 Write true sentences with the past simple (affirmative or negative) of the verbs in brackets.
1 People _____ the scalpel for the first time around 3000 BC. (use)
2 The Japanese _____ acupuncture. (invent)
3 People _____ false teeth before 700 BC. (wear)
4 False teeth _____ between 700 BC and AD 1770. (change)
5 Zacharias Jansen _____ the first microscope. (make)
6 His microscope _____ objects ten times bigger than their real size. (show)

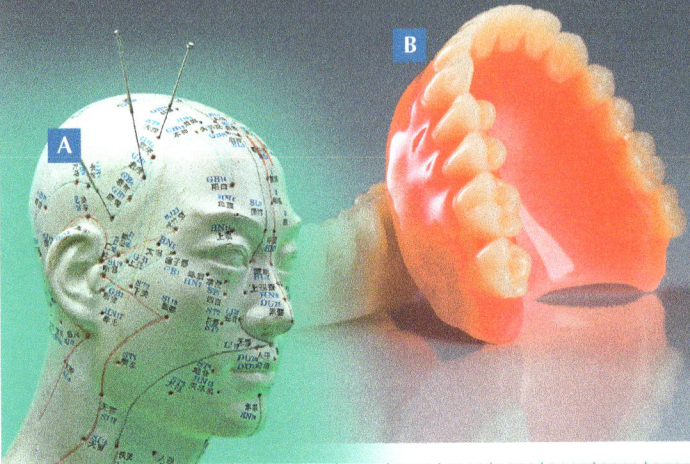

Medical Inventions

1 The scalpel is one of the oldest inventions in medicine. It is a small, light and very sharp knife. People used it for the first time around 3000 BC in the area of modern Iraq. The scalpel <u>did not change</u> very much for 4,000 years.

2 The Chinese invented acupuncture needles around 2000 BC. At first, they did not make needles from metal, but from stone. Today, people in China and other countries use acupuncture for many illnesses.

3 People in southern Italy invented the first false teeth in about 700 BC. They used pieces of bone, or sometimes second-hand human teeth! After that, false teeth did not change for the next 2,500 years until, in 1770, a Frenchman called Alexis Duchateau first used porcelain – a hard, white material that we still sometimes use today.

4 Zacharias Jansen from Holland made the first microscope in about 1590. Through it, objects appeared nine times bigger than their real size, but it did not give a very clear picture. Jansen did not use his invention very much because people at that time did not want to look at small things!

MEDICAL INVENTIONS 9.2

LISTENING

6a Look at the photo below. What is this machine, do you think?
a an MRI scanner
b an X-ray machine
c a microscope

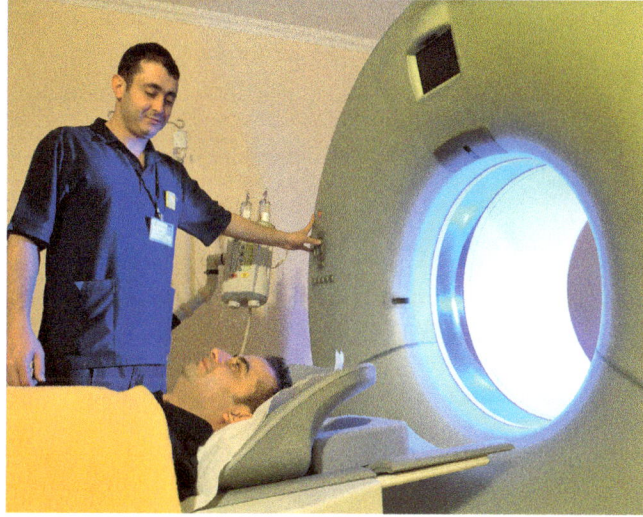

6b [9.4] Listen to the first part of a radio interview and check your answer.

7a Are these sentences true or false, do you think?
1 The machine looks inside you.
2 It can only take a picture of your head.
3 It's dangerous.
4 German scientists invented it.
5 Hospitals first used it in the 1980s.

7b [9.5] Listen to the rest of the interview and check your answers.

8 Listen again and complete these sentences.
1 The scanner can show both the hard parts and the _soft parts_ of the body.
2 It can take a picture of the _____ body.
3 In the 1950s, Felix Bloch _____ the importance of NMR for looking inside the human body.
4 Raymond Damadian and his team built the first full-body MRI scanner in _____.
5 In _____, hospitals around the world bought their first MRI scanners.
6 The scanner isn't good for people who don't like _____ _____.

9 Researching the topic Can you think of any other important medical inventions? Find out something about one of them and tell your group.

GRAMMAR
PAST SIMPLE: QUESTION FORM

10 Look at these two questions and choose the correct words in the rules below.

Did Felix Bloch **invent** the MRI scanner?
When **did** they **build** the first scanner?

1 Past simple questions use the past form of *do / have*.
2 *Did* always comes *before / after* the subject of the question.
3 The main verb comes *before / after* the subject.
4 The main verb is in *the infinitive (without to) / the past simple (affirmative)*.

GRAMMAR TIP

Notice the short answer.
Did you see him there? – Yes, I did. / No, I didn't.
Did they arrive on time? – Yes, they did. / No, they didn't.

➡ Language reference and extra practice, pages 118–119

11 Put the words in the correct order to make questions. Ask and answer the questions with a partner. Check your answers on page 144.
1 Thomas Edison / TV / invent / Did / ?
2 make / Europeans / the first paper / Did / ?
3 did / invent / Wilhelm Röntgen / What / ?
4 the Americans / When / on the Moon / did / land / ?
5 Where / first arrive / did / in America / Christopher Columbus / ?

SPEAKING

12 Work with a partner. Take turns to talk about your first experiences of the topics from this box. Answer your partner's questions. Then listen to your partner's experiences and ask questions.

travel alone   go abroad   eat foreign food
cook a meal   play a sport   hold a baby
move to a new house   win something
organise a party   fly   vote

A: *I first travelled alone when I was eighteen.*
B: *Did you like it? How did you feel? What happened?*

▶ MEET THE EXPERT

Watch an interview with Odette Aguirre, an acupuncturist, about the benefits of acupuncture.
Turn to page 129 for video activities.

9.3 SCENARIO
EVERYDAY INVENTIONS

PREPARATION

1 Match these objects with the photos (A–E). How often do you use them?

1. mirrors
2. balloons
3. Post-it® notes
4. tin cans
5. umbrellas

2a 9.6 Listen to the introduction to a radio programme and complete this information.

1. the title of the programme: *The Nation's _____ Everyday _____*
2. the phone number of the radio show: 0810 _____

2b Listen again. Then complete the description of the programme below with the words in the box.

| choose | history | information | normal |
| opinion | texting | | |

This programme gives the ¹_____ of inventions that people use in their ²_____ lives. We learn some important ³_____ about the inventions. Each week, the presenter gives her ⁴_____ about the inventions and, after the programme, the listeners ⁵_____ their favourite invention by ⁶_____ a phone number.

3a How much do you know about the history of the umbrella? Do you think these sentences are true or false?

1. People first used umbrellas in places like India, Egypt and China.
2. At first, only rich and important people used umbrellas.
3. The British made the first umbrella for the rain.
4. In Europe, for many years, only men used umbrellas. Women did not like them.
5. The first umbrella shop opened in London.

3b 9.7 Listen to the first part of the radio programme and check your ideas.

4 9.8 The presenter gives four reasons for voting for the umbrella. What are the reasons, do you think? Choose four reasons from the list, then listen to the rest of the programme and check.

1. It is one of the oldest everyday inventions.
2. It is a good simple design.
3. It has three different uses.
4. Umbrellas can be very colourful.
5. Umbrellas are not expensive.
6. They are easy to carry.

9.3 EVERYDAY INVENTIONS

KEY LANGUAGE
GIVING REASONS

5 [9.9] Look at these reasons from the programme. Complete the sentences, then listen and check.
1. Well, the _____ important reason _____ that it's one of the oldest inventions in the world.
2. Secondly, the umbrella is a great invention _____ it's got several different uses.
3. Vote for the umbrella _____ umbrellas bring colour to our grey, rainy streets.
4. My _____ reason _____ that umbrellas are very cheap to make.

6 You can put many different things before the phrases *reason is that* and *because*. Complete the table with the words or phrases in the box.

~~a very good~~   ~~they are popular~~   another
one   people buy umbrellas   the main
umbrellas are useful   buy an umbrella

A very good		They are popular	
_____	reason is (that) …	_____	because …
_____		_____	
_____		_____	

PRONUNCIATION

7a Stressed words Look at these phrases. Underline the words that are different in each phrase.
1. <u>An important</u> reason is that …
2. A good reason is that …
3. The second reason is that …
4. One reason is that …
5. Another reason is that …
6. The main reason is that …

7b [9.10] Listen to the phrases from Exercise 7a. Which word has the most stress in each phrase?

8 Ask and answer these questions with a partner. Use the phrases from Exercises 6 and 7a.
1. Why are you learning English?

I'm learning English because I like the language. The main reason is that I want a better job.

2. Why do people join clubs?
3. Why do people go to university?
4. Why do people play sport?
5. Why do people have pets?
6. Why do people go abroad on holiday?

TASK
GIVING A SHORT PRESENTATION

9a Work with a partner. You are the presenters of the radio show. Prepare a short talk about an everyday invention. Follow the instructions below.

Pair A: Look at page 147.   Pair C: Look at page 137.
Pair B: Look at page 145.   Pair D: Look at page 139.

Make sure you
- give a short introduction to the invention – perhaps an interesting fact, or a description of the invention
- give three facts about the invention
- give some reasons for voting for this invention
- make a final comment.

Look at Audio scripts 9.7 and 9.8 on pages 154–155 for examples.

USEFUL PHRASES

My invention is …
Here are my three facts.
Firstly, … Secondly, … Finally, …
The first/second/main reason is that …
So, why vote for … ?

9b Now work in groups of four students. Each group has an A, B, C and D student. Give your talk to the other students in your group.

10 Vote for your favourite invention and say why you like it.

D

E

9.4 STUDY AND WRITING SKILLS

WINDS FROM THE EAST: Chinese inventions

The Chinese invented many things that we use today, long before they appeared in the West.

The Chinese invented paper in the second century BC. Over a thousand years later, in the twelfth century AD, Europeans first made paper. Another example is matches: the Chinese had matches in the sixth century, but Europeans did not use them until the nineteenth century. Paper money is another Chinese invention: Europeans first made it in Sweden in 1661, but the Chinese invented it 800 years earlier, in the ninth century.

Knowledge of other inventions came along the 'Silk Road', linking East and West, and more information came by sea. Sailors brought Chinese ideas to the Arabian Gulf and northern Africa and, from there, they spread north to Europe. Travellers like Marco Polo (1254–1324) also brought stories of Chinese inventions back to Europe.

STUDY SKILLS
MAKING NOTES WHILE READING

1 Discuss these questions with a partner.
1 When do you make notes?
2 How do you make notes?
3 Do you think you are good or bad at making notes? Why?

2 Making notes There are different ways of making notes. There is no correct or incorrect way. Read the article above and complete the two different kinds of notes.

3 Note-making style Study the notes and answer these questions.
1 Do we use words like *a*, *the* and *in* in notes?
2 What do these symbols mean?
  a ⇨   b +   c "   d C.

4 Which kind of notes do you prefer, A (the word web) or B? Why?

5 Look at the article about Leonardo da Vinci on page 71. Make notes on it. Compare your notes with a partner. Can you make your notes better?

A
1 _____ 2nd C. BC
2 _____ e.g. Marco Polo
paper 12th C.
matches 3 _____
CHINA — 4 _____ Road — EUROPE
matches 19th C.
paper money 5 _____
by sea via Arabian Gulf + 6 _____
paper money 7 _____

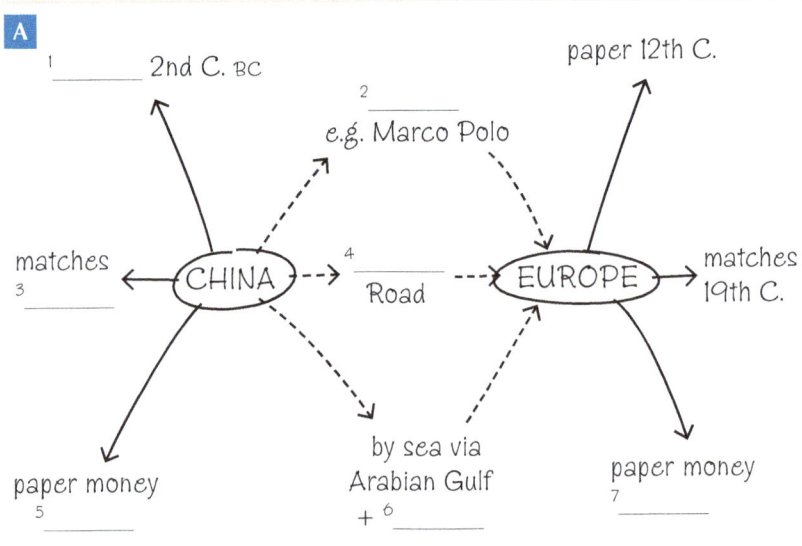

B CHINESE INVENTIONS

Chinese invented 1_____ 2nd C. BC   Europe 12th C.
   "   "   matches 2_____   "   19th C.
   "   "   paper money 9th C.   "   AD 1661

WAYS TO EUROPE
• 3_____ Road
• by sea, China ➔ Arabian 4_____ + northern Africa ➔ Europe
• 5_____, e.g. Marco Polo

76

STUDY AND WRITING SKILLS 9.4

WRITING SKILLS
A SHORT BIOGRAPHY

6 Discuss these questions with a partner.
1 Do you know the names of any women inventors?
2 Why are most inventors men, do you think?

7a Look at these events in the life of Lady Ada Lovelace and number them in the correct order. Discuss your order with your partner.

Lady Ada Lovelace
the world's first woman in computers

a	At the age of thirteen, she produced a design for a flying machine.	☐
b	She began work with Charles Babbage.	☐
c	Lord Byron left England forever.	☐
d	She died in 1852.	☐
e	Her parents (the poet Lord Byron and Anne Milbanke) separated.	2
f	She married William King (later Lord Lovelace) and they had three children.	☐
g	She developed the idea of using binary numbers (0,1) and understood many ideas that we use in computer programming today.	☐
h	Ada Byron was born in 1815 in Piccadilly, London.	☐
i	She met the mathematician and inventor Charles Babbage for the first time.	5

Charles Babbage's analytical engine

7b `9.11` Listen and check your answers.

8 Linkers Look at the underlined phrases in Audio script 9.11 on page 155. Complete the table with the linking words.

at the same time	next
at that time	after

9 Read the text about Madam C J Walker and choose the best linking words.

Madam C J Walker (Sarah Breedlove)
the first African–American woman millionaire

Sarah Breedlove was born in Louisiana, USA, in 1867. Her parents died when she was seven years old. ¹*After / Next / Later* their death, she went to work in the cotton fields. Seven years ²*during / then / later*, in 1881, she married Moses McWilliam. Four years ³*then / after that / next*, her only daughter – Lelia – was born. In 1887, her husband died and she got a job washing clothes. ⁴*During / Then / Later* the 1890s, she lost some of her hair. In 1905, she married Charles Walker and changed her name to Madam C J Walker. She developed and sold new haircare products. In 1908, she opened a training college in Pittsburgh, and ⁵*before / during / then*, in 1910, she built a factory in Indianapolis. She became a rich woman and gave money to help other African–Americans. When she died in New York State in 1919, she was the richest African–American woman.

10 Use the information below to write a short biography.

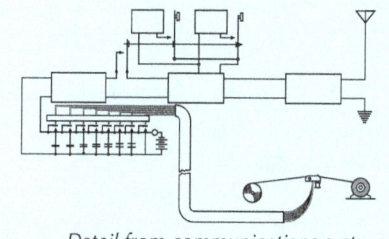

Detail from communications system

Hedy Lamarr – Hollywood star and communications expert

1913 – born in Vienna, Austria
1929 – went to acting school in Berlin
1932 – acted in the European art film `Extase' / became famous
1933 – married Fritz Mandl, the first of her six husbands / during her marriage / learnt many things about weapons from her husband (he sold weapons to Adolf Hitler before World War II)
1937 – left her husband / went to Paris, London, to the US
1938 – made her first film in America (Algiers) / became a Hollywood star / people called her the most beautiful woman in the world
1940 – met George Antheil (a composer)
1942 – they developed a radio communications system for submarines
1966 – wrote a book about her life, `Extase and Me'
2000 – died in Florida, in the US

11 Evaluating In your opinion, which of these inventors had:
a the most interesting life?   b the hardest life?

10 Money
10.1 KEEPING IT SAFE

IN THIS UNIT

GRAMMAR
- *should, shouldn't*
- *have to, don't have to*

VOCABULARY
- money (nouns incl verb phrases)

SCENARIO
- asking for and giving opinions
- doing an opinion survey

STUDY SKILLS
- making notes during a talk

WRITING SKILLS
- formal writing (an online form)

'There are people who have money, and people who are rich.' Coco Chanel, 1883–1971, French fashion designer

VOCABULARY
MONEY (NOUNS)

1a Look at the words and phrases in the box. Check any new words in your dictionary. Which two are *cash*?

| cashpoint | cheque | coin | credit card |
| note | PIN | purse | wallet |

1b Make true sentences, using the words above. Compare with a partner.
1. I've got / I haven't got a lot of _____.
2. I don't often use _____.
3. There are a lot of _____ in my _____.
4. It's easy/difficult to remember my _____.
5. I always destroy old _____.
6. _____ is/are more useful to me than _____.

READING

2 Look at the poster on the right. Where can you see it?

3 Are these sentences about the talk true or false?
1. The talk is for all students of the university.
2. The talk is only about money.
3. Sue Cutler works for the university.
4. The talk is on Wednesday morning.
5. There is nothing to eat or drink there.

Sheffield Metropolitan University

INTERNATIONAL STUDENTS!
ARE YOU NEW TO THIS CITY?

Are you worried about:
- keeping your money safe?
- going out at night?
- using taxis alone?
- people stealing your phone?

Come to a talk by Sue Cutler, Sheffield Met International Student Welfare Officer

Staying safe: looking after yourself and your money

Wednesday 3 October
Peak Building Lecture Theatre, 4 p.m.
Tea and biscuits from 3.30 p.m.

Everyone welcome!

KEEPING IT SAFE 10.1

LISTENING

4 ▶10.1 Read these sentences, then listen to the first part of Sue's talk and choose the best summary.
1 The city is dangerous and it's important to be very careful with your money.
2 The city is safe, but it's important to be careful with your money.
3 The city is safe, so it's not important to be careful with your money.

5 ▶10.2 Listen to the rest of Sue's talk and fill the gaps.
1 You should be careful in _____ places.
2 You should keep your _____ safe.
3 You shouldn't keep your _____ in your back pocket.
4 You shouldn't carry a lot of _____.
5 You shouldn't take your money out in _____ _____ places.

6 Look at what these people say. Do they follow Sue's advice?
1 'I can never remember my PINs, so I keep them on a piece of paper in my wallet.'
2 'I always carry my wallet in my inside jacket pocket.'
3 'I don't like cheques or credit cards, so I always carry a lot of cash.'
4 'I sometimes check how much money I've got in my purse when I'm on the bus.'

GRAMMAR
SHOULD, SHOULDN'T

7 Look at these examples and explanations, then answer the questions below.

examples	explanations
You **should** be careful.	It's the right thing to do.
He **shouldn't** put his money in his back pocket.	It isn't the right thing to do.
Should I wear a money belt?	Is it the right thing to do?

1 Do we add -s to *should* after *he*, *she* and *it*?
2 Can you think of another verb with grammar like this?

➡ Language reference and extra practice, pages 120–121

8 Complete the sentences with *should* or *shouldn't* and the verb in brackets.
1 *Should I keep* this money? I found it in the street. (I / keep)
2 _____ to that restaurant on your birthday – the food is really bad. (you / go)
3 Max lost his wallet yesterday. _____ more careful with his money. (he / be)
4 _____ a new camera. Her other camera is only six months old. (she / buy)
5 'Someone stole my purse from my car.' '_____ the police.' (you / tell)
6 _____ all our money on a round-the-world trip or on a swimming pool in the garden? (we / spend)

9 Problem-solving Look at some more problems below for international students in the UK. Give them advice with *should* and ideas from the box.

don't use your computer late at night
go out in a group   join a sports club
watch TV and practise listening

1 'I don't know any British people.'
2 'I can't understand what British people say.'
3 'I don't feel safe in the city.'
4 'I send emails to my friends back home until 2 a.m., and then I can't sleep.'

SPEAKING

10a Work with a partner. Read about Nadia below, then think of some advice for her.

From nadiaj@awll.com
To   Student Advice Service

I'm a student in London. This is a very expensive city and I don't get a lot of money – my parents pay my university fees but they can't afford to give me any extra money. I have a part-time job in a restaurant, but it doesn't pay very much. I'm using my credit cards a lot and now I'm in debt. What should I do?

Nadia

10b Look at page 140 and check your advice. Then discuss advice for the other people on that page.

WRITING

11 Work with a partner. Write a reply to one of the people on page 140.

10.2 BUSINESS LOANS

VOCABULARY
MONEY (VERB PHRASES)

1 Complete the definitions below with the phrases in the box.

borrow money (from someone)   charges you interest
earn money   get a loan   lend money (to someone)
pay back

1 When you _____, you get money from your job.
2 When you _____, you get some money from someone and return it later.
3 When you _____ some money, you return the money that you borrowed before.
4 When you _____, you give someone some money and he/she returns it later.
5 When you _____, you borrow money, for example from a bank.
6 When a bank _____, you pay back more money than you borrowed.

READING

2 Look at the FAQs (Frequently Asked Questions) page for Start-Up Loans and answer these questions.
1 Who does Start-Up Loans help?
2 What does Start-Up Loans do?

START-UP LOANS

Helping young people to start a business
Low-interest loans and great business advice

FAQs

Is a loan from us the same as a loan from a bank?
No, it isn't. Banks don't usually lend money to young people because they don't have jobs or houses. Banks also charge a lot of interest (10%). The government provides the money for Start-Up Loans. This means you don't have to have a job or house, and we don't charge much interest (6%).

How much money can you borrow?
You can borrow anything from £250 to £25,000. The average loan is £2,500.

Who can borrow money from us?
He/She …
• has to be between 18 and 30 years old.
• has to live in the UK.
• has to have a good business plan.
• doesn't have to be British.
• doesn't have to own a house.

---

3 Are the sentences about the text true or false?
1 The interest rate is lower than a bank's one.
2 A person needs a house to get a loan.
3 Most people borrow £25,000.
4 A seventeen-year-old person can get a loan.
5 A Spanish person living in the UK can get a loan.

GRAMMAR
HAVE TO, DON'T HAVE TO

4 Match the sentences (1–4) with the correct explanations (a or b).
1 She doesn't have to do it.
2 He has to do it.
3 We have to do it.
4 You don't have to do it.

a It is necessary.
b It isn't necessary.

GRAMMAR TIP

Notice the question form.
Does he/she have to … ?
Do I/you/we/they have to … ?

➥ Language reference and extra practice, pages 120–121

5 Complete these sentences with the correct form of *have to* (affirmative, negative or question form) and a verb from the box.

check   give   keep   pay   pay   ~~show~~   use

1 When you open a bank account, you *have to show* some identification.
2 When you borrow money from a friend, you _____ interest.
3 In a foreign country, you _____ foreign currency because you can use a credit card.
4 The bank _____ your money safe.
5 _____ the bank manager _____ my loan application?
6 How much interest _____ I _____ ?
7 A bank manager _____ you a loan – he/she can choose.

6 What are the differences between these jobs? What do/don't the people have to do?

a doctor   a footballer   a musician   a pilot
a police officer   a student   a teacher

A teacher has to prepare lessons. A teacher doesn't have to wear a uniform.

START-UP LOANS

BUSINESS LOANS

10.2

Elena, 24: Tangle Dress Design

I have a women's fashion-design business and I make designer clothes for individual customers. The dresses cost about £300. My customers get a personal service and my designs are a lot cheaper than other designer dresses!

I have a degree in Digital Fashion Design and I worked in Dubai for a fashion company before I opened my shop in England. My job in Dubai gave me useful experience. I wanted to start my own business, but the banks didn't lend me any money. I spent six months doing market research, and I used my savings to open my shop one month ago. I then borrowed £2,500 from Start-Up Loans, and I am using it to pay the rent for the shop and to pay for my website.

What advice can I give? Well, you have to do your market research because you have to know what your customers want. Also, you have to have a lot of energy. It's not easy to start your own business. In five years' time, I want to have five shops, so I have to work hard now!

READING

7a Work with a partner to read about two people who started their business with a loan.

Student A: Read about Elena (above) and answer the questions below.
Student B: Read about Graeme on page 146 and answer the questions.

1. What is the name of Elena's business?
2. What does she do?
3. What is different about her business?
4. What training and experience did she have before she started her business?
5. How helpful were the banks?
6. How much did she borrow, and what is she doing with the loan?
7. How many pieces of advice does she give? What are they?
8. What is her ambition?

7b Use your answers from Exercise 7a and tell your partner about the young person and his/her business.

SPEAKING

8a Work with a partner. You work for Start-Up Loans. Read and share information about four people and their business ideas.

Student A: Look at the information on page 142.
Student B: Look at the information on page 144.

Then tell each other about the business ideas and take notes.

8b Evaluation Discuss the four people and their business ideas.

1. What do you think of the ideas?
2. Is the young person a good person to start that business?
3. Are they ready?
4. Choose the two best businesses to receive loans.

9 Do you have a business idea, or a different ambition? What do you have to do to make that business or ambition happen?

10.3 SCENARIO
IN MY OPINION

PREPARATION

1 Do you agree or disagree with these quotes? How true are they: definitely true, partly true or not at all true?

1 'Money can buy you happiness.' *Anon*
2 'Time is more valuable than money.' *Jim Rohn*
3 'You can be young without money, but you can't be old without it.' *Tennessee Williams*
4 'Money makes the world go round.' *Kander and Ebb, from the musical 'Cabaret'*

2a 10.3 A bank is doing a survey about money. Listen to an interview and answer these questions.

1 What is the relationship between David and Katie, do you think?
2 Which person is more careful with their money, David or Katie?
3 Which person are you more similar to?

2b Listen again. Are these sentences true or false?

1 David thinks that you can spend too much money with a credit card.
2 Katie likes to buy things immediately.
3 Katie never saves any money.
4 David says he is saving money for a holiday.
5 David thinks that borrowing money from friends is a very bad idea.
6 Katie thinks that it is a good idea to borrow a lot of money from friends.
7 Katie never gives money to charity.
8 David gives money to charity every month.

KEY LANGUAGE
ASKING FOR AND GIVING OPINIONS

3 10.4 Complete these questions and answers from the interview. Then listen and check.

1 'What's your opinion about _____ credit cards?'
   'Well, personally, I _____ that they're a bad idea.'
   'Well, in my _____, they're great.'
2 'Do you _____ _____ saving money is important?'
   'Erm, yes, I suppose _____ _____, …'
   'Oh yes, _____.'
3 'Do you think that borrowing money from friends is a _____ _____?'
   'Oh, no, not at _____.'
   'Well, I'm not _____.'
4 'Do you agree that people _____ ___ money to charity every month?'
   'No, not at all. I _____ that the government _____ look after everyone.'
   'Well, yes, I _____.'

10.3
IN MY OPINION

PRONUNCIATION

4a 🔊 10.5 **Stressed words** Listen to part of the interview again and answer these questions.
1. Which word is stressed most in each question below? Underline the correct words.
   a 'OK, madam, and do you think that saving money is important?'
   b 'And sir, do you think that saving money is important?'
2. Which question means 'Tell me about this topic'?
3. Which question means 'I want to know your opinion'?

4b Listen again and repeat the two questions.

5 Work with a partner. Ask and answer the questions in Exercise 3. Remember to change the stress when you say the question the second time.

A: *Do you think that saving money is important?*
B: *Oh yes, definitely. And do you think that it's important?*
A: *No, not at all. I think that you should spend your money while you can!*

TASK
DOING AN OPINION SURVEY

6 Work with a partner and make a questionnaire about money. Choose from these ideas and complete the questionnaire below.
- give money to homeless people
- borrow money for a computer
- students pay for university
- directors earn a very high salary
- buy expensive clothes
- parents give children pocket money
- children work
- save money for retirement

Section A — Notes
1 What's your opinion about _____ ?
2 What's your opinion about _____ ?

Section B (tick one ✓)   Yes   No   Not sure/Don't know
3 Do you think that _____ is important?
4 Do you think that _____ is a good idea?
5 Do you agree that _____ ?
6 Do you agree that _____ ?

7a With your partner, make copies of your questionnaire and interview as many other students as you can. Make notes of the answers.

USEFUL PHRASES

I think that …	Personally, I think …
I don't know.	Yes, I suppose it is.
In my opinion, …	I'm not sure.
Yes, definitely.	No, not at all.

7b Share your notes with your partner.

Three students think that we should save money for our retirement. Two students think that it isn't necessary …

8 Write a short paragraph about the results of your survey. You can use tables to show some of the information. Show your results to other students.

Four students think that giving money to homeless people is important. Two students think that it isn't a good idea and one student isn't sure.

83

10.4 STUDY AND WRITING SKILLS

STUDY SKILLS
MAKING NOTES DURING A TALK

1a Look at the photos. What ways of banking do they show?

1b How do you, your family and your friends manage your bank accounts? Do you often go to a branch of your bank(s), or do you manage your accounts in another way?

2a ▶10.1 Watch a talk about bank accounts. How many different ways of banking do Kathy and Paul mention? What are they?

2b First impressions are important! What is your first impression of Paul and Kathy? Tick (✓) the statements you agree with. Then compare with a partner.
1 They speak clearly.
2 They are enthusiastic.
3 They are young.
4 They are good-looking.
5 They look honest, so I can trust them.
6 I am happy to open an account with their bank.

3a ▶10.2 Watch the part of the talk about online banking again. Complete the notes with one word per gap.

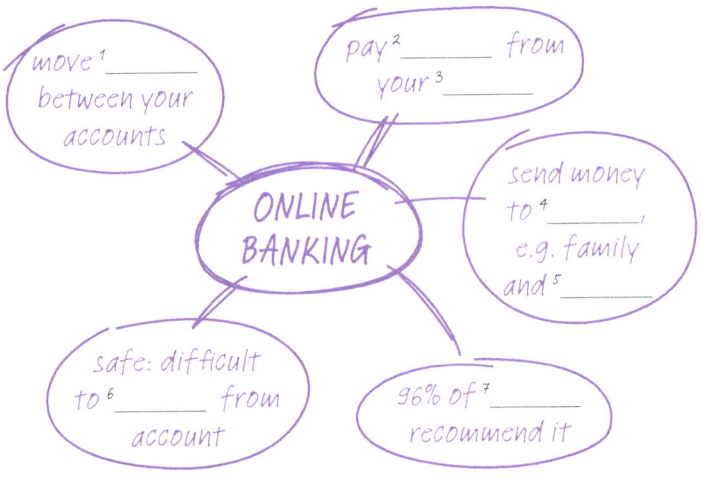

3b *Introducing extra information* Which words and phrases introduce extra information? (Do they have a similar meaning to *and*?) Watch again, then check Video script 10.2 on page 156. Where do we often put these words and phrases in the sentence?

4a ▶10.3 Watch the next part of the talk. Make notes, then compare your notes with a partner.

4b Use your notes to write a short paragraph about the way of banking in Exercise 4a. Use the words from Exercise 3b to introduce extra information.

5 *Evaluation* Can you think of advantages and disadvantages of these different ways of banking? Which way of banking do you prefer?

84

STUDY AND WRITING SKILLS 10.4

WRITING SKILLS
FORMAL WRITING (AN ONLINE FORM)

6 Read Liliana's complaint to her bank. Complete gaps 1–3 with sentences a–c.
a Could you please refund the difference (£8)?
b I am writing about a problem with a recent international money transfer.
c However, £30 is the charge for an urgent transfer.

Make a complaint online
Please use this form if you have an account with us.

Please tell us a few details about yourself.

Title:	Ms
First name:	Liliana
Family name:	Betancor
First line of your address:	17 Market Street
Account number:	65427494
Daytime telephone number:	01765 247857
Email address:	lilibet@aoll.com
Please contact me:	in writing

What is your complaint about?
Please tell us in your own words what went wrong

¹_____. On 4th January, I made an online transfer of £500 from my UK bank account to my Colombian account. This was a normal transfer, not an urgent transfer.

When I checked my account statement, I noticed that you charged me £30 for this service.

²_____. As I mentioned, my transfer was not an urgent transfer. The cost for a normal transfer is £22. In addition, the transfer took five working days, when you say that it should only take between two and four working days.

What can we do to put things right?

I am afraid that I am unhappy with this situation.
³_____.
Thank you very much. I look forward to hearing from you.

Important
Please note that we do not contact customers to ask for their full security details.

SUBMIT YOUR COMPLAINT

---

7 Choose the correct answer (a, b or c).
1 What is Liliana's main problem?
  a The Colombian bank charged the wrong amount of money.
  b The English bank moved the money to the wrong bank account.
  c The English bank charged the wrong amount of money.
2 What does Liliana want?
  a She wants the bank to give her £8.
  b She wants the bank to give her £22.
  c She wants the bank to give her £30.

8 Put these topics in the order Liliana writes about them.
a what she did ☐
b the problems she had ☐
c her reason for writing ☐

9 In formal writing, we do these things. Find examples in the form.
1 We don't usually use short forms and contractions.
2 We use polite and formal language.

10a **Linkers** In formal writing, we often use *that* to link two clauses. (We don't usually use *that* in informal writing.) Where can you put *that* in these sentences? Read the form to check.
1 I noticed you charged me £30 for this service.
2 I am afraid I am unhappy with this situation.

10b Put these words in the right order to make sentences.
1 was / I / it / thought / free / that / .
2 charge / said / the / he / was / £100 / that / .
3 realised / I / was / there / mistake / that / a / .
4 you / hope / that / can / I / me / help / .
5 am / I / that / unhappy / happened / this / .

11 Write a complaint to the National Bank of England about <u>two</u> problems in the table. Use Liliana's complaint as a model.

subject	charge (bank said)	final charge
credit card application	no charge	£20
travel money (foreign currency)	no charge	£25
loan application	no charge (January special offer)	£50

11 Homes

11.1 MY HOME, MY CASTLE

IN THIS UNIT

GRAMMAR
- will, won't
- be going to

VOCABULARY
- compound nouns

SCENARIO
- checking understanding
- asking for information about accommodation

STUDY SKILLS
- examination skills

WRITING SKILLS
- an informal email

'A small house will hold a hundred friends.' African proverb

READING

1 Work with a partner and answer these questions.

1. Describe the area where you live.
2. Do you feel safe in your area / in your home?
3. Look at the photo in the article. What is this place, do you think?

2 Read the article quickly and choose the best answer (a, b, c or d).

The article tells us about gated communities
a in the future.
b now.
c now and in the future.
d in the future, now and in the past.

3 Read the article again. Which of these ideas are in it?

1. Gated communities existed a long time ago.
2. Gated communities will have a lot of facilities.
3. You can find these communities in many places around the world already.
4. They are expensive to live in.
5. There is no crime in them.
6. Some people are against gated communities.

Separate lives

A What kind of homes will we live in twenty or thirty years from now? Some people think that many of us will live in 'gated communities'. There will be high walls and fences around our houses and flats. Security guards will control the entrances. Inside, there will be parks and play areas for children, supermarkets, business centres and travel agencies, restaurants, gyms and golf courses.

B These gated communities already exist in many countries. Some of them are like small towns, and in Brazil, some even have their own schools. Of course, they aren't cheap places to live in: at Beverley Park, in Los Angeles, houses cost between twelve and thirty-two million dollars.

C It's clear why people want to live in them. In Johannesburg, South Africa, sixty-five percent of residents feel unsafe in their homes at night. In many cities, public spaces like parks are sometimes dangerous. A gated community gives people a feeling of security and, naturally, people want to feel safe.

D But not everyone is happy about a future of gated communities, including some top police officers. They say that the people in the communities won't mix with people outside. Also, the gap between rich and the poor will increase, and society will become more dangerous.

MY HOME, MY CASTLE 11.1

4 Match sentences 1–5 with a paragraph from the article.
1 People are nervous these days.
2 There will be cameras everywhere.
3 They say that people in the communities are too similar.
4 They will check people, bicycles and cars as they come in.
5 They are more common in the Americas and Africa than in Europe or Australia.

5 *Exploring the topic* Do you think that gated communities are a good idea?

VOCABULARY
COMPOUND NOUNS

6a Look at these compound nouns (noun + noun). Find three more compound nouns in the article.

security guards   play areas   business centres

6b Match nouns from box A with nouns from box B to make ten compound nouns. You can use some nouns more than once. Which of these things can you see in your area?

A car   internet   police   post   railway
   shopping   sports   swimming   tennis   theme

B café   centre   court   office   park
   pool   station

car park, …

GRAMMAR
WILL, WON'T

7 Look at the first and last paragraphs of the article and answer these questions.
1 Why do we usually use *will* and *won't (will not)*?
   a To talk about what is generally true in the present
   b To talk about what happened in the past
   c To talk about what we know or think about the future.
2 Do we add *-s* to *will* after *he, she, it* or *there*?
3 Do you know any other verbs with grammar like this?

➜ Language reference and extra practice, pages 122–123

8 Complete these sentences with *will* or *won't (will not)* and a verb from the box.

be   change   have   have to   live   meet

1 Gated communities _____ high walls.
2 There _____ safe places where children can play.
3 People outside _____ people inside.
4 Poor people _____ in these communities.
5 People in these places _____ leave the community very often.
6 The communities _____ society in some ways.

9 Put the words in the right order to make questions. Then ask and answer the questions with a partner.

In the year 2100,
1 families / be / will / smaller than / now / bigger / or / ?
2 any fish / there / will / in the sea / be / ?
3 the internet / use / people / will / ?
4 people / all their life / will / keep / all their teeth / ?
5 India / will / be / the most important country / ?
6 will / love / in relationships / be important / ?

PRONUNCIATION

10 11.1 *Contractions* Listen and complete these sentences. Then practise saying them.
1 I'll _____ rich.
2 You'll _____ three children.
3 She'll _____ a sports car.
4 He'll _____ alone.
5 It'll _____ them happy.
6 We'll _____ excellent English.
7 They'll _____ to Australia.

SPEAKING

11 *Speculating* Work with a partner. Discuss some ideas about your lives in the future.

Student A: Look at page 145 and follow the instructions.
Student B: Look at page 146 and follow the instructions.

11.2 SMART HOUSE

SPEAKING

1 Describe your home to your partner.
1. What kind of building is it?
2. How many rooms are there?
3. What is there in the rooms?
4. How much technology is there in your home?

READING

2a Read the house-building company's brochure. Complete the titles (A–D) with the words in the box.

fun   energy   safer   environment   convenience

2b Which of the design features do you think definitely, may or probably don't need computer or internet technology to work?

3a Match these design features to categories A–D in the brochure.
1. wind turbines
2. living roof / roof garden
3. swimming pools
4. outdoor security lighting
5. electric car- and bike-charging points
6. home cinema and computer-games room

a modern home, your dream home

These days, you can build your own home and you can make it your dream home. With modern technology, you can enjoy the perfect home. Here are some of the modern design features that we can offer you in your new home.

A Save ¹_____, save the ²_____
- Smart energy meters: know exactly how much energy you are using.
- Solar panels: make electricity from the sun.
- Automatic lighting: it turns on and off when you enter and leave a room.

B Enjoy more ³_____
- Computer-controlled food shopping: never forget to buy milk again.
- Smartphone-controlled heating: make your house warm before you get home.

C Have more ⁴_____
- Multi-room entertainment system: big-screen TVs, internet and music in every room.
- Saunas and steam rooms: the healthy and hot way to relax.

D Feel ⁵_____
- Security camera system: check your house when on holiday.
- Fingerprint door locks: never use keys again.

3b Work with a partner. Describe the design features in Exercise 3a.

wind turbine – this means you can make electricity from the wind.
If you have this, you can …

3c How many compound nouns (noun + noun) can you find in the brochure and Exercise 3a?

LISTENING

4 Rachel and her husband, Simon, want to build a new house. Look at the plan for their new house, and features A–H. Which of the design features in the brochure and Exercise 3a did they choose?

5a 11.2 Listen to Rachel talking about plans for her new house. Which of the features (A–H) does she discuss? Which features do they decide to have?

5b Rachel gives reasons for her decisions. Listen again and complete these reasons.
1. … because we want to _____ how much electricity we _____.
2. That means we can _____ our energy costs and help _____ the environment.
3. We think it doesn't _____ much money and we're not that _____!
4. They're really expensive and they use a lot of _____!
5. If we do that, we can _____ TV, DVDs and _____ the internet in every room.
6. … because I often _____ my keys.
7. We need one because he's going to _____ an electric car soon.

GRAMMAR
BE GOING TO

6a Read these sentences from the conversation and answer the questions below.
a I'm going to have a big screen in the kitchen!
b You're going to build a new house.
c He's going to buy an electric car soon.
d We're going to put a wind turbine on the roof.
1. Are the sentences about the past, present or future?
2. Are the sentences about definite plans/intentions or possible ideas/predictions?
3. What is the main verb in each sentence?
4. *I'm going to = I am going to*. What about *you're/he's/we're/they're going to*?

6b Find all the examples of this grammar in Audio script 11.2 on page 156. How do we make questions and negative sentences with this grammar?

➥ Language reference and extra practice, pages 122–123

SMART HOUSE 11.2

7 Complete these plans with the correct form of *be going to* and the verbs in brackets.

1 I _____ an electric bike soon. (buy)
2 She _____ the electric car because she can't drive. (not use)
3 They _____ a swimming pool because they're expensive. (not have)
4 _____ they _____ a TV screen in the bathroom? (put)
5 When _____ the builders _____ the house? (finish)
6 Why _____ they _____ a living roof? (have)

PRONUNCIATION

8a 11.3 Contractions We often use contractions with *be going to* (*He's going to …*). In the negative, you have two choices: *He's not going to …* or *He isn't going to …* Listen to seven sentences with contractions and repeat them.

8b Work with a partner and practise saying affirmative and negative contractions with different subject pronouns. Use *to be going to* and verb phrases from the box.

| put a TV in the bedroom | save energy |
| have a security camera system | use solar panels |

SPEAKING

9a You are going to design your own modern dream home. First, can you remember the fifteen modern design features from this lesson? Close your book and write them down.

9b Check your list with a partner, and then look at the brochure and Exercise 3a. How many did you remember, and spell, correctly?

10a Design your dream home. Choose seven design features from the list, and add two more ideas of your own. Draw a picture.

10b Explaining decisions Tell your partner about the plans for your new home. How big is it going to be? What modern design features is it going to have? Why are you going to have those things?

WRITING

11 Write a short description of your plans for your new home.

▶ MEET THE EXPERT

Watch an interview with Godson Egbo, an architect, about homes of the future.
Turn to page 130 for video activities.

89

11.3 SCENARIO
FINDING A FLAT

PREPARATION

1 Put the words in the box into three groups: rooms, furniture, equipment.

armchair   bathroom   bedroom   chair   cooker
cupboard   desk   dining room   dishwasher
fridge-freezer   kitchen   living room   sofa
table   wardrobe   washing machine

2 Imagine you are going to work or study in another country. Think about where you would like to live. Put these things in order of importance to you. Then compare your ideas with your partner.

The place should have:
- large bedrooms
- a garden or balcony
- a good-quality bathroom
- a large kitchen
- modern furniture
- large windows

It should be:
- in a quiet road
- near public transport
- near a supermarket
- near restaurants and cafés
- in a central location
- near a park

3a 11.4 Colleen is a student in Dublin. Her university is in the city centre. She and a friend are looking for a flat, so she phones an accommodation agency. Listen and answer these questions.

1. How many rooms does each flat have?
2. How much are the weekly rents?
3. Does Colleen decide to rent one of them?

3b Listen again and complete Colleen's notes.

Flat:	One	Two
Number of bedrooms:	1_____	11_____ large bedrooms
Other rooms:	kitchen, living room, 2_____	small 12_____, dining room, living room, large 13_____
Floor:	3_____	14_____ – no lift
Garden:	4_____	no
Bedrooms:	no furniture	bed, 15_____, wardrobe
Kitchen:	5_____, 6_____	cooker, 16_____, washing machine
Living room:	7_____	17_____
Dining room:	no	18_____, chairs
Public transport:	metro station: 8_____-min walk away (20 mins to city centre)	bus stop: 19_____ mins away (45 mins to city centre)
Local area/ facilities:	supermarket, 9_____, other shops	nice and quiet, local shops
Rent:	10€_____ per person per week	20€_____ per person per week

11.3 FINDING A FLAT

TASK
ASKING FOR INFORMATION ABOUT ACCOMMODATION

7a Work with a partner to find out about flats.

Student A: You are a student in Ireland and you are looking for a flat to share with a friend. Phone the accommodation agency and find out about a flat. (Check when you are not sure about something.) Complete the form below.
Student B: You work in an accommodation agency. Look at page 147.

7b Change roles. Do the role-play again.
Student A: Now you work in the accommodation agency. Look at page 132.
Student B: Phone the accommodation agency and complete the form below.

KEY LANGUAGE
CHECKING UNDERSTANDING

4 Listen again and complete these questions from the conversation. Check your answers with Audio script 11.4 on pages 156–157.
1 Could you _____ that, please?
2 _____, there's a cooker, a fridge-freezer and a washing machine. Is that _____?
3 I'm sorry, could you say that _____?
4 _____ that 15 or 50 minutes?
5 I'm sorry, _____ you say 19 or 90 euros?

PRONUNCIATION

5 **11.5** **Stressed words** When you check information, you stress the words you want to check. Listen to questions 4 and 5 from Exercise 4. Which words have the most stress?

6a Complete the questions below to check the bold information in Student A's sentences.
1 A: It's on the **fourth** floor.
   B: I'm sorry, was that the _fourth_ or the _fifth_ floor?
2 A: The rent is one hundred and **fifty** euros.
   B: Did you say one hundred and _____ or _____?
3 A: It's got a **living** room.
   B: Was that a _____ _____ or a _____ _____?
4 A: **There's** a sofa in the living room.
   B: Did you say _____ _____ or _____ _____ a sofa?
5 A: It **hasn't got** a balcony.
   B: Did you say it _____ or _____ got a balcony?

6b **11.6** Listen and check. Then practise the questions and answers with your partner. Remember the stress.

```
Flat (address):      ......................................................
Bedrooms:            ......................................................
Other rooms:         ......................................................
Floor:               ......................................................
Garden:              ......................................................

Furniture/Equipment
  kitchen:           ......................................................
  bedrooms:          ......................................................
  living room:       ......................................................
  dining room:       ......................................................
Public transport:    ......................................................
Local facilities:    ......................................................
Rent:                € ............ per person per week
```

USEFUL PHRASES
How can I help?
I'm looking for …
Let's see …
What floor is the flat on?
I'm afraid there isn't …
What furniture is there?
Would you like to see the flat?
What about the local area?
How much is the rent?
Thanks for your help.

8 You want to share a flat with your partner. Your university is in the city centre. Look at the information about the four flats in Exercise 3b and Exercise 7 and choose the best flat for you to share.

91

11.4 STUDY AND WRITING SKILLS

STUDY SKILLS
EXAMINATION SKILLS

1 Developing self-awareness Discuss these questions with a partner.
1. Do you like examinations and tests? Why?/Why not?
2. What was the last exam you did? When was it?
3. How did you feel before, during and after the exam?

2 Do you know these words connected with exams? Check them in your dictionary.

| to pass an examination   to fail an examination |
| instructions   a practice test   to relax/relaxation |
| to revise/revision |

3a Before the exam Look at these ideas about preparing for an exam. Which do you do? Which do you think are good ideas?
1. 'I find out everything I can about the exam or test.'
2. 'I make a revision plan.'
3. 'I don't revise all day. I study in the morning and relax in the afternoon.'
4. 'I revise with a group of my classmates.'
5. 'I do a lot of practice tests. Every time you do a practice test, you get better.'
6. 'I always start my revision a long time before the exam.'
7. 'I usually study at the same time every day.'
8. 'I always study in a quiet place.'
9. 'I like to go to a party the night before the exam.'
10. 'I drink a lot of coffee on the morning of the exam.'

3b Discuss the ideas with a partner. Decide on two or three things that both of you will try in the future.

4 It is important to relax and take breaks when you are revising. Look at these relaxation techniques. Add four or five more to the list.

| watching TV   walking   playing tennis   yoga |

5 During the exam Look at the 'golden rules' below. Fill the gaps with the words in the box.

| watch   take   do (x3)   make   read   spend |

1. _____ the instructions carefully.
2. _____ what the questions ask you to do.
3. Don't _____ a long time on one or two difficult questions. Come back to them later.
4. _____ sure that your writing is easy to read.
5. Don't _____ other students working.
6. Don't _____ the exam too quickly and make careless mistakes.
7. Don't _____ the exam too slowly, and not finish. Answer all the questions.
8. _____ time at the end of the exam (about ten minutes) to check your answers (information, grammar, spelling, etc.).

6 After the exam Which of these things do you do after an exam? Which are good things to do?
1. Think about which questions you answered well (or badly).
2. Think about how you used your time.
3. Think about how you can prepare better next time.
4. Worry about mistakes you made in the exam.
5. Continue to study hard.

STUDY AND WRITING SKILLS 11.4

WRITING SKILLS
AN INFORMAL EMAIL

7 Look at the photo. What is happening? What is the reason, do you think?

8a Read Carla's email quickly and check your answers. Do you do this in your country? What is the relationship between Carla and Erdem, do you think?

8b Read the email again. Are these sentences true, false or the email doesn't say?
1. Carla is happy with her new flat.
2. Carla is living alone in her new flat.
3. You have to get a taxi from the station.
4. Erdem is going to go to the party.

9 Look at Carla's email and the formal writing on page 85. What are the main differences between the two texts? (Think about language, punctuation, etc.)

10 Look at the email again and complete the lists below with the phrases in the box.

| ~~Hello,~~ ~~How are you?~~ ~~Take care.~~ Bye for now |
| Dear …   How are things?   Love   Hi |
| How's life?   See you soon   Hope you're OK |

1. Greetings: *Hello,*
2. Opening phrases: *How are you?*
3. Endings: *Take care.*

11 Directions Find words in the email to complete these sentences.
1. Go _____ on for 300 metres.
2. My house is _____ the right.
3. _____ the number 39Y bus to Enfield Town station.
4. _____ down the hill.
5. _____ right at the traffic lights.

12 Linkers We can use *when* to join sentences, and often use it for directions. Find the example of *when* in the email. Then match sentence beginnings 1–3 with endings a–c.
1. When you get off the bus,
2. When you get in the taxi,
3. When you get to my house,
a. park your car in the next street on the left.
b. walk to the traffic lights.
c. ask the driver to take you to Wood Green.

13 Write an email to a friend, inviting him or her to a party at your house (see the map on the right). Use the email as a model to help you.

Subject: party   inbox 6

Hello Erdem,

How are you? I'm in my new flat now, and I'm really enjoying it.

I'm going to have a housewarming party on Saturday 28th June, starting about 8 p.m. Can you come? A lot of our group will be here (I hope!), as well as some old friends. I'm going to cook something very special – it's a secret! We can also celebrate the end of exams!

My new address is:
147 Wood Green Road
London
NN22 9DT.

It's really easy to get here. Take the underground to Wood Green station. You can walk from there. When you come out of the station, turn left and go up the hill. Turn right at the traffic lights – then you're on my road. Go straight on for about 200 metres. The building is on the left.

Hope to see you on Saturday 28th. By the way, my new home number is 0228 888 0563.

Take care

Carla

12 Travel

12.1 GLOBAL NOMADS

IN THIS UNIT

GRAMMAR
- present perfect
- present perfect and past simple

VOCABULARY
- using verbs as nouns (gerunds)

SCENARIO
- taking long turns
- recounting experiences

STUDY SKILLS
- learning outside the classroom

WRITING SKILLS
- a travel blog

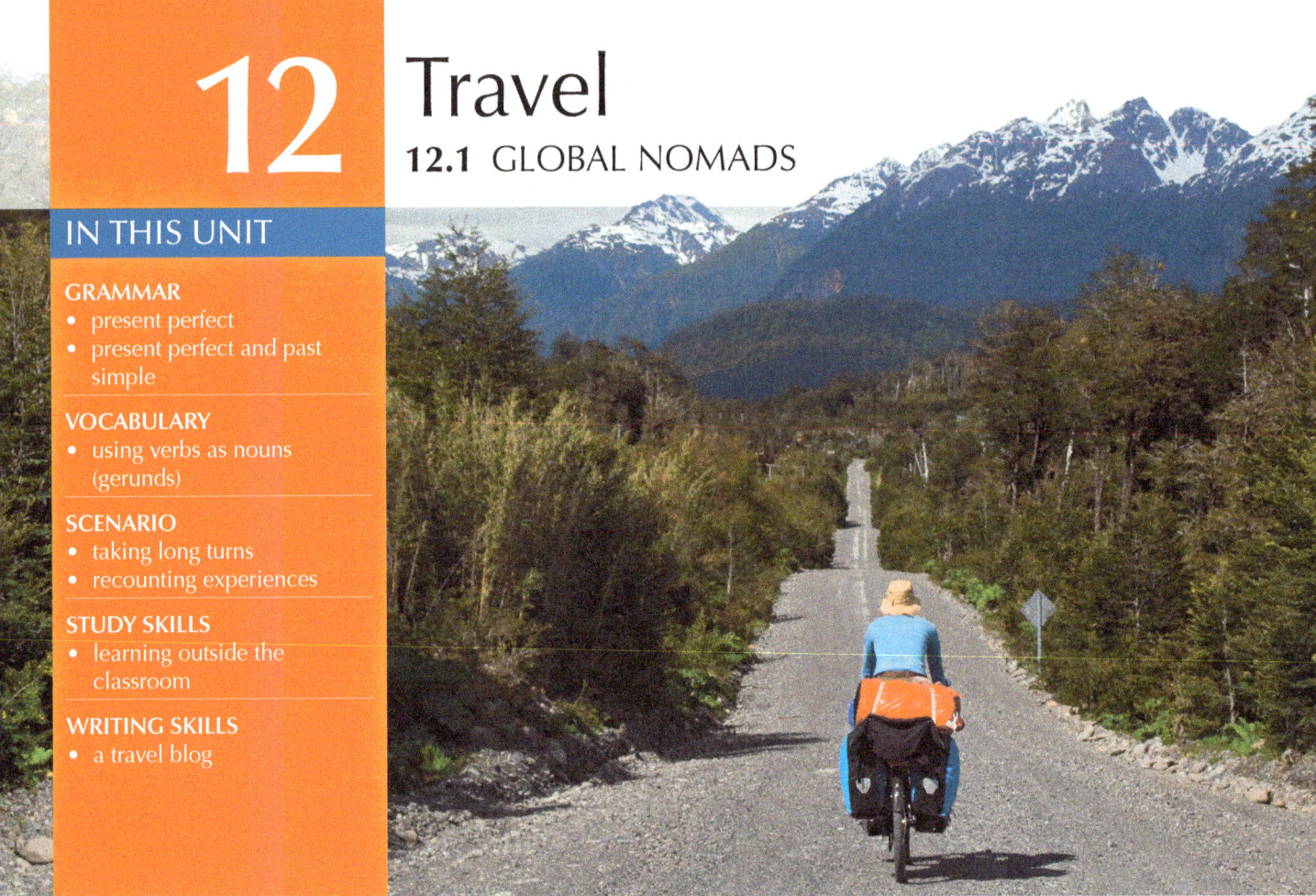

'Experience, travel – these are an education in themselves.' Euripides, 480–406 BC, Greek playwright

LISTENING

1 Which country would you like to live in, apart from your own? Why?

2a 12.1 Listen to an interview with Kirsty, a student with experience of living abroad. In general, is she happy or unhappy about her time abroad?

2b Listen again and complete the form.

Experiences of living abroad

Name: *Kirsty Andrews*
Countries: ¹_____, *Oman and* ²_____.
Favourite country: ³_____
Reason: ⁴_____, _____
Languages: *A little* ⁵_____.
Work experience: *None.*
Changes (in the person):
Knows more about differences between ⁶_____.
Doesn't think that her way is best.
Problems: *Seeing old* ⁷_____.
Future:
Wants to live in a ⁸_____ *country, and in* ⁹_____ *America.*

GRAMMAR
PRESENT PERFECT

3 Look at these sentences. When exactly did Kirsty live abroad?

A: Have you ever lived abroad?
B: Yes, I have. I've lived in a lot of countries.

When we talk about an experience in the past, but we don't say when we did it, we use the present perfect.

4 Look at Audio script 12.1 on page 157 and complete this table.

	subject + have	past participle
+	I ¹_____/we've/you've/they've he's/she's/it's	worked
–	I/we/you/they ²_____ he/she/it hasn't	³_____
?	⁴_____ I/we/you/they ⁵_____ he/she/it	(ever) worked?

➥ Language reference and extra practice, pages 124–125

GRAMMAR TIP

Regular past participles are the same as the past simple form of the verb (see page 158).
I worked – I have worked

94

GLOBAL NOMADS

12.1

5a Complete these sentences with the present perfect of the verb in brackets.
1. We _____ a lot of interesting places. (visit)
2. I _____ a lot in the last ten years. (change)
3. She _____ to people from a lot of countries. (talk)
4. He _____ films in different languages. (watch)
5. They _____ house several times. (move)

5b 12.2 Listen and check your answers. Then repeat the sentences.

5c Use the sentences in Exercise 5a to ask a partner questions.

A: *Have you visited a lot of interesting places?*
B: *Yes, I have. / No, I haven't.*

READING

6 **Understanding reasons** Read the website below. Why are these people writing? Choose the best reason.
1. to find new friends
2. to practise their English
3. to communicate with other people like themselves

7 Answer these questions with *Nina, Maria* or *Andy*. You can use each name more than once.

Who
1. has lived in the most countries?
2. has a good relationship with his/her parents?
3. has no problems meeting people?
4. doesn't feel comfortable anywhere?
5. is the most successful person, do you think?

8 According to the website, what are the advantages and disadvantages of being a 'global nomad'? Are there more advantages or more disadvantages?

> **GRAMMAR TIP**
>
> Many common verbs have irregular past participles.
> to have → had
> to see → seen

9a Find the past participles of these verbs in the website.

to grow   to do   to feel   to become

9b Use your dictionary or the verb list on page 158 to find the past participles of the verbs in Exercise 10.

→ Language reference and extra practice, pages 124–125

SPEAKING

10 Work with a partner. Ask and answer questions using the ideas below. Then think of some other questions to ask your partner.

drive a sports car   eat Indian food   fly at night
live away from home   read a travel book
travel on a boat   visit another continent
work/study with someone from another country

A: *Have you ever driven a sports car?*
B: *Yes, I have. / No, I haven't.*

HAVE YOUR SAY ...

Children of the wind

Children of the wind (or global nomads) are people who have grown up abroad because of a parent's job. They've often had a good life, with large homes and nice holidays, and they're well-educated, international citizens of the twenty-first century. However, they often feel different from other people and can't stay in one place for a long time. Are you a global nomad? What's your experience?

By: Nina Rendquist (mail)   Posted on: 26 October

I'm from Sweden, but I left the country when I was six. I've lived in Saudi Arabia and the Philippines. I don't feel at home anywhere, but I think that I've done a lot. Because of my past, I'm good at learning new skills and meeting people.

By: Maria (mail)   Posted on: 27 October

Nina, I really understand you. I spent my childhood saying hello and goodbye. I'm from Argentina, but my parents took us from one country to another: Malaysia, Nigeria, Russia. Now I'm living in Paris. I feel I'm a stranger everywhere, but I'm independent and strong. I've travelled, I've seen the world and I speak three languages.

By: Andy (mail)   Posted on: 29 October

Like you, I'm proud to be a global nomad – I've lived in Kuwait, Venezuela and Kazakhstan. Sometimes I've felt lonely, but I'm comfortable with people from all over the world. And I've become really close to my mum and dad – they're like my best friends.

12.2 JOURNEYS OF A LIFETIME

SPEAKING

1 Discuss these questions with a partner.
1 Do you usually go abroad for your holiday or work?
2 Which five countries would you like to visit? Why?
3 Are there many travel programmes on TV in your country?
4 Do you watch many of them? Which ones, and why do you like them?

READING

2 Simon Reeve is a TV travel-programme presenter. Complete Simon's magazine interview below with questions a–f.

a Which countries have you visited?
b How many travel shows have you made?
c What have you learnt from your different trips?
d What's the best place that you've visited?
e When did you become a travel-show presenter?
f Have you done any unusual or dangerous things?

3 Answer these questions.
1 What things does Simon show us in his programmes?
2 When did he go to Kazakhstan?
3 Where did he go for his ninth TV series?
4 Where does he hope to go in the future?
5 In what year did a camel chase him?
6 Where did he meet the San people?
7 In what way are people the same all over the world?

Discovering the world
with Simon Reeve

Simon Reeve has visited many countries and he has become one of our most popular TV travel-show presenters. His programmes are different to other ones because he goes to unusual countries and he shows us more than the tourist attractions. From his programmes, we also learn about the people in the countries, the way of life, the politics and the wildlife. I asked him about his fascinating work.

by Stuart McCarthy

1 _____

I started to work as a TV presenter in 2003. Before that, I was a political journalist and writer. In my first travel show, I visited countries in central Asia, such as Kazakhstan.

2 _____

I've made nine travel TV series. In three of those shows, I travelled round the world in a circle – they were very long journeys! In my most recent series, I went to Australia.

3 _____

Perhaps you should ask which countries I haven't visited! I think I've travelled to more than 110 countries, but I haven't been to the North and South Poles. Perhaps I'll go there soon.

4 _____

Oh, definitely. I've eaten lots of unusual food. Eating sheep's eyes was very strange for me. A camel has chased me. That happened when I made my first TV show, and it felt more dangerous than when I was in the middle of a war in Somalia!

5 _____

Ah, one of my favourite places is the Kalahari Desert in southern Africa. I went there in 2007. It's really beautiful and a lot greener than a typical desert. I met the San people there, and I learnt a lot from them.

6 _____

The most important thing that I've learnt is that human beings are very special animals. We can change and live in any environment. Also, in all these different places, with all these different ways of life, our children are always the most important things for us.

96

JOURNEYS OF A LIFETIME 12.2

GRAMMAR
PRESENT PERFECT AND PAST SIMPLE

5a Look at these sentences and answer the questions below.

1 I started to work as a TV presenter in 2003.
2 I've travelled to more than 110 countries.
3 I've made ten TV series.
4 I went there in 2007.

a Which sentences give the time when Simon Reeve did something?
b Which tense do we use when we give the time we did something?
c Which tense can we use when we do not give the exact time we did something?

5b Find all the examples of this grammar in the interview. How do we make questions and negatives?

GRAMMAR TIP
I've been = I've gone and I've come back

➜ Language reference and extra practice, pages 124–125

6a Complete this personal travel history with the present perfect or the past simple.

I ¹ _have visited_ (visit) many different countries, but I ² _____ (not go) to South America and Africa – I hope to go there soon. I first ³ _____ (go) abroad in 2001. I went to France with my school and two years later, I ⁴ _____ (visit) Spain – my favourite country. I also love Asia. I ⁵ _____ (work) in China and I ⁶ _____ (visit) Thailand and Japan. I ⁷ _____ (work) in China in 2008 – I ⁸ _____ (have) a wonderful time because it ⁹ _____ (be) so different from my country. Finally, last year, I ¹⁰ _____ (study) at film school in New Zealand – that was great!

6b Write a short travel history about yourself or someone you know.

SPEAKING

7a Work with a partner. Ask and answer questions about your travel experiences. Complete the tables at the back of the book.

Student A: Use the table on page 145.
Student B: Use the table on page 146.

A: Have you ever visited another country?
B: Yes, I have. I've been to Britain.
A: When did you go there?
B: Last year. I went with my family.
A: Did you have a good time?

7b Speaking from notes Tell the class about your partner's experiences.

Mehmet's visited Britain. He went there last year with …

VOCABULARY
USING VERBS AS NOUNS (GERUNDS)

4a Complete this sentence with a single word. Then find the sentence in the interview and check your answer.

_____ sheep's eyes was very strange for me.

4b 12.3 When we want to use a verb as a noun, we often add *-ing* to the infinitive. Look at these sentences about Simon's experiences. What do you think the missing words are? Listen and check.

1 _____ football in Argentina was fantastic.
2 _____ about life in the desert was interesting.
3 _____ the sun rise over the Indian Ocean was unforgettable.
4 _____ with sharks was scary.
5 _____ the animals in Africa was amazing.
6 _____ a horse in Kazakhstan was great fun.

4c Write similar sentences about experiences from your life and the activities you do, using verbs as nouns. Compare your ideas with a partner. Use adjectives from Exercise 4b and the box below.

| superb | easy | boring | strange | wonderful |
| exciting | difficult | | | |

Learning English is easy.

12.3 SCENARIO
AROUND THE WORLD

PREPARATION

1 Work with a partner and discuss these places. Have you ever been to or seen any of them? What do you know about them? Which continents are they on?

1. Heathrow Airport
2. the North Pole
3. the South Pole
4. Table Mountain
5. the Great Pyramid
6. the Taj Mahal
7. the Great Wall of China
8. Angkor Wat
9. Mount Fuji
10. Uluru (Ayers Rock)
11. Easter Island
12. the Grand Canyon
13. Machu Picchu
14. the Empire State Building
15. the Amazon Forest
16. the Djenne Mosque

2a `12.4` Listen to a woman talking about one of the places above. Which place is it?

2b Listen again. What does she say about it? Make notes on these topics.
1. when she saw the building
2. first view of it
3. visits to it
4. reasons for liking it

KEY LANGUAGE
TAKING LONG TURNS

3a Listen again and complete these sentences.
1. 'The tallest building? Well, _____ _____ _____, I haven't seen …'
2. 'I first saw the building from the plane. _____ was fantastic.'
3. 'It's different from most tall buildings _____ it's made of bricks.'
4. 'Other tall buildings are all glass, _____ it's very different …'
5. 'It's very different, and _____ _____ I think that it looks beautiful.'
6. 'Well, _____ _____? Oh yes, I also went up the building at night.'

3b Match the words and phrases in Exercise 3a to these functions.
1. showing you are looking for ideas
2. linking sentences and ideas together

3c Listen again and read Audio script 12.4 on page 157. Can you find more thinking and linking language?

4 Work with a partner and practise talking for one minute, then swap roles.

Student A: Talk about your last holiday for about one minute. Use the Key language.
Student B: Listen to your partner. Which of the Key language does he/she use?

TASK
RECOUNTING EXPERIENCES

5a Choose six places from Exercise 1 that you would like to visit. Choose from at least three continents. Write the places and their numbers below.

- _____ ☐
- _____ ☐
- _____ ☐
- _____ ☐
- _____ ☐
- _____ ☐

5b Work with a partner and practise giving short talks. Play the board game. In the game, you travel around the world and visit the sixteen places from Exercise 1. On your trip, you have to talk about different topics for 30 seconds. Read the rules.

RULES

- You need one or two dice and two counters.
- Everyone starts at Heathrow Airport (number 1 on the map).
- Throw your dice and move your counter the correct number of spaces. You can move in any direction.
- When you reach a tourist attraction (2–16), you have to stop and talk about a topic for thirty seconds. The topics for each place are below.
- When you land on one of the six places you chose in Exercise 5a, tick the box next to it.
- When you have visited all of your six places, you have to return to Heathrow and talk about the final topic. The winner is the first person to return to Heathrow Airport.

TOPICS FOR YOUR TALKS
1. the journey that you have just made in the game
2. the coldest place that you have ever been to
3. the quietest place that you have ever been to
4. a famous person, dead or alive, that you admire
5. the hottest place that you have ever been to
6. the most beautiful building that you have ever seen
7. food from other countries that you have eaten
8. an old religious building that you have been to
9. a mountain that you have been to
10. a sport that you have played
11. some art (paintings/statues) that you have seen
12. an American film that you have seen
13. an ancient culture that you have learnt about
14. the tallest building that you have seen
15. an animal that you have looked after or known
16. a national festival that you have been to

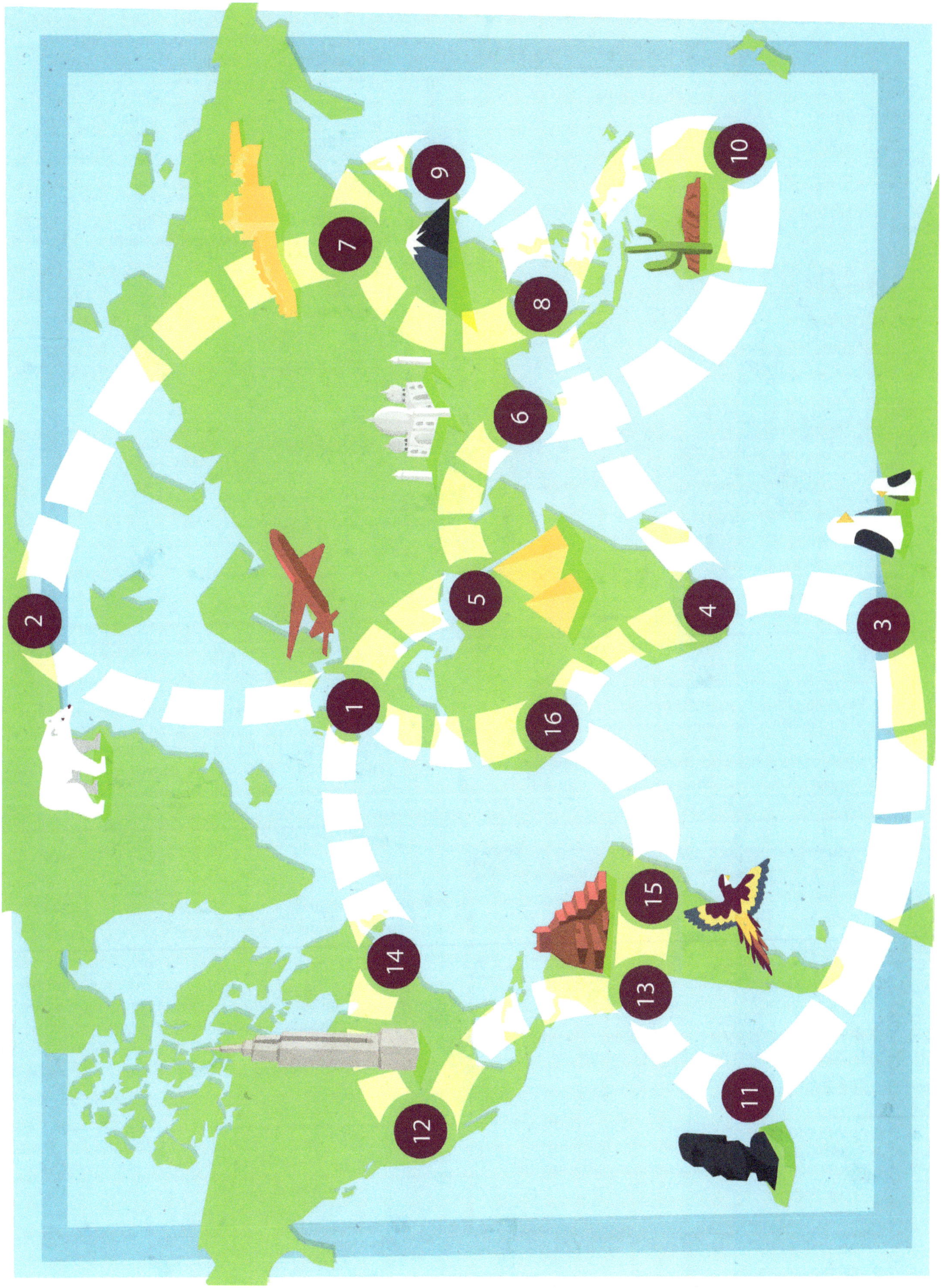

12.3 AROUND THE WORLD

12.4 STUDY AND WRITING SKILLS

STUDY SKILLS
LEARNING OUTSIDE THE CLASSROOM

1 Ways of practising English You can practise your English outside the classroom in many different ways. How often do you do these things outside the classroom?

- use the internet in English
- watch DVDs/films in English
- use apps on your mobile phone
- revise your classwork
- listen to songs in English

www.longmandictionaries.com

2 Many students ask for learning advice on the internet. Look at these questions. Can you give any advice?

1 How can I learn vocabulary?
2 How can I improve my listening?
3 Is it better to learn alone or with friends?

3 Match the teacher's advice below with the questions in Exercise 2. Have you done any of these things?

A You should do things with the words. Make vocabulary cards and put them in your house so you can see them every day. Put vocabulary in groups and make sentences with them.

B I think you should do both: on your own, you can practise at your speed, but with friends, you can practise speaking and test each other.

C The internet is perfect because you can usually listen again and again. Also, listen to songs; you can usually get the song words from the internet to help you.

4a ▶12.1 **Using technology to learn** Watch the teacher giving a talk about using technology to learn English. Which of these things does he talk about? Does he mention any of the things in the photos on this page?

radio programmes   blogs   TV   chat rooms
language-learning websites   video clips

4b Watch again and make notes on the advice. Make notes in the form of a word web, using these headings. Then compare your notes with Video script 12.1 on page 157.

- writing practice
- listening practice
- language-learning sites

5a Complete the quote below with the words in the box.

say   do   read   see   hear   say   see

The important thing is to do lots of different things:
'We remember 20 percent of what we read,
30 percent of what we hear,
40 percent of what we ^{1}_____,
50 percent of what we ^{2}_____,
60 percent of what we do and
90 percent of what we ^{3}_____, ^{4}_____, ^{5}_____, ^{6}_____ and ^{7}_____. (Flanagan 1997)
So, follow my advice and enjoy practising your English outside the classroom.'

5b ▶12.2 Watch the end of the talk to check your ideas.

6 The teacher would like to know your opinions about the talk. Give him a score from 1 to 5 (1= *no/not very*, 5 = *yes/very*). Then discuss your opinions with a partner.

- interesting
- confident
- intelligent
- well-educated
- smart/well-dressed
- friendly

7 Evaluating ideas Look again at all the advice in this Study skills section. Which are the best ideas, do you think? Compare your answer with a partner.

STUDY AND WRITING SKILLS 12.4

WRITING SKILLS
A TRAVEL BLOG

8 Discuss these questions with a partner.
1. What kind of writing do you do on holiday?
2. Do you send postcards to people?
3. Do you send text messages?
4. Do you write a travel diary or blog?

9a Look at this list of things that we can write about in a travel blog. Which of them can you find in Hussein and Ranya's blog?

famous buildings		food	health
hotels	activities	people we meet	
interesting places		jobs	leisure
money	TV	the weather	

9b What is the main topic of each post in the blog?

10 The blog uses a number of different tenses. How many can you find?

11 Are Hussein and Ranya enjoying their trip? Find words or phrases in the blog that show this.

12 Adjectives These sentences come from two other blogs. Who is having the worst holiday?

Yurika	Sandro
The food isn't very good.	The food is disgusting.
The weather is very bad.	The weather is terrible.
The people aren't very nice.	The people are horrible.
The hotel is unpleasant.	The hotel is awful.

13 Imagine you are on holiday or on a trip. Write a travel blog. Use the model in Exercise 9a to help you. Use a variety of tenses and adjectives.

Posted on 25 Apr

We arrived here in Singapore yesterday. The city is busy, but very modern and clean. Communicating with people has been easy, because English is the official language here. It's a good chance for us to practise! Tomorrow we're going to visit the Botanic Garden.

Posted on 26 Apr

The Botanic Garden is beautiful – with lots of unusual plants and animals. There's even an area of rainforest! While we were there, there was a huge storm. We stayed in a shelter and couldn't go anywhere because the rain was so heavy. For two hours, we just waited and chatted. Finally, the storm passed! It's been very hot, but now it's a bit cooler.

Posted on 28 Apr

Ranya loves the shops here, but we haven't bought much because we're going to Bali soon and we don't want to carry a lot of things with us.

Posted on 29 Apr

Every evening, we have dinner outside in a food market. We've eaten Chinese, Indian and Malay food – it's all amazing! We think this is one of the best places in the world for food!

Posted 30 Apr

Changi Airport is really nice – full of trees, plants and flowers – inside the terminal! We've had a great time in Singapore and we're looking forward to the next part of our trip!

1 LANGUAGE REFERENCE

GRAMMAR

G1 TO BE (AFFIRMATIVE)

	contraction	full form
I	'm	am
he/she/it	's	is
you/we/they	're	are

For speaking, use contractions with *I, he, she, it, you, we, they*.
   I'm a student.
   It's cold in winter.

Use *to be* with jobs, adjectives and descriptions.
   He's a teacher.
   The bus is noisy.
   Buses are expensive in the city.

G2 TO BE (NEGATIVE)

	contraction	full form
I	'm not	am not
he/she/it	isn't/'s not	is not
you/we/they	aren't/'re not	are not

New York isn't a capital city.
You aren't a teacher.

G3 TO BE (QUESTIONS)

Am	I ... ?
Is	he/she/it ... ?
Are	you/we/they ... ?

Use full forms (not contractions) to ask questions.
   Is it expensive?
   Are you a teacher?

Use full forms (not contractions) for short answers with *yes*.
   'Is London old?' 'Yes, it is.' ✓
   'Is London old?' 'Yes, it's.' ✗

Use contractions for short answers with *no*.
   'Is São Paulo a small city?' 'No, it isn't.'
   'Are the restaurants famous?' 'No, they aren't.'

G4 THERE IS, THERE ARE (+ ANY)

singular		
	contraction	full form
+	there's	there is
–	there isn't / there's not	there is not
?		Is there ... ?
Short answers +		Yes, there is.
–		No, there isn't.

plural		
	contraction	full form
+		there are
–	there aren't any	there are not any
?		Are there any ... ?
Short answers +		Yes, there are.
–		No, there aren't.

Use *there is / there are* to say what is or isn't in a place. *There is* and *there are* introduce places and things.
   There's an airport in the city.
   There are people on the bus.

Use *any* with *there aren't* and *Are there ... ?*
   There aren't any cars in Venice.
   Are there any cinemas in the city?

Use *a lot of* for large numbers.
   There are a lot of people in Mumbai.
   There are a lot of boats in the harbour.

Use full forms for short answers with *yes*.
   'Is there an opera house?' 'Yes, there is.' ✓
   'Is there an opera house?' 'Yes, there's.' ✗

Use contractions for short answers with *no*.
   'Are there any famous buildings?' 'No, there aren't.'

KEY LANGUAGE

KL SAYING WHERE PLACES ARE

B A C   (A is) between (B and C).
A B   (A is) next to (B).
B c   (C is) in (B).
A ← → B   (B is) opposite (A).
A B   (A is) on the left of (B).
B C   (C is) on the right of (B).

VOCABULARY

V1 CITIES
Beijing, Istanbul, Jakarta, Lagos, London, New York, Mexico City, Shangai, Tokyo

V2 ADJECTIVES
bad, beautiful, big, cheap, cold, dry, expensive, good, hot, new, noisy, old, quiet, small, ugly, wet

V3 PLACES IN A CITY
airport, beach, bookshop, bridge, building site, bus station, canal, car park, church, cinema, college, concert hall, fountain, gardens, harbour, library, market, mosque, mountain, museum, park, post office, public toilets, railway station, shopping centre, swimming pool, temple, theatre, tourist information centre, university, zoo

EXTRA PRACTICE 1

G1 **1** Write the correct form of *to be*. Use contractions if possible.

1 I __'m__ a teacher.
2 She _____ a student.
3 We _____ from New York.
4 Poland and the UK _____ in Europe.
5 Brazil _____ famous for football.
6 She _____ in Kraków, in Poland.
7 Istanbul and New York _____ noisy cities.

G2, 3 **2** Are the verbs correct (✓) or incorrect (✗)? Correct the wrong forms.

1 'My friend aren't ugly!' ✗ *isn't*
2 'We aren't in Brasilia – we're in São Paulo.'
3 'Is Tokyo a small city?' 'No, it isn't. It's big.'
4 'Are the restaurants good?' 'No, they are.'
5 'Japan isn't a cheap country.'
6 'Are you Spanish?' 'No, I am. I'm French.'

G2, 3 **3** Match questions 1–6 with answers a–f.

1 Is it cold in winter? _____
2 Are you a student? _____
3 Are we in the east of the city here? _____
4 Are the summers dry? _____
5 Is Maria on the phone? _____
6 Is he cold? _____

a No, I'm not.
b Yes, she is.
c Yes, it is.
d No, he isn't.
e Yes, they are.
f No, we aren't.

G4 **4** Write the missing word in sentences 1–5.

1 There _'s_ a famous opera house in Sydney.
2 There not any cars in Venice.
3 'Is there a film at the cinema today?' 'No, isn't.'
4 In Chicago, there any good theatres?
5 In Kyoto, there are a lot old buildings.

G1–4 **5** Choose the correct words.

'Hello, my name ¹*is / am* Laura. ²*I'm / I's* from Auckland. Auckland ³*am / is* a city on the north island of New Zealand. There ⁴*is / are* 1.3 million people here, but it ⁵*aren't / isn't* the capital city. In the summer, it's hot and there are ⁶*any / a lot of* boats on the sea. The city is famous for boats! ⁷*Is / Are* there any boats in your city?'

KL **6** Look at the map and match 1–5 with a–e.

1 The bookshop is
2 The university is
3 The bus station is
4 The market is
5 The park is

a next to the library.
b on the left of the map.
c opposite the market.
d on the left of the university.
e between the bookshop and the bus station.

7 Look at the map again. Where's the library?
The library is _____.

8 Speaking practice Work with a partner. Ask and answer these questions.

Where is
- your language school?
- your classroom?
- your teacher?

V1 **9** Which are capital cities?
London   Kraków   Istanbul   New York   Tokyo   São Paulo

V2 **10** Write the vowels (*a, e, i, o, u*) in the adjectives.

1 The mountains are b _e a u t i f u_ l.
2 It's h _ t at the beach.
3 The library is q _ _ _ t.
4 This is a b _ g shopping centre.
5 Is the museum _xp _ ns _ v _?
6 Marco's is a n _ w restaurant.
7 My coffee is c _ ld.
8 The buses are ch _ _ p.

V3 **11** Write these words in the table.

~~museum~~   bus   cinema   market   temple   railway   bookshop   shopping centre

Buildings	Stations	Shopping
museum		

LANGUAGE REFERENCE

GRAMMAR

G1 PRESENT SIMPLE (AFFIRMATIVE)

| I/you/we/they | like |
| he/she/it | likes |

The present simple verb is in the infinitive form (*live*, *work*) after *I*, *you*, *we* and *they*.
  We **live** in New York.
  They **work** for a shop.

Add *-s* to the verb after *he/she/it*.
  He **lives** in New York.
  She **works** for a shop.
  She **buys** clothes for the shop.

In verbs ending in a consonant + *-y*, the *-y* changes to *-ies* after *he/she/it*.
  He **flies** to Rome.
  She **studies** at university.

In the verbs *go* and *do*, *-o* changes to *-oes* after *he/she/it*.
  The train **goes** to London.
  Philip **does** a boring job.

The verb *have* becomes *has* after *he/she/it*.
  Maria **has** an interesting job.

Use the present simple to talk about things that are generally true.
  I **like** the city.
  We **live** in Berlin.

Use the present simple to talk about things that happen again and again.
  Stephen **designs** houses.
  The pilots **fly** from Paris to New York.

G2 PRESENT SIMPLE (NEGATIVE)

	contraction	full form
I/you/we/they	don't like	do not like
he/she/it	doesn't like	does not like

Use *do* or *does* + *not* to form the negative in the present simple.
  You **don't like** airports.
  They **do not speak** English.
  He **doesn't go** to the cinema.
  She **does not drink** coffee.

For speaking, use contractions.
  My father **doesn't work**. ✓

Don't use *don't/doesn't* with the verb *to be*.
  He ~~doesn't be~~ a teacher. ✗
  He **isn't** a teacher. ✓

G3 PRESENT SIMPLE QUESTIONS (YES/NO)

| Do | I/you/we/they | work? |
| Does | he/she/it | |

Use *do* or *does* to form a question in the present simple.
  Do you **live** in France?
  Does she **study** Arabic?

Use short answers with *yes/no* questions.
  'Do you work in an office?' 'Yes, **I do**. / No, **I don't**.'
  'Does she have a lesson now?' 'Yes, **she does**. / No, **she doesn't**.'

G4 PRESENT SIMPLE QUESTIONS (QUESTION WORDS)

| What | do | I/you/we/they | have? |
| | does | he/she/it | |

  What languages **do** they **study**?
  What **do** you **do**?
  What job **does** she **have**?

Don't use *do/does* with the verb *to be*.
  What ~~does~~ your favourite subject ~~be~~? ✗
  What's your favourite subject? ✓
  What ~~does~~ it ~~be~~? ✗
  What is it? ✓

KEY LANGUAGE

KL ASKING FOR INFORMATION

What information do you want?
Where is it?
Is it (in the city centre)?
What are (the working hours)?
What does (an office assistant) do?
What (qualifications/skills) do I need?

VOCABULARY

V1 JOBS AND PLACE OF WORK

accountant, businessperson, doctor, fashion buyer, lawyer, lecturer, pilot, web designer

company, court, hospital, office, plane, shop, university

V2 STUDYING; UNIVERSITY

campus, canteen, course, exam, halls of residence, international students' office, lecture theatre, lecturer, librarian, library, professor, qualification, score, staff, student, subject, tutor

V3 OFFICE WORK

communication, email, event, filing, internet, letter, meeting, photocopier, photocopying, salary, skill, work duties, working hours

(to) answer, (to) do, (to) go to, (to) organise, (to) send, (to) use, (to) write

EXTRA PRACTICE 2

G1 **1** Write the verb in brackets in the correct form.
1. I _work_ in a hospital. (work)
2. You _____ in China. (live)
3. Marco _____ from Holland. (fly)
4. Jake and Sandro _____ at Oxford University. (study)
5. He _____ computer programs. (buy)
6. The boat _____ from Spain to Morocco. (go)
7. She _____ a modern computer. (have)
8. We _____ fashion designers. (meet)

G2 **2** Choose the correct form.
1. They *don't / doesn't* live in India.
2. Raul *don't / doesn't* go on holiday every year.
3. She *isn't / doesn't* a pilot.
4. I *don't / not* like horse-riding.
5. We *aren't / don't* work in the city centre.
6. You *doesn't / don't* have lunch at one.
7. We *aren't / don't* like noisy offices.
8. I *don't / doesn't* go to university.

G1, 2 **3** Speaking practice Write sentences for yourself. Tell a partner.

I like _____.
I don't like _____.
I speak _____.
I don't speak _____.
I'm a _____.
I'm not a _____.
I _____.
I don't _____.

G3, 4 **4** Write the words in sentences 1–8.

| ~~do~~ | do | don't | is | does | what |
| what | don't | where | are | doesn't | |

1. '_Do_ you work in Spain?' 'No, I _____.'
2. '_____ languages do you speak?' 'English and Spanish.'
3. '_____ you a student?' 'Yes, I am.'
4. '_____ Ricardo have a lesson now?' 'No, he _____.'
5. _____ subjects do you study?
6. _____ he a student or a teacher?
7. _____ are the halls of residence? Are they in the city centre?
8. '_____ Raul and Sophie work in the same shop?' 'No, they _____.'

KL **5** Complete the conversation at an employment agency with a–e.
a What
b ~~where is~~
c what does
d what are
e Is it

A: I like the website manager job, but [1] _b_ the office?
B: It's in the city.
A: OK. [2] _____ in the centre?
B: Yes, it is.
A: And [3] _____ the working hours?
B: Nine to five.
A: [4] _____ skills do I need?
B: You don't need any skills. They organise training.
A: So [5] _____ a website manager do?
B: Well, you work with …

V1 **6** What's the job?
1. 'I work in a hospital.' _doctor_
2. 'We fly from Sydney to Singapore.' _____
3. She works in a court. _____
4. He designs websites. _____
5. 'I teach in a university.' _____
6. 'I buy clothes for a big shop in Seoul.' _____

V1, 2 **7** Match the words below and complete sentences 1–5.

live — of 100
give — in halls of residence
do — classes
go — a course
score — to university

1. She doesn't _____. She's in a flat.
2. I want to _____ in English for business.
3. Do you _____ or to school?
4. Does your college _____ in English?
5. I need a _____ in the exam.

V3 **8** Write the words in the job advertisement.

~~working hours~~ qualifications filing duties salary

Part-time office help
- A local company needs extra help.
- [1] Working hours: 11.00–14.00
- [2] _____: $1,400 per month
- Work [3] _____: photocopying and [4] _____. Also some computer work.
- You don't need any [5] _____ or experience. We give training.

105

3 LANGUAGE REFERENCE

GRAMMAR

G1 QUESTION WORDS

What asks about a thing or an idea.
  What's your favourite country?
  What do you study at university?

Who asks about a person.
  Who's your manager?
  Who do you know in the class?

Where asks about a place.
  Where do you live?
  Where's the restaurant?

When asks about a time.
  When is the party?
  When do you start work in the morning?

How asks about the way we do something.
  How do you travel to work?
  How do you study languages?

Why asks about the reason for something.
  Why do you want to go home?
  Why do you want to meet Julia?

Which asks about a choice between a few things, usually two or three.
  Which do you study, English or Spanish?
  Which do you like, tea or coffee?

Sometimes we use *What … ?* and *Which … ?* with a noun.
  What subjects do you study?
  What cities do you visit?
  Which language do you speak, Chinese or English?
  Which qualification do you have, a degree or a certificate?

G2 ADVERBS OF FREQUENCY

100% ← ·············· 50 ·············· → 0%

always   usually   often   sometimes   occasionally   never

Put the adverb after the verb *to be*.
  He's **always** at work.
  The sea **is never** cold here.

With other verbs, put the adverb before the verb.
  I **sometimes work** in the evening.
  They **often play** tennis.

Ask about routines and habits with *How often … ?*
  '**How often** do you go to the cinema?' 'Occasionally.'
  '**How often** do you see whales in the sea?' 'We never see them.'

G3 G3 EXPRESSIONS OF FREQUENCY

every
once a
twice a   day / week / month / year
three times a

Put the expression after the verb and other words.
I read the newspaper **every day**.
We go to a restaurant **once a week**.
Our family has a holiday **twice a year**.

! once a week = weekly
We meet once a week = We meet weekly.

KEY LANGUAGE

KL1 MAKING SUGGESTIONS
Have you got any ideas?
Let's (have a sponsored cycling event).
Any ideas for (Saturday night)?
Why don't we have a (music event)?
What about (Saturday afternoon and morning)?
What about a (wildlife art and photography competition)?

KL2 RESPONDING TO SUGGESTIONS
Positive response (+)
OK.
That sounds fun/good.
That sounds interesting.
Good idea!
Great idea!
Fantastic!/Excellent!

Negative response (–)
I don't want to do that.
That sounds boring.
I'm not sure.

VOCABULARY

V1 VERBS CONNECTED WITH WATER
boil, change, drink, freeze, swim, wash, waste

V2 ADJECTIVES
beautiful, boring, fun, great, happy, interesting, popular, sad

V3 NATURE
an animal, a beach, a cactus, a camel, a desert, a dolphin, a kangaroo, a koala bear, a national park, a panda, a plant, a rainforest, a rock, sand, the sea, a seal, a shark, a tree, a turtle, wildlife

V4 CLASSROOM OBJECTS
blackboard, CD player, chair, computer, coursebook, DVD player, English–English dictionary, notebook, pen, pencil, whiteboard

V5 CLASSROOM LANGUAGE
answer, check, close, know, make, mean, open, repeat, stop, understand, work

EXTRA PRACTICE 3

G1 1 Complete questions 1–8 with a question word.
1 _____ do you like, water or milk?
2 _____ do people travel to work in your city?
3 _____ does he like Kraków?
4 _____ does Jos fly to?
5 _____ job does he have?
6 _____ city do they like, Atlanta or New York?
7 _____ does she start work?
8 _____ do you know at the party?

2 Speaking practice Make questions and ask a partner.
1 What languages / speak?
   What languages do you speak?
2 What cities / like?
3 Why / study English?
4 Where / live?
5 How / travel to school?
6 When / go to sleep?
7 Who / your English teacher?

G2, 3 3 Read about Youna. Choose the correct adverb or expression of frequency in sentences 1–6.

Youna is a fashion buyer in Seoul, in South Korea. She works for a clothes shop and goes to work in her car every day. She goes to other countries twice a month and buys clothes. But she doesn't wear the clothes. 'They're for the shop.' She doesn't often have free time, but on Saturdays she always plays tennis. 'I like to cook but I don't often have time.'

1 She *always / occasionally* goes to work in her car.
2 She *never / often* visits other countries.
3 She *usually / never* wears the clothes.
4 She *occasionally / never* has free time.
5 She plays tennis *once a week / monthly*.
6 She *sometimes / usually* cooks.

4 Are sentences 1–8 correct (✓) or incorrect (✗)? Correct the wrong sentences.
1 I see always the turtles. ✗ *I always see …*
2 They are never at work.
3 I every week play tennis.
4 How often do you eat at restaurants?
5 We occasionally meet for coffee.
6 He always is at school.
7 Do you often London visit?
8 We talk on the phone twice a week.

KL1, 2 5 Write the verb in brackets in the correct form.
A: What about ¹ *going* (go) to the cinema on Friday?
B: That ² _____ (sound) fun. What's the film?
A: It's *Star Fight*.
B: Oh no! I ³ _____ (not/want) to see that. Why ⁴ _____ we _____ (not/go) to a different film?
A: It's the only film this week. What about ⁵ _____ (have) dinner on Saturday?
B: Good idea! Let's ⁶ _____ (meet) at 7.00.

V1 6 Write these words in the table.

boil   cactus   camel   dolphin   drink
freeze   kangaroo   koala bear   panda   plant
rainforest   sea   shark   swim   tree   turtle
waste   wildlife

Animal words	Vegetation words	Water words
_____	_____	_____
_____	_____	_____
_____	_____	_____
_____	_____	_____
_____	_____	_____
_____	_____	_____
_____		

V4, 5 7 Match the words 1–8 with the words in the box to make combinations.

answers   ~~board~~   board   book   book
in pairs player   the question

1 black   *board*
2 check   _____
3 work   _____
4 note   _____
5 DVD   _____
6 white   _____
7 course   _____
8 answer   _____

8 Is each combination in Exercise 7 one, two or three words?

V1–4 9 Complete the adjective for sentences 1–6.
1 The desert looks b*eautiful* in the morning.
2 She is h_____ when she swims with turtles.
3 The guided tours are p_____ – lots of visitors go on them.
4 The job on Kangaroo Island sounds i_____.
5 Some people think football is b_____ but I don't!
6 The university music events are g_____ fun – the bands are usually very good.

4 LANGUAGE REFERENCE

GRAMMAR

G1 ARTICLES

a/an
The article *a/an* means *one*. We usually use *a/an*, not *one*.
   I have **a** video. (= I have one video.)

Use *a/an* with a singular noun, and to talk about a person's job.
   Hong Kong is **a** noisy city.
   George Lucas is **a** director.

Use *an*, not *a*, when the noun begins with a vowel sound (*a, e, i, o, u*).
   Monaco is **an** expensive city.
   He's **an** actor.
   But note **an** hour.

We usually say *a/an* with the schwa (/ə/).
   an actor – /ən'æktə/

the
Use *the* with singular or plural nouns, to talk about a specific person or thing. We know *who* or *what*.
   The history teacher at my school is good.
   (= There is only one history teacher at the school.)
   The Songkran Water Festival starts **the** Thai New Year.
   (= There is only one Songkran Festival, and one New Year.)
   The actors and directors meet here.
   (= We know which actors and directors.)

We usually say *the* with the schwa (/ə/): *the* (/ðə/) director, but before a vowel, it is the strong form /iː/: *the* (/ðiː/) actor.

No article
Don't use articles with plural nouns, when you talk about people or things in general.
   Love stories are boring.
   Dolphins are famous for big jumps.

! Known specific = **The children** are in the garden.
General = **Children** are welcome at this hotel.

G2 CAN, CAN'T

Use *can* for ability.
   Jack goes skiing. He's very good. = Jack **can** ski.
   Sheila doesn't swim. She never swims. = Sheila **can't** swim. / Sheila **cannot*** swim.
   * The full form of *can't* is *cannot*.

Use *can* for permission (what is allowed).
   Only full-time students **can** use the library.

Use *can* for possibility (what is possible).
   You **can** watch television in the clubroom.

Put *can* before the main verb.
   He **can** ski. ✓   He ski can. ✗

Don't use *to* after *can*.
   I **can use** a computer. ✓   I can to use a computer. ✗

Don't use *do/does* in a question with *can*.
   Can she ride a bike? ✓   Does she can ride a bike? ✗

Don't use *do/does* in a negative sentence with *can*.
   We **can't** go to the gym today. ✓
   We don't can go to the gym today. ✗

Don't add *-s* to *can* in the *he/she/it* form.
   Rosa **can** run a marathon. ✓
   Rosa cans run a marathon. ✗

KEY LANGUAGE

KL1 ASKING FOR INFORMATION
Can I help you?
Can/Could you give me some information about (the resort)?
Can/Could you tell me about (the accommodation)?
Is there (a kids' club)?
Are there any (restaurants)?
Can I (play other sports)?

KL2 ANSWERING POLITELY

Saying *yes* politely	**Saying *no* politely**
Yes, certainly.	No, I'm afraid not.
Yes, of course.	I'm sorry. I'm afraid you can't.
	No, I'm afraid there isn't/aren't.

VOCABULARY

V1 TYPES OF FILM
action/adventure film, actor, animation, comedy, director, historical film, horror film, love story, musical (n), romantic comedy, science fiction (film), thriller, war film, western

V2 LEISURE ACTIVITIES, SPORTS
dance, do aerobics, do yoga, go hiking, go mountain biking, go running, go scuba diving, go swimming, go to a fitness club, go windsurfing, play basketball, play football, play tennis, ride a bike, ski, work out in a gym

V3 HOLIDAY RESORTS AND ENTERTAINMENT
double room, family room, kids' club, painting class, satellite TV, sea view

V4 FRACTIONS AND PERCENTAGES; APPROXIMATION
fifth, fraction, half, percent, quarter, third, about, exactly, nearly, over

EXTRA PRACTICE 4

G1 **1** Match 1–5 with a–e.
1. Abbas Kiarostami is a ___d___.
2. Ariel Mateluna is an _____.
3. I like _____.
4. The _____.
5. *Blackboards* is an _____.

a actor
b President is on TV
c interesting film
d ~~film director~~
e horror films

2 Write *a*, *an*, *the* or Ø (no article).

A: Do you often listen to ¹__Ø__ American groups?
B: Yes. In fact, I have ²_____ new CD by ³_____ American group. There's ⁴_____ song about ⁵_____ woman in New York. It's really good and ⁶_____ singer is beautiful.
A: Can I listen to it?
B: Yes, of course.

3 Correct the mistakes with articles in sentences 1–8.
1. Dee is shop assistant in a big department store.
   a shop assistant
2. Festival in February in my city is really exciting.
3. I really enjoy the thrillers.
4. Let's take children with us to the party.
5. My father is a accountant.
6. A director of this film is very good.
7. 'Where's Luke? Is he home?' 'Yes, he's in a garden.'
8. Let's meet in cinema in King Street.

G2 **4** Find the extra word in each sentence.
1. He can to sing.
2. Can does she ride a motorbike?
3. We doesn't can't go to the gym.
4. Louis can make makes films.
5. Sorry, I can't to play tonight.
6. Can you do tell me about the course?

5 Speaking practice Ask a partner questions with the words.
1. Can / speak / foreign language?
   Can you speak a foreign language?
2. Can / ride / motorbike?
3. Can / do / yoga?
4. Can / make / webpage?
5. Can / run / marathon?
6. Can / play / the drums?

KL1,2 **6** Complete the conversation in a hotel with a–h.

a Are there any
b Yes, certainly.
c No, I'm afraid not.
d there isn't
e Can you tell me
f Can I
g Is there
h ~~Could you give me some~~

A: Hello. ¹__h__ information about your hotel?
B: ²_____ What do you want to know?
A: ³_____ about the facilities? ⁴_____ a swimming pool?
B: ⁵_____ But there is a sauna and a fitness club.
A: Great. And is there a restaurant?
B: No, I'm afraid ⁶_____.
A: ⁷_____ good restaurants in the city?
B: Yes, of course. There are lots.
A: OK. ⁸_____ book a room?
B: Certainly.

V1 **7** Write the type of film in sentences 1–5.

historical ~~love story~~ thrillers animations westerns

1. She likes romantic comedies with a good *love story*.
2. My children like all _____, especially Wallace and Gromit.
3. A lot of boys like _____ with American cowboys.
4. I like _____ films because I learn about the past.
5. _____ are exciting.

V2 **8** Match the verb with the activity.

	1	aerobics
	2	swimming
do	3	football
play	4	yoga
go	5	running
	6	basketball
	7	tennis

V3 **9** Write words from V3 in this table.

Accommodation	Entertainment
_____	_____
_____	_____
_____	_____

V4 **10** Say these fractions and percentages.

¼   40%   ½   ¾   100%   ⅕

5 LANGUAGE REFERENCE

GRAMMAR

G1 COMPARATIVE ADJECTIVES

Use comparatives to compare one person or thing with another person or thing (or to compare groups of people or things).

adjective	comparative
slow	slower (than)
fast	faster (than)
modern	more modern (than)
important	more important (than)

Add *-er* to most one-syllable adjectives.
   A bicycle is slow**er**. (→ G3, *Spelling rules*)

Add *than* after the comparative adjective.
   A bicycle is slower **than** a car.

Put *more* in front of most two-syllable adjectives and all adjectives with three syllables or more.
   The new office is **more modern than** the old office. ✓
   The new office is ~~moderner than~~ the old office. ✗
   Underground trains are **more expensive than** buses.

❗ Note these irregular comparative adjectives.
   good – **better**   bad – **worse**

   Marco's English is **better than** my English. ✓
   Marco's English is ~~gooder than~~ my English. ✗
   The coffee here is **worse than** at the restaurant. ✓
   The coffee here is ~~badder than~~ at the restaurant. ✗

G2 SUPERLATIVE ADJECTIVES

Use superlatives to compare one person or thing with several people or things (more than two).
   He's **the oldest** in the class.
   My car is **the fastest** on the road.

We can also compare one group with other groups.
   Buses are **the cheapest** way to travel.

adjective	superlative
slow	the slowest
fast	the fastest
modern	the most modern
important	the most important

Add *-est* to most one-syllable adjectives.
   You have **the slowest** car. (→ G3, *Spelling rules*)

Use the article *the* before a superlative.
   Singapore is **the cleanest** city in south-east Asia. ✓
   Singapore is ~~a cleanest~~ city in south-east Asia. ✗

Use *most* in front of most adjectives with two syllables and all adjectives with three syllables or more.
   It's **the most beautiful** city in Europe.

❗ Use *in Europe* / *in the world* / *in my class* after superlatives, not *of*.

❗ Note these irregular superlative adjectives.
   good – **best**   bad – **worst**

   Marco's English is **the best** in the class.
   This film is **the worst** at the cinema this week.

G3 SPELLING RULES FOR COMPARATIVES AND SUPERLATIVES

Some comparative and superlative adjectives change their spelling.

Add *-r* or *-st* to one-syllable adjectives ending in *-e*.
   My sister is nice**r** than my brother.
   He's the nice**st** of my brothers.

With two-syllable adjectives ending *-y*, change *-y* to *-i* and add *-er* or *-est*.
   This city is ug**lier** than London.
   London Heathrow is the bus**iest** airport in the world.

With most one-syllable adjectives with a consonant + vowel + consonant spelling, double the last consonant and add *-er* or *-est*.
   big – big**ger** – big**gest**
   wet – wet**ter** – wet**test**
   sad – sad**der** – sad**dest**

   The UK is ~~weter~~ than Turkey. ✗
   The UK is wetter than Turkey. ✓
   The UK is one of the wettest countries. ✓

KEY LANGUAGE

KL BUYING A TICKET

Traveller
Can you tell me about (the British Airways flight)?
When does it leave?
When does it arrive?
How long does it take?
How much does it cost?
Is it a good (airline)?
I'd like to book (the British Airways flight), please.

Travel agent
Would you like (standard or business class)?
How would you like to pay?
Would you like to (make a booking)?

VOCABULARY

V1 TRANSPORT
bicycle/bike, boat, bus, car, ferry, lorry, motorbike, plane, ship, taxi, train, tram, underground/metro (train)

V2 FLYING
airline, aisle seat, arrival time, business class, flight, in-flight service, return ticket, standard class, window seat

(to) depart, (to) land, (to) leave

V3 WRITTEN WORK
draft, final copy, order, paragraph, sentence, topic sentence, word web

(to) add, (to) join

EXTRA PRACTICE 5

G1 1 Write the adjectives in sentences 1–8 in their comparative forms.
1. Business class is *more comfortable* than standard class. (comfortable)
2. Kraków in Poland is _____ than Warsaw. (beautiful)
3. Buses are _____ than trams in my city. (cheap)
4. London is _____ than New York. (old)
5. My new car is _____ than my old car. (good)
6. In the city centre, a bicycle is _____ than a car. (fast)
7. Madrid is _____ than London in the summer. (hot)
8. I think the German language is _____ than English. (easy)

G2 2 Write the adjectives in sentences 1–8 in their superlative forms.
1. Mount Everest is the *highest* mountain in the world. (high)
2. Planes are the _____ means of transport. (fast)
3. Boats are the _____ means of transport. (comfortable)
4. Maths is my _____ subject at school. (bad)
5. The world's _____ spy is James Bond. (good)
6. Is the President of the USA the _____ person in the world? (important)
7. I'd like to book the _____ flight. (short)
8. Sam is the _____ man that I know. (romantic)

G1, 2 3 Speaking practice Make sentences about these subjects with the comparative and superlative form.
1. Drinks: tea / coffee / water
   I think tea is better than coffee. – But water is the best drink!
2. Animals: whales / elephants / penguins
3. Places: deserts / mountains / sea
4. Countries: Brazil / Japan / Poland
5. Sport: football / tennis / golf
6. Films: musicals / horror films / comedy films

G3 4 Find the extra letter in each sentence.
1. Ice cream is nice**o**er than bread.
2. Walking is easyier than running.
3. Tickets on aeroplanes are more expensiver than trains.
4. Blue whales are the bigggest type of whale.
5. My English is worser not better!
6. Is he a bestter actor than Tom Cruise?
7. London is the busyiest city in the UK.
8. Six o'clock is the lattest time you can come.

KL 5 Match questions 1–6 with responses a–f.
1. When does it arrive? _b_
2. Would you like to make a booking? _____
3. Is it a good airline? _____
4. How long does it take? _____
5. How would you like to pay? _____
6. How much does it cost? _____

a. 539 Australian dollars.
b. ~~At 8.00 in the evening.~~
c. Yes, please.
d. Seven hours.
e. Oh yes. It's the best.
f. By credit card.

V1 6 Complete sentences 1–6 with words from V1. Make them true for you.
1. I go to work by _____.
2. I can/can't ride a _____.
3. We usually go by _____ when we go on holiday.
4. In my city, _____ are the cheapest means of transport.
5. And _____ are the most expensive means of transport.
6. I like travelling by _____.

V2 7 Match 1–6 with a–f.
1. I don't want a window seat, _f_
2. Is that a _____
3. Would you like business _____
4. When does it depart and _____
5. This is departures, but _____
6. Please board the plane _____

a. when does it arrive?
b. return ticket?
c. you need arrivals.
d. half an hour before departure.
e. or standard class?
f. ~~I'd like an aisle seat.~~

V3 8 Match a word or phrase in V3 with definitions 1–5.
1. This is usually first in a paragraph. _____
2. This is the last draft of your writing. _____
3. It's a group of sentences. _____
4. You join these to make a paragraph. _____
5. This is a way of organising ideas. _____

6 LANGUAGE REFERENCE

GRAMMAR

G1 COUNTABLE AND UNCOUNTABLE NOUNS

Nouns can be countable or uncountable.

countable nouns	uncountable nouns
banana doctor car phone hotel	water bread garlic sand oil

	countable nouns	uncountable nouns
Use of *a/an*	can have *a/an* in front of them: **A doctor** works in a hospital.	do not have *a/an* in front of them: **Garlic** is good in salad.
Plural form	can have a plural form: **Doctors** work in hospitals.	do not have a plural form and only use singular verbs: **Bread is** good for you.
some and *any* (→ G2 below)	can have *some* or *any* in front of the plural: **Some** restaurants are expensive. There aren't **any** hotels in the town.	can have *some* or *any* in front of them: **Some** olive oil is expensive. Is there **any** milk on the table?

Some nouns can be countable and uncountable, with different meanings.
> I like **chicken** for dinner. (uncountable)
> **A chicken** can run fast. (countable)

G2 SOME AND ANY

Use *some* in affirmative sentences.
> Yes, there are **some** strawberries.
> Yes, there is **some** milk.

Use *any* in negative sentences.
> No, there aren't **any** nuts.
> No, there isn't **any** oil.

Usually use *any* in questions.
> Are there **any** planes to Zurich today?
> Is there **any** bread?

! Use *some* in questions to ask for or offer something.
> Can you give me **some** information?
> Would you like **some** chocolate?

See also *Key Language: Requests and offers*.

G3 MUCH, MANY, A LOT OF

Use *many* and *a lot of* with countable nouns.
> London has **many** buses
> London doesn't have **a lot of** trams.

Use *much* and *a lot of* with uncountable nouns.
> We have **a lot of** public transport.
> We don't have **much** public transport.

Use *many* and *a lot of* in both affirmative and negative sentences.

> I write **a lot of** emails to friends.*
> I write **many** emails to friends.
> I don't write **many** emails to friends.
> I don't write **a lot of** emails to friends.

* *A lot of* is more common than *many* in affirmative sentences. *Many* is quite formal.

Use *much* in negative sentences, not in affirmative sentences.
> There **isn't much** water in the desert. ✓
> There is ~~much~~ water in the sea. ✗

Use *much*, *many* and *a lot of* in questions.
> Have you got **much** money in the bank?
> Have you got **many** vegetables?
> Do you eat **a lot of** chocolate?

Use *How many* for questions with countable nouns and *How much* with uncountable nouns.
> How many computer games have you got?
> How much exercise do you do?

G4 HAVE GOT

Use *have got / has got* in informal spoken British English. It means the same as *have/has*.
> I**'ve got** three brothers.
> I **have** three brothers.

! American English does not use *have got / has got*.

KEY LANGUAGE

KL REQUESTS AND OFFERS

Requests
We would like / We'd like (some bread), please.
I would like / I'd like (some water).
Can/Could we have (some tea)?

Offers
Would you like (fish or meat)?

! we would = we'd
I would = I'd

Could is more polite than *can*.

Use *some* in offers and requests.
> Would you like **some** coffee?

VOCABULARY

V1 FOOD AND DRINK

banana, beans, (roast) beef, biscuit, blueberry (-berries), bread, broccoli, burger, cabbage, cake, carrot, caviar, cheese, chicken, chilli con carne, chips, chocolate, coffee, coffee bean, corn, couscous, crisps, curry, desserts, egg, fast food, fish, fruit, garlic, green tea, ice cream, kebab, lamb, meat, milk, noodles, nut, olive oil, orange, pasta, (red) pepper, pizza, potato(es), rice, rice cakes, salmon, salt, sardine, sausages, strawberry (-berries), sugar, sushi, tea, tomato(es), vegetable

V2 HEALTH AND NUTRITION

brain, diet, energy, health, heart, illness, medicine, memory, vegetarian, vitamin

EXTRA PRACTICE 6

G1 1 Write these nouns in the table.

~~food~~   city   coffee   cinema   pilot   money
rain   film   rice   vitamin

countable nouns	uncountable nouns
___	*food*
___	___
___	___
___	___
___	___

2 Sentences 1–5 are incorrect. Write them again.
1. A bread is good for you.
   Bread is good for you.
2. We work in office.
   _____
3. Green teas is a super drink.
   _____
4. Nurse work in hospitals.
   _____
5. An olive oil is good on salad.
   _____

G2 3 Write *some* or *any* in sentences 1–10.
1. _Some_ cars are expensive.
2. Are there _____ rooms at the hotel?
3. She doesn't have _____ free time.
4. There aren't _____ good restaurants in the city centre.
5. He has _____ ice cream.
6. Do you have _____ qualifications?
7. There's _____ parking at the back of the hotel.
8. There are _____ children in the street.
9. I'm sorry, there aren't _____ taxis at the moment.
10. Can I have _____ milk in my tea, please?

G3 4 Read this interview and choose the correct words.

A: Hi, Irina. Tell me about your city of St Petersburg in Russia.
B: It's a beautiful city. It has ¹*a lot of / ~~much~~* old buildings, like the castle. ²*Much / Many* tourists visit it.
A: Do you often go there?
B: No, I'm a student at the university and so I don't have ³*many / much* free time.
A: What do people do in the evening?
B: ⁴*Much / A lot of* people go to cafés and restaurants.
A: How ⁵*much / many* cafés are there in St Petersburg?
B: I don't know exactly, but there are ⁶*a lot of / much* them!

5 Speaking practice Complete questions 1–4 with your own words. Ask a partner.
1. Do you drink a lot of _____?
2. Have you got much _____?
3. How much _____?
4. How many _____?

G4 6 Complete sentences 1–5 with the correct form of *have got*.
1. Mark _has got_ two brothers.
2. His oldest brother _____ a big house in the country.
3. He _____ a beautiful wife, too.
4. But they _____ any children.
5. They _____ two horses.

KL 7 You are in a café. Complete the conversation below with a–f.
a can
b would you like
c I'd
d could we
e ~~would you~~
f would like

WAITER: Hello, ¹_e_ like some drinks?
YOU: Yes, please. ²_____ like a cola and my friend ³_____ some orange juice.
WAITER: OK. And ⁴_____ a sandwich or something to eat?
YOU: Yes, ⁵_____ have the pasta, please? And ⁶_____ we also have a salad with it?

V1 8 Find words in V1 to complete the table.

fruit	meat	fish	vegetables	drinks
banana				

9 Speaking practice Ask and answer with a partner.
Which food is popular in your country?
What's your favourite food in the table in Exercise 8?

V2 10 Re-order the letters in italics to make a word.
1. I don't like meat. I'm a *angetevari*. _vegetarian_
2. Garlic is a natural *cinmedie*. _____
3. She has a healthy *tied* of fish, vegetables and fruit. _____
4. Green tea can protect you from *silnels*. _____
5. Eat blueberries. They help your *moremy*. _____

7 LANGUAGE REFERENCE

GRAMMAR

G1 PRESENT CONTINUOUS

Use the present continuous to describe an action happening now or around now.
   They're playing tennis at the moment.
   Angie can't come to the phone – **she's sleeping**.
   I'm reading a really good book at the moment.

We also sometimes use the present continuous to describe a changing situation.
   Our business **is growing** very quickly.

Affirmative sentences

subject	verb *to be*		verb + *-ing*
	contraction	full form	
I	'm	am	
you/we/they	're	are	working
he/she/it	's	is	

   I'm buying a new pair of jeans.
   We're buying a car.
   It's raining.

Negative sentences

subject	verb *to be*		verb + *-ing*
	contraction	full form	
I	'm not	am not	
you/we/they	aren't	are not	waiting
he/she/it	isn't	is not	

   I'm not watching the film now.
   You aren't studying Spanish at the moment.
   She isn't trying on the suit.

G2 PRESENT CONTINUOUS AND PRESENT SIMPLE

The present continuous describes an action happening now. The present simple describes things that happen again and again.
   I'm learning English at the moment. ✓
   She does exercise every day. ✓
   They ~~watch~~ TV now. ✗

! We normally use adverbs of frequency (*always*, *usually*, *never*, etc.) with the present simple and not with the present continuous.
   I always get up at 6 a.m. ✓
   ~~I'm usually getting up~~ at 6 a.m. ✗

We don't use the continuous form with some verbs, e.g. *want*, *know*, *understand*, *like*.
   I want a glass of water now. ✓
   ~~I'm wanting~~ a glass of water now. ✗

G3 PRESENT CONTINUOUS QUESTIONS

Yes/No questions

verb *to be*	subject	verb + *-ing*
Am	I	
Are	you/we/they	leaving?
Is	he/she/it	

Wh- questions

question word	verb *to be*	subject	verb + *-ing*
What	am	I	doing?
Why	are	you/we/they	leaving?
Where	's (is)	he/she/it	going?

Questions in the present continuous can start with the verb *to be* or with a question word.
   Are you leaving now?
   When are you leaving?

The verb *to be* usually comes before the subject.
   Is she working in Beijing?
   Where **is she** working?

If the subject is the question word *what* + noun, the verb *to be* comes after.
   What changes are happening in town centres?

KEY LANGUAGE

KL GIVING ADVANTAGES AND DISADVANTAGES

What are the advantages/disadvantages?
Are there any advantages/disadvantages?
There are two main advantages/disadvantages.
The first/second is that ...
One/Another advantage is that ...
The disadvantage is that ...
I think / don't think (it's a nice place).
This means that ...
This is more ...
I think X is better because ...

VOCABULARY

V1 THINGS WE BUY
books, clothes, DVDs, electronic items (cameras, MP3 players, etc.), food, furniture, goods, make-up, shoes, stationery

V2 SHOPS AND SHOPPING
bookshop, consumer, customer, discount, hypermarket, internet shopping, market, online shopping, price, product, service, shoe shop, (department) store, supermarket, window shopper, the sales

(to) ask for, (to) buy, (to) check, (to) go (shopping), (to) look for, (to) order, (to) pay for, (to) shop, (to) spend (time/money), (to) try on

V3 US ENGLISH
downtown, highway, motel, shopping mall, store

EXTRA PRACTICE 7

G1 **1 Complete sentences 1–8 with these verbs in the present continuous.**

~~talk~~   sit   go   buy   not/work   do   not/rain   meet

1. He _'s talking_ on the phone at the moment.
2. They _____ a new house.
3. Prices _____ up again at the local supermarket.
4. She _____ some visitors at the station this morning.
5. We _____ our homework.
6. The computer _____. There's a problem.
7. You _____ in my chair.
8. It _____ now, it's sunny!

G2 **2 Choose the correct verb.**

My day ¹ *is / is being* always busy. For example, at the moment ² *I organise / I'm organising* dinner for some visitors from Japan. They ³ *visit / are visiting* my country for the week. My assistant usually ⁴ *help / is helping* me, but today ⁵ *she does / she's doing* a training course. Our visitors ⁶ *stay / are staying* in a hotel near the office, so ⁷ *I try / I'm trying* to book a restaurant. We often ⁸ *eat / are eating* in a good Indian restaurant near here, so maybe that's a good idea.

G3 **3 Write the words in the correct order to make questions.**

1. is / friend / driving / your
   Is your friend driving?
2. are / what / doing / you
   _____?
3. are / phoning / you / who
   _____?
4. going / are / where / they
   _____?
5. are / how / feeling / you
   _____?

G2, 3 **4 Match questions 1–6 with responses a–f.**

1. Do you often come here? _d_
2. Are you always busy? ____
3. Is he studying? ____
4. Where's he studying? ____
5. Are people buying online these days? ____
6. What do you want? ____

a. Yes, he is.
b. No, I'm not.
c. Yes, they are.
d. ~~Yes, I do.~~
e. A pen, please.
f. At the University of Hong Kong.

KL **5 Complete the conversation with sentences a–g.**

a. The second is that it's more expensive than in the city.
b. There are disadvantages in that.
c. This means that they cost more money.
d. Another is that it's more beautiful.
e. So where do you think?
f. What are the advantages in that?
g. I don't think it is.

A: I'm bored with the city. I'd like to move nearer to the sea.
B: The sea ... I don't know. ¹____
A: Really? What are they?
B: The first is that it's often cold. ²____
A: ³____ Houses here are more expensive.
B: Not these days. A lot of people want a house near the beach. ⁴____
A: Well, OK, not the sea. ⁵____
B: Let's move to the mountains.
A: ⁶____
B: One advantage is that it's cheaper. ⁷____

V1,2 **6 Choose the correct verb.**

1. How much did you *buy / pay* for the book?
2. I often *shop / spend* £100 at the hypermarket.
3. Did you *try / pay* on the suit?
4. She always *buys / checks* the prices.
5. They *buy / check* food on the internet.
6. We can't *pay / spend* any more time and money.

7 Read these definitions and write the word.

1. a shop that sells all types of food _____
2. a person who buys in a shop _____
3. using a computer to shop _____
4. something that you can buy _____
5. chairs and tables, for example _____
6. a very large example of the shop in number 1 _____
7. how much you pay for something _____
8. pens, pencils and notebooks, for example _____

V3 **8 Complete the table.**

US English	UK English
gas station	¹_____ station
² _____	motorway
parking lot	³_____ park
⁴ _____	hotel (for motorists)
downtown	town ⁵_____
shopping ⁶_____	shopping centre
⁷ _____	shop

8 LANGUAGE REFERENCE

GRAMMAR

G1 PAST SIMPLE OF TO BE

Use the past simple to talk about events and situations that are finished.

affirmative (+)	negative (–)		question (?)
	contraction	full form	
I was	I wasn't	I was not	Was I … ?
he/she/it was	he/she/it wasn't	he/she/it was not	Was he/she/it … ?
you/we/they were	you/we/they weren't	you/we/they were not	Were you/we/they … ?

I **was** late this morning.
You **were** in the hospital last week.
The city **wasn't** important in 2000 BC.
She **wasn't** at the shop on Saturday.
'**Was** the food expensive?' 'No, it **wasn't**.'

! Normally, we use *wasn't/weren't*. Use the full form *was not / were not* in formal English.

Use *there was/were* to describe something or a situation in a place in the past.

affirmative (+)	negative (–)		question (?)
	contraction	full form	
there was	there wasn't	there was not	Was there … ?
there were	there weren't	there were not	Were there … ?

There was an old city in the desert.
'**Were there** many people at the conference?' 'No, there **weren't**.'

! Use short answers for past simple *to be* questions.
'**Were you** early for school?' 'No, **I wasn't**.'
'**Was there** someone at the airport?' 'Yes, **there was**.'

G2 COULD, COULDN'T

Use *could/couldn't* to talk about ability and possibility in the past.
In the past, only some people **could** read and write. Now, most people can read.
My grandparents **could** walk to their work. Now we usually drive to work.

Use *could* for *can* in the past simple.
I **can't** go tonight. → I **couldn't** go last night.

Use the infinitive without *to* after *could* or *couldn't*.
People **couldn't visit** the country. (✓)
People couldn't ~~to~~ visit the country. ✗
People couldn't ~~visits~~ the country. ✗

! Use short answers for *could* questions.
'When you were one, **could you** walk?' 'Yes, **I could**. / No, **I couldn't**.'

KEY LANGUAGE

KL1 POLITE REQUESTS

Could you …	help me, please? give us (a map of the museum), please? take a photo of us?
Could you tell me …	how much it is? where (the cloakroom) is? when (the next film) is? how old it is?

A: How can I help you?
B: Could you tell me (where the cloakroom is), please?
A: Here, on the right.
B: Oh yes, I see it. Thank you.
A: Not at all. / You're welcome.

! We also use *Can you … ?*
but *Could you … ?* is more polite.

KL2 RESPONDING TO POLITE REQUESTS

Positive responses
Certainly.
Yes, of course.
That's no problem.

Negative responses
I'm afraid not.
I'm afraid I can't do that.

VOCABULARY

V1 BUILDINGS

cloakroom, courtyard, door, entrance, furniture, garden, gate, ladder, lift, painting, roof, room, wall, window

V2 VERB + PREPOSITION

chat to, focus on, go on (a trip), move on to, read about, stay in, talk to

V3 DESCRIBING OBJECTS

circle, circular, heavy, leather, length, light, long, metal, narrow, plastic, rectangle, rectangular, short, square (adj, n), weight, wide, width, wood

(to) lengthen, (to) weigh, (to) widen

EXTRA PRACTICE 8

G1 1 Complete the three conversations with *was, wasn't, were* or *weren't*.

A: Sorry I ¹*was* late this morning.
B: That's OK. ²____ your bus late?
A: No, it ³____. My train ⁴____ late.
___

C: I didn't know it ⁵____ Jan and Pierre's birthdays last weekend.
D: Yes, they ⁶____ 25.
C: ⁷____ they at the restaurant on Saturday?
D: No, they ⁸____. They ⁹____ in Paris for the night!
___

E: When ¹⁰____ your chemistry exam?
F: Last Tuesday.
E: ¹¹____ it OK? ¹²____ there any difficult questions?
F: There ¹³____ two difficult questions, but it ¹⁴____ OK.

2 Write questions with *was* or *were* for these answers.

1 *Were you late for the class*?
  No, I wasn't late for the class.
2 _____?
  No, the teacher wasn't here.
3 _____?
  I was at the cinema yesterday evening.
4 _____?
  Yes, it was a very good film.
5 _____?
  I was with my brother.

3 Speaking practice Work with a partner. Ask and answer questions with the words below.

| holiday | exam | party | lesson | visit to the dentist |

When was your last _____?
Where was your _____?
How was your _____?

G2 4 Choose the correct word.

1 He couldn't *sees / see* the film.
2 I'm afraid I *couldn't / can't* come tonight.
3 'Could they ski when they were children?' 'Yes, they *could / couldn't*.'
4 Ten years ago, it was safe in the city. You *can / could* walk in the streets at night.
5 Now we *can / could* phone anywhere in the world, but my parents *can't / couldn't* when they were young.
6 Sorry we *couldn't / can't* come last night.
7 Computers *can / could* do anything these days!

KL1, 2 5 Write the words in questions 1–7.

| help | when | ~~how~~ | can | give | where | what |

1 Could you tell me *how* much it is?
2 Could you tell me ____ this means, please?
3 How ____ I help you?
4 Could you ____ me, please?
5 Could you tell me ____ the next show is?
6 Could you ____ us the menu, please?
7 Could you tell me ____ the cloakroom is?

6 Now match questions 1–7 in Exercise 5 with responses a–g.

a Yes, of course. At 5.30 p.m. _5_
b No, I'm afraid I can't. Ask your teacher. ___
c Certainly. What's the problem? ___
d Yes, I can. It's £5. ___
e Of course. Down the stairs and turn left. ___
f I'd like a new shirt, please. ___
g Yes, of course. Here it is. ___

V1 7 Someone is describing a new house. Write in the words.

| painting | ~~room~~ | garden | gate | window | door |

'This is a large ¹ *room* and you can see the mountains through that ²____. The ³____ on the wall is by a local artist. Let's go through this ⁴____. Outside there's a small courtyard and you go through this metal ⁵____ into a ⁶____ with plants and flowers.'

V2 8 Write the prepositions in sentences 1–6.

| on | on | onto | in | ~~to~~ | about |

1 I like to chat *to* my friends on the phone.
2 When do you go ____ holiday?
3 I'd like to focus ____ Phil's new idea at this meeting.
4 Did you read ____ the Chinese economy?
5 I usually stay ____ a hotel when I'm on a business trip.
6 Before I move ____ the next topic, are there any questions?

V3 9 Choose the correct word.

1 I'd like a *long / length* table.
2 This *wooden / wood* chair is beautiful.
3 Why is a CD *circular / circle*?
4 How *wide / width* is this room?
5 The field for baseball isn't a *rectangular / rectangle*. You're thinking about football.
6 How much does the baby *weight / weigh*?

9 LANGUAGE REFERENCE

GRAMMAR

G1 PAST SIMPLE (AFFIRMATIVE, REGULAR VERBS)

Use the past simple to talk about finished events and times in the past.

I **worked** in Singapore in 1989.
She **lived** in Cape Town last year.
They **stayed** in a hotel last night.

With regular verbs, add *-ed* to the infinitive to make the past simple.
cook – cook**ed**
enjoy – enjoy**ed**

For verbs ending in *-e*, add *-d*.
invite – invit**ed**
live – liv**ed**

❗ Note these spelling changes.
study – stud**ied**
carry – carr**ied**
travel – travel**led**

G2 PAST SIMPLE (IRREGULAR VERBS)

Many common verbs in the past simple are irregular.
do – **did**
drive – **drove**
go – **went**
have – **had**
sit – **sat**

I **sat** at the doctor's for two hours last week.
We **drove** across Europe when we were students.

→ Irregular verb list page 158

❗ Don't add *-ed* to the infinitive or to the past form of an irregular verb.
I went to the meeting yesterday. ✓
I goed to the meeting yesterday. ✗
I wented to the meeting yesterday. ✗

G3 PAST SIMPLE (NEGATIVE AND QUESTIONS)

Negative sentences

subject	did + not		infinitive without *to*
	contraction	full form	
I/he/she/it/you/we/they	didn't	did not	change.

I **didn't go** out last night.
The letter **didn't arrive** this morning.
They **didn't leave** for two days.

❗ When we speak, and for informal writing, we use *didn't*, not *did not*.

❗ Do not use *didn't* with the verb *to be*.
I didn't be born in 1992. ✗
I **wasn't** born in 1992. ✓

Questions

question word + *did*	subject	infinitive without *to*
(What) did	I/he/she/it/you/we/they	say?

Did he phone the police?
When **did you move** house?
Where **did they live** before?

For short answers, use *did/didn't*.
'**Did** you play tennis with her?'
'Yes, **I did.** / No, **I didn't.**'
'**Did** we agree to this price?'
'Yes, **we did.** / No, **we didn't.**'

❗ Do not use *did* with the verb *to be*.
When did you be born? ✗
When **were you** born? ✓

KEY LANGUAGE

KL GIVING REASONS

The most important reason is that …
The first/second reason is that …
The main reason is that …
One/Another reason is that …
My final reason is that …
Firstly/Secondly/Finally, …
It's important/useful because …

VOCABULARY

V1 MEDICAL SCIENCE AND MACHINES

acupuncture needles, bones, equipment, examinations, experiment, false teeth, lab(oratory), medicine, microscope, MRI scanner, scalpel, scientist, skin, teeth, tools, treatment, waiting room, X-ray machine

V2 (EVERYDAY) INVENTIONS AND MACHINES

balloon, diving suit, helicopter, high heels, mirror, parachute, Post-it® note, radio, robot, telescope, tin can, umbrella

EXTRA PRACTICE 9

G1, 2 **1** Write the past simple form of verbs 1–12.
1. enjoy *enjoyed*
2. go _____
3. return _____
4. build _____
5. hold _____
6. work _____
7. drive _____
8. stand _____
9. help _____
10. study _____
11. travel _____
12. invent _____

2 Complete sentences 1–8 with verbs from Exercise 1 in the past simple.
1. I _____ from Brazil an hour ago.
2. She _____ me to carry this.
3. Many famous people _____ at Bologna University.
4. The children _____ the film.
5. Five of us _____ from Cádiz to Madrid in a really small, uncomfortable car.
6. Doctor Grey _____ in this laboratory.
7. Leonardo da Vinci _____ over 100 machines.
8. They _____ the palace in 1706.

G3 **3** Each sentence has one word missing. Find the missing word in the box and write it in.

| ~~did~~ | did | did | did | drive | not | was | where |

did
1. I / not play tennis last weekend.
2. They did see him. Did you?
3. Did you here in your car?
4. What time you leave?
5. Did you live before you lived in Morocco?
6. 'Did they say "yes"?' 'Yes, they.'
7. My brother not born in hospital.
8. Some of our friends not come to the party last night.

G1–3 **4** Correct sentences 1–6.
1. I ~~carryed~~ this shopping all the way from the supermarket. *carried*
2. He sitted in the hospital for two hours.
3. The Romans wored false teeth.
4. They didn't to like the food.
5. Did you enjoyed the film last night?
6. She didn't was interested in the conversation.

5 Speaking practice Work with a partner. Compare answers to questions 1–5 with your partner.
1. When did you leave school/university?
2. What did you do last weekend?
3. Where did your mother and father meet?
4. Why did you choose this course?
5. How long did you spend at school?

KL **6** Complete phrases 1–4 about university with your own ideas.
1. The most important reason for going to university is _____
2. Another reason is that you _____
3. It's also important _____
4. My final reason is that _____

7 Now match reasons a–d with phrases 1–4 in Exercise 6. Are they the same as your reasons?
a. receive a qualification. _____
b. because you learn about life. _____
c. you meet lots of interesting people! _____
d. that it's good for your education. _____

V1 **8** Complete the table with three parts of the body and two machines.

| ~~bones~~ | needles | medicine | skin | laboratory |
| scanner | teeth | tool | microscope | |

parts of the body	machines
bones	_____
_____	_____
_____	

V1, 2 **9** Make words from V1 and V2. Match 1–10 with a–j.
1. chewing   a. heels
2. diving   b. teeth
3. high   c. suit
4. Post-it®   d. machine
5. tin   e. room
6. MRI   f. needles
7. false   g. gum
8. acupuncture   h. can
9. X-ray   i. scanner
10. waiting   j. note

10 LANGUAGE REFERENCE

GRAMMAR

G1 SHOULD, SHOULDN'T

Use *should* when something is the right thing to do.
> You **should** keep your money in a bank.
> He **should** call me when he gets home.

Use *shouldn't* when something isn't the right thing to do.
> You **shouldn't** drive over 70 kilometres per hour.
> We **shouldn't** eat there. It's expensive.

Use *Should* + subject to ask the question 'is something the right thing to do?'.
> **Should I** come to the doctor with you?
> **Should we** take some money?

! Don't add -s to *should* after *he*, *she* or *it*.
> She **should** buy a new car. ✓
> She ~~shoulds~~ buy a new car. ✗

! Use the infinitive of the main verb without *to* after *should*.
> They **should use** a cash machine. ✓
> They should ~~to~~ use a cash machine. ✗

G1 HAVE TO, DON'T HAVE TO

Use *have to / has to* when something is necessary.
> My university is expensive, so I **have to** work in the summer holiday.
> She **has to** buy some new clothes because she's got a new job.

Use *don't have to / doesn't have to* when something isn't necessary.
> We **don't have to** fly there. We can take the train.
> The game **doesn't have to** end now. I can play for another half hour.

Use *Do* + subject + *have to* to ask the question 'is something necessary?'.
> **Do you have to** leave now?
> **Does he have to** pay cash?

KEY LANGUAGE

KL ASKING FOR AND GIVING OPINIONS

Asking for opinions
What's your opinion about (saving money)?
Do you think that (it's important)?
Do you agree that (it's a good idea)?

Giving an opinion
In my opinion, (it's a good idea).
I think that (it's a bad idea).
Personally, I think (we shouldn't do it).

Agreeing
Yes, definitely.
Yes, I suppose it is.

Showing uncertainty
I'm not sure.
I don't know.

Disagreeing
No, not at all.

VOCABULARY

V1 MONEY
cash, cashpoint, cheque, coin, credit card, debt, note, PIN, purse, wallet

V2 VERBS AND PHRASES CONNECTED WITH MONEY
borrow money (from someone), (can) afford, charge (you) interest, earn money, get a loan, lend money (to someone), pay back, refund, save

V3 BANKS
bank account, branch, cashpoint, interest rate, online banking

EXTRA PRACTICE 10

G1 **1** Write some advice for these problems. Use *should* and the words in brackets.

1 My boss isn't nice to me.
(you / get / new job)
You should get a new job.

2 I live in an ugly city.
(you / move / more beautiful)
_____.

3 My bank charges a lot of interest.
(you / change / account)
_____.

4 He often loses his wallet.
(he / be / careful)
_____.

5 He borrowed money from me. He didn't pay me back.
(you / ask / money)
_____.

6 Shopping at the supermarket is slow.
(you / shop / internet)
_____.

2 Write two sentences giving advice for these problems. Use *shouldn't* in the first sentence and *should* in the second. Invent the second piece of advice.

1 I'm always late for work.
You shouldn't be late for work.
You should get up earlier   .

2 They go out all the time and never study.
_____.
_____.

3 He smokes a lot.
_____.
_____.

4 We watch about six hours of television a day.
_____.
_____.

5 She spends all her money on clothes.
_____.
_____.

3 Write *Should … ?* questions for the answers given.

1 Should I *tell him* ?
No, it's OK. I can tell him.

2 Should we _____?
No, we can take the car. I don't want to walk.

3 Should he _____?
Yes, I think he can do the exam this term.

4 Should she _____?
Yes, a credit card is a good idea.

G2 **4** Write the correct form of *have to* (affirmative, negative or question) in sentences 1–9.

1 I *have to* phone a friend. Can I use your phone?
2 The taxi is here. We _____ leave now.
3 It's OK. You _____ pay for the meal. We can pay.
4 It's very busy now, so he _____ work long hours.
5 A birthday present _____ be expensive. It can be special and cost very little.
6 _____ we _____ decide now? I'd like time to think about the problem.
7 There isn't a lesson today, so we _____ go to school.
8 I don't like Bill. _____ you _____ invite him?
9 How much interest _____ she _____ pay on the loan?

KL **5** Complete the conversation with phrases a–h.

a No, not
b Do you think
c ~~What's your opinion~~
d Personally
e not at all
f I'm not sure
g definitely
h Do you

A: ¹ *c* about students having jobs, Ben?
B: ² _____, I think they should have a part-time job.
C: ³ _____. Students shouldn't work, really. Students have to study. They should have time.
B: But in my opinion, they have time to study and work. There are many countries where this happens.
A: ⁴ _____ that students should pay for their education, then?
B: Yes, ⁵ _____. I don't use education, so why should I pay for other people?
A: Wow! ⁶ _____ agree with that, Carol?
C: ⁷ _____ at all. I think this country should have qualified people, so we all have to pay for that.
A: Definitely. That's right, Ben, isn't it?
B: No, ⁸ _____ …

V1, 2, 3 **6** Complete sentences 1–9 with these pairs of words.

a know / number
b pay / credit
c lend / dollars
d afford / insurance
e write / cheque
f charge / interest
g earn / money
h ~~get / cash~~
i get / loan

1 I need to *get* some *cash* from the cashpoint.
2 They _____ more _____ than me, but I do the same job.
3 Can I _____ by _____ card?
4 Can we _____ a _____ from the bank for a new car?
5 Can you _____ me ten _____? I left my wallet at home.
6 The banks _____ about 20 percent _____ on overdrafts.
7 I can't _____ house _____. It's too expensive.
8 Do you _____ your account _____?
9 You _____ a _____ for £200 and send it to us.

121

11 LANGUAGE REFERENCE

GRAMMAR

G1 WILL, WON'T

We use *will* (*'ll*) and *will not* (*won't*) for what we <u>know</u> about the future.
   In 2050, **I'll** be 67 years old.
   It **won't** be dark at 5 p.m. in October.

We use *will* (*'ll*) and *will not* (*won't*) for what we <u>think</u> about the future.
   I think China **will** produce the most food in the future.
   People **won't** watch TV in the future. I believe they **will** use the internet for films and entertainment.

Use contractions *'ll* and *won't* for speaking and informal English.
   In 2050, **I'll** be 67 years old.
   People **won't** watch TV in the future.

Use *Will/Won't* + subject to ask questions.
   Will the climate become warmer?
   Won't grey whales completely disappear?

Use the infinitive without *to* after *will*.
   People **will live** longer in the future. ✓
   People will ~~to~~ live longer in the future. ✗

❗ Don't add *-s* to *will* after *he*, *she*, *it* or *there*.
   She **will** have to change jobs. ✓
   She ~~wills~~ have to change jobs. ✗

G2 BE GOING TO

Use *be going to* to talk about plans and intentions. These plans and intentions are not certain.

	subject + *be* (+ *not*)	going to	verb
+	I'm he's/she's/it's you're/we're/they're	going to	start
–	I'm not he/she/it isn't you/we/they aren't	going to	
?	*be* + subject Am I Is he/she/it Are you/we/they	going to	start?

I'm going to have a holiday in the summer.
He's going to call me in five minutes.
She **isn't going** to do it.
We **aren't going** to borrow any money next year.
Is the teacher **going** to use the book in this lesson?
Are they **going** to change the timetable?

❗ *She isn't going to …*
= *She's not going to …*

❗ The plans and intentions can be personal or impersonal.
   I'm going to lend him some money.
   The bank **is going** to lend him some money.

KEY LANGUAGE

KL CHECKING UNDERSTANDING

Could you repeat that, please?
I'm sorry, could you say that again?
So there are (two bedrooms). Is that right?
Was that (13 or 30)?
Did you say (14 or 40)?

VOCABULARY

V1 COMPOUND NOUNS

business centre, car park, gated community, internet café, play area, police station, post office, railway station, security guard, shopping centre, sports centre, swimming pool, tennis court, theme park

V2 SMART HOUSES

automatic lighting, big-screen TV, computer-controlled food shopping, computer games room, design feature, electric car/bike-charging point, fingerprint door locks, home cinema, living roof / roof garden, modern feature, multi-room entertainment system, outdoor security lighting, sauna, security camera system, smart home, smart (energy) meter, smartphone-controlled heating, solar panel, steam room, swimming pool, wind turbine

(to) save energy, (to) save the environment, (to) feel safer, (to) have more convenience, (to) have fun, (to) switch/turn off, (to) switch/turn on

V3 HOME AND FURNITURE

armchair, balcony, bathroom, bed, bedroom, bookcase, chair, cooker, cupboard, desk, dining room, dishwasher, flat, floor, fridge-freezer, garden, kitchen, lift, living room, sofa, table, wardrobe, washing machine, window

V4 EXAMS AND TESTS

exam(ination), instructions, practice test, relaxation, revision, test

(to) fail (an exam), (to) pass (an exam), (to) relax, (to) revise

EXTRA PRACTICE 11

G1 1 Read this dialogue between a presenter and a professor in a TV programme. Complete the dialogue with *will*, *'ll* or *won't*.

PRES: Today I'm talking to Professor Brumsfeld about the future of transport. First of all, Professor, what kind of cars ¹ _will_ we drive in the future?
PROF: Some people think we ² _____ fly in our cars, but it won't happen. I really don't think so.
PRES: So, what ³ _____ we do?
PROF: Well, cars ⁴ _____ use petrol because the world ⁵ _____ have any petrol. So we need something else. Some scientists think we ⁶ _____ use hydrogen. The advantage is that this is cleaner than petrol and better for the environment.
PRES: So ⁷ _____ these cleaner cars save the planet from global warming?
PROF: No, they ⁸ _____. We ⁹ _____ need to do many other things for that.

2 Speaking practice Ask a partner *Will you ... when you're older?* questions with the words below.

1 children
   Will you have children when you're older?
2 another country
   _____
3 excellent English
   _____
4 new car
   _____
5 Mars or the Moon
   _____

G2 3 Write the words in the right order to make *be going to* sentences.

1 a / going / I'm / have / to / shower / .
   I'm going to have a shower.
2 you / to / TV / going / are / watch / ?
   _____
3 he / anything / isn't / going / new / to / do / .
   _____
4 is / to / visit / John / his / grandmother / going / ?
   _____
5 aren't / change / going / our / to / we / plans / .
   _____
6 Bertrand and Tijana / build / a / are / going / house / to / ?
   _____
7 going / about / find / out / they're / to / flight / times / .
   _____
8 are / we / recycle / going / what / to / ?
   _____

KL 4 A student phones about an advert for a computer. Complete the conversation between the seller (S) and the student (ST) with these words in gaps 1–5.

~~right~~   say   repeat   it   was

ST: You have a computer for sale. Is that ¹ _right_?
S: ᵃ_Yes, that's right_.
ST: Is ² _____ a desktop or a laptop?
S: ᵇ_____
ST: How old is it?
S: ᶜ_____
ST: Did you ³ _____ eight or 18 months?
S: ᵈ_____
ST: And how much is it?
S: ᵉ_____
ST: Could you ⁴ _____ that, please?
S: ᶠ_____
ST: ⁵_____ that 200?
S: ᵍ_____
ST: Oh, OK. Can I come and have a look at it?

5 Now complete the dialogue in Exercise 4 with these responses in lines a–g.

~~Yes, that's right.~~   A laptop.   Eighteen.
I'd like £200.   Yes, it was.
Two hundred pounds.   About 18 months.

V1 6 What word is missing from each group to make compound nouns?

1 business, shopping, sports _____
2 car, theme _____
3 police, railway _____

V3 7 Find words in V3 to write next to these headings.

1 bedroom: _wardrobe,_ _____
2 kitchen: _____
3 living room: _____

V4 8 Write the words in sentences 1–6.

revise   practice   pass   relaxation   revision   fail

1 I _____ grammar every day because I have a test once a week.
2 She didn't do any _____. That's the reason she failed.
3 I'm sure that Klaus will _____ his exam. He's very good at English.
4 But it's possible that Elena will _____ the exam, as her English isn't very good.
5 The teacher gave us a _____ test today.
6 _____ the night before an exam is the best way to prepare.

123

12 LANGUAGE REFERENCE

GRAMMAR

G1 PRESENT PERFECT (REGULAR VERBS)

We use the present perfect when we talk about an experience in the past, but we don't say when we did it.

	subject + *have* (+ *not*)		past participle
	contraction	full form	
+	I've/you've/we've/they've	I/you/we/they have	worked
	he's/she's/it's	he/she/it has	
–	I/you/we/they haven't	I/you/we/they have not	
	he/she/it hasn't	he/she/it has not	
	have + subject		
?	Have I/you/we/they		(ever) worked?
	Has he/she/it		

! Note that regular past participles are the same as the past simple form of the verb (add *-ed* to the end of the infinitive).
I**'ve visited** a lot of countries.
She**'s talked** to the class.
We **haven't studied** the present perfect.
My father **hasn't changed** a lot in the last twenty years.
Have you ever **watched** a musical at the theatre?
Has he phoned about the flat?

Use short answers (without the main verb) to answer questions.
'**Have you** talked to your teacher?' 'Yes, **I have**. / No, **I haven't**.'

G2 PRESENT PERFECT (IRREGULAR VERBS)

Many common verbs are irregular, and the past simple and the past participle can be different.
eat – ate – eaten
write – wrote – written
drive – drove – driven
be – was/were – been
go – went – gone
do – did – done

I**'ve eaten** sushi.
They**'ve driven** a sports car.

! I've been to France. = I've gone to France and I've come back.
He's gone to France. = He's gone and he hasn't come back.

➡ Irregular verb list page 158

G3 PRESENT PERFECT AND PAST SIMPLE

We use the present perfect when we don't give (or don't know) the exact time we did something. We use the past simple when we give (or know) the exact time we did something.
He**'s travelled** to many countries.
In 1990, he **travelled** around the world.

We add more information with the past simple.
I**'ve been** to Mexico twice. I **went** there **in 1997** and then I **went** again **in 2003**. I **stayed** there **for three months** that time.

! Do not use past time adverbs (*yesterday, last night, a year ago*) with the present perfect.
He's travelled through the jungle last year. ✗
He**'s travelled** through the jungle. ✓
He **travelled** through the jungle **last year**. ✓
I've eaten sushi last night. ✗
I**'ve eaten** sushi in Japan. ✓
I **ate** sushi **last night**. ✓
Have you finished the essay at the weekend? ✗
Have you finished the essay? ✓
Did you finish the essay **at the weekend**? ✓

➡ Irregular verb list page 158

KEY LANGUAGE

KL LINKERS, SEQUENCERS AND FILLERS

also, let me see, perhaps, so, then, well, what else?

VOCABULARY

V1 ADJECTIVES

amazing, ancient, awful, beautiful, boring, clean, close (to people), cold, comfortable (with different people), confident, dangerous, different, difficult, disgusting, easy, exciting, famous, fantastic, fascinating, favourite, friendly, global, great fun, heavy (rain/storm) hot, horrible, huge, important, independent, intelligent, interesting, international, lonely, lucky, national, perfect, poor, political, proud, quiet, religious, scary, smart, special, strange, strong, superb, tall, terrible, tourist, unforgettable, unpleasant, unusual, well-dressed, well-educated, wonderful

V2 USING VERBS AS NOUNS

communicating with people, learning about life (in the desert), learning new skills, meeting people, riding a horse, seeing the sun rise, swimming with sharks, watching football, watching the animals

EXTRA PRACTICE 12

G1 1 Write these verbs in sentences 1–8 using the present perfect.

~~learn~~ drive go look watch eat talk be

1 They _have learned_ a lot with the new teacher.
2 _____ you _____ at the holiday photos?
3 _____ she _____ a Porsche?
4 They _____ Spanish food but not Japanese food.
5 _____ you _____ that new TV travel programme?
6 _____ they _____ about our new idea?
7 I _____ very busy.
8 Michael _____ to Bermuda. He doesn't want to come back.

G2 2 Correct the verbs in sentences 1–6.

1 Sally has never ~~drove~~ a Lamborghini.   _driven_
2 Have you ever see a dolphin?
3 Russell has went to the hospital. He'll be back at 6.00.
4 We haven't have dinner. Would you like to eat with us?
5 Have you ever growed flowers in your garden?
6 David Attenborough has maked a lot of TV programmes about the natural world.

G3 3 Choose the correct verb form.

1 I _made / have made_ a cake for us yesterday morning.
2 Can we give these customers a table? They _went / have been_ here many times before.
3 We _ate / have eaten_ alligator on holiday in Florida last year.
4 She _left / 's left_ for work at 8.30.
5 I don't think he _was / 's ever been_ to the opera.
6 My football team _didn't play / hasn't played_ very well last Saturday.
7 You _didn't meet / haven't met_ my sister. This is her first visit.
8 My parents _have never been / never went_ abroad. They want to go to Australia this year.

4 Match questions 1–5 with responses a–e.

1 Did you spend your childhood in the country? _b_
2 Have you ever studied Chinese? _____
3 Were you ever lonely? _____
4 Have you ever been to the house in Florence? _____
5 Did you have a good time last night? _____

a No, I haven't.
b ~~No, I didn't. We moved to the city when I was two.~~
c Yes, we have. We've been several times.
d Yes, I did. It was a great evening.
e Yes, I was sometimes.

KL 5 Write the words in gaps 1–4 in this dialogue.

perhaps   also   so   ~~let~~

A: What's the hottest place you've ever been to?
B: ¹ _Let_ me see. Erm … ² _____ it was when I went on holiday to India. We went to Delhi and then the south. That was hot. What about you?
A: Well, I've been to the Sahara desert, ³ _____ that was the hottest.
B: I'm sure!
A: I've ⁴ _____ been to Mexico, but it wasn't as hot as the desert.

V1 6 Write the missing vowels (a, e, i, o, u) in the adjectives.

1 This food tastes d_i_sg_u_st_i_ng. Send it back.
2 Eating sheep's eyes was an unf_rg_tt_bl_ experience.
3 Budapest is a f_sc_n_t_ng city.
4 The people were very proud and _nd_p_d_nt. They didn't need outside help.
5 I'm not a w_ll-_d_c_t_d person but I have a very good job.
6 I was in a car accident yesterday. It was a very _npl__s_nt experience.

V1 7 Match the verbs to the nouns, then complete sentences 1–5.

watching	the sun
learning	the animals
~~riding~~	~~a horse~~
communicating	with people
seeing	about different cultures

1 _Riding a horse_ in the Grand Canyon was an amazing but scary experience.
2 _____ in English online is an enjoyable experience – you can learn a lot.
3 _____ in the Amazon Forest was a fantastic experience – I took lots of photos.
4 _____ is a definite advantage of travelling.
5 _____ go down over Uluru is a beautiful sight – the colours are fantastic.

▶ MEET THE EXPERT

1 LESSON 2

1 Work with a partner. Answer these questions.
1 A megacity is a city with a population of 10 million people or more. True or false?
2 Think of ONE megacity in each of these countries:

Brazil China India Indonesia Japan
Mexico Nigeria Thailand Turkey
the United States (USA)

3 Are there any megacities in your country?

2 Watch the video. Tick (✓) the words you hear.

exciting place   lovely beaches
population   museums
modern   nice parks
jobs   noisy
schools or universities a crowded train
sport   expensive

3 Watch again. Choose the best answer.
1 The population of Mexico City is over *12 / 20 / 27* million.
2 There are over *13 / 30 / 33* million people in Tianjin, China.
3 There are a lot of *centres / opportunities / good apartments* in megacities.
4 There is an old *museum / park / temple* in the centre of Mexico City.
5 *Education / Transport / Home* life in megacities is a problem.

4 Can you remember? What is the order of the information in the video? Number these things from 1 to 4 (1 = the first thing on the video).

a bad things about megacities
b megacities in different countries
c information about Adam
d good things about megacities (including Mexico City)

5 Work with a partner. Answer these questions.
1 What are the good things about megacities? What are the bad things?

Megacities are exciting …

In megacities, there are a lot of …

2 Are you from a megacity? If not, would you like to live in a megacity? Why / Why not?

2 LESSON 1

1 Discuss these questions with a partner.
1 Look at the pictures below. Do you know the names of these airlines? Which countries are they from?

2 Which airlines are from your country?
3 Are there any airports in/near your city?
4 What are your favourite airports and airlines?

2a Watch the interview with Chris Holt, a pilot from the UK. Tick (✓) the places Chris talks about. Which is his favourite place?

Delhi   Dubai   London   Mexico City
Mumbai   Rio de Janeiro   Seoul   Toronto

2b Watch the interview again. Match these statements with one of the places in Exercise 2a.
1 The people are friendly.
2 The temperature is 50 degrees.
3 The temperature is minus (–) 30 degrees.
4 The food is fantastic.
5 There are mountains and strong winds.
6 It is four and a half hours ahead of London.

3 Watch again. Are these statements true or false?
1 Chris lives very near London's Heathrow Airport.
2 In his job, he sometimes says one or two words in the local language.
3 He doesn't like his job.
4 Every day is the same.
5 His daughter is 12 years old.
6 He plays golf.

4 Do you remember any other information from the interview about Chris's job or his home life?

5 Write down two good things and two bad things about Chris's job. Then compare your ideas with a partner's. Would you like to do Chris's job? Why?/Why not?

6 Imagine you are a pilot like Chris *or* that you do another job (for example, a doctor, a lecturer, a businesswoman/man). Think of some ideas and make notes about your job and home life. Then tell your partner.

I live in …
In my job, I …
I don't …
I …

3 LESSON 2

1 Discuss these questions.

1 Do you sometimes watch nature documentaries on TV or the internet? Can you remember any?
2 Do you have a favourite wildlife show?
3 Do you sometimes read magazines about nature and wildlife? Can you remember any photos or images from them?
4 Do you take photos of nature and wildlife?

2 David Stevenson is a professional wildlife photographer. Look at the statements below (A–G). Which four of them do you think are true? Watch and check.

A His pictures are in magazines and newspapers.
B Working days are similar and he usually gets a good shot.
C It is good to know how different animals behave.
D There is good light for photography at the end of the day.
E Some animals don't often see people, so they can be nervous.
F He never takes photos in zoos or parks.
G He uses a helicopter to go up mountains for photo-shoots.

3a Watch the interview again and complete these extracts. Compare your answers with a partner's.

1 The thing I like about working with _____ is that …
2 Before I go to _____ anything, I always …
3 The best time for _____ is …
4 There isn't really a _____ day …
5 Understanding where animals _____ is very important if …
6 The thing that I enjoy about _____ wildlife photography is that …
7 I also work in two of the best _____ in the UK …

3b Match these endings (A–G) to the sentence openings in Exercise 3a. Watch and check your ideas. Take more notes. What else do you remember from the video?

A … try to have a plan.
B … it's always unpredictable.
C … the people that come to me to learn are always very enthusiastic.
D … for me in my photography.
E … you're a wildlife photographer.
F … in the beginning and the end of the day.
G … to teach wildlife photography.

4 Think about one of your hobbies, interests or pastimes. Use the sentence openings from Exercise 3a and share your ideas.

The thing I like about … is that …
The best time for … is …
Before I …, I always …
Understanding … is very important if …
There is/isn't really a …
The thing that I enjoy about … is that …
I also …

4 LESSON 1

1 Discuss these questions.

1 Do you sometimes watch American movies?
2 Can you name any American movies, actors or directors?
3 Do you know these names, things or places?

| Hollywood | Martin Scorsese | Leonardo DiCaprio |
| Oscar | Robert de Niro | Shutter Island |

2 Watch the interview with Lynda Myles, a film producer. Which of these topics does Lynda *not* talk about?

A Lynda's opinion of Martin Scorsese and his films
B Martin Scorsese's childhood
C Scorsese's film school education
D Three key films by Scorsese
E The Oscar awards
F Actors
G Documentary films
H Future films

3a From your memory of the interview, are these sentences about Martin Scorsese true or false? Compare with a partner.

1 He makes personal films about important issues.
2 He grew up in a quiet area.
3 Music is important in his films.
4 He was ill as a child.
5 As a child, he liked reading storybooks.
6 He often went to the cinema.
7 He has received many Oscars in his long career.
8 He often works with the same actors.
9 He also makes documentaries about sports stars.

3b Watch the interview again and check your answers.

4a Think of successful people from your country, in the following areas. Write their names.

Film and theatre _____
Literature _____
Music and dance _____
TV and radio _____
Art and fashion _____
Architecture _____

4b Compare your list with a partner's. Talk about the people on your lists.

MEET THE EXPERT

5 LESSON 2

1 What do you know about these places and sights in London?

Big Ben   The River Thames   The London Eye
Trafalgar Square   Greenwich   The Olympic Park
Buckingham Palace   Camden Market   Oxford Street

2a Watch the interview with Chloe Couchman, an expert on London tourism. Which of the things below does she talk about?

buses   museums   tourist/visitor attractions   boats
markets   rivers   taxis   modern buildings   parks

2b What can you and your partner remember about each topic?

3a Watch the interview again and complete these notes with single words.

> Thames clipper (1)_____ : see many sights on the river
> Greenwich:
>   a) a royal connection:
>   (2)_____ Henry VIII
>   (3)_____ Elizabeth I
>   b) the Royal Naval (4)_____
>   c) the measurement of (5)_____
> Greenwich market: (6)_____ and second-hand clothes,
>   Tuesday – (7)_____
> The Observatory: look at the (8)_____
> The Fan museum: fans from different (9)_____
> The Millennium Dome: (10)_____ on the roof

3b Would you like to go to London? Are there other cities you want to visit? Discuss with a partner.

4a Prepare to talk about different places that you know. Look at the types of place below and think of three places for each one. Write the names.
A historic building: _____
A modern building: _____
A museum: _____
A market: _____
An entertainment centre: _____
A river or green area: _____

4b Prepare to talk about some of the places. Describe them. Why do you like them? Make notes in your notebook.

4c Listen to your partner talk about his/her places. Take notes. Tell him/her about your places.

4d Find a new partner and tell him/her about your first partner's places. Use your notes to help you.

6 LESSON 2

1 Discuss these questions with a partner.
1 Do you ever cook?
2 How do you learn about cooking?
3 What do you like cooking?
4 Who do you know who is a good cook?
5 Can you cook food from different countries?

2 Watch the interview with Nikita Gulhane, the owner of an Indian cookery school in London. In what order does he talk about these things?

A Family social occasions: births, marriages
B His early family life
C Where he and his family are from
D Different food from different parts of one country
E Food and welcoming people
F Food and religion

3a What can you remember about the topics in Exercise 2? Watch the interview again and complete these extracts.

1 … I always had an important role in getting the evening _____ out. And that's something which, that sense of sharing and passing on is something which I do with my ____ today.
2 … on the _____ coast of India. And we, there the food is particularly famous for being very _____, very spicy …
3 … to part of London which had a lot of Punjabi people, people from _____ India, and there the things I love eating are the _____, the tandoori naans, er, the tandoori chicken …
4 … when a _____ is born, then this is a time of great joy, the things which people like to give are – they tend to be _____ really …
5 … what we tend to eat are the _____ foods, but we're just cooking for large amounts of people, anything up to a _____ or more people.
6 Do you have something _____ for them to eat? Have you got certain snacks available? Can you make something very _____ for them?

3b Match the topics in Exercise 2 to the extracts in Exercise 3a. What else do you remember from the interview?

4a Prepare to talk about food in your life. Think about these topics.

Family meals   Food at birthdays   Cooking
Food at festivals and ceremonies   Food at school/college

4b Discuss the topics in Exercise 2 with a partner.
Who does the cooking in your family?
Tell me about typical family meals.
What happens on birthdays?

128

8 LESSON 1

1 What do you know about these ancient civilisations? Did you study them in school?

Egyptian Mayan Sumerian Ancient Greek
Ancient Chinese (Qin and Han dynasties) Roman
Aztec Ancient India

2a Watch the interview with Mark Weeden, a lecturer at the School of Oriental and African Studies in London. Tick the words that you hear.

writing art law cities music
farming mathematics king business
wars literature education

2b Compare your answers with your partner's. How do the words connect to the Sumerian civilisation? What can you remember?

3 Watch the interview again and complete these notes with single words.

> Sumer: (1) _____ Iraq
>
> Invented (2) _____, mathematics, (3) _____ practice and codes
>
> Writing: (4) _____ shapes in clay
>
> Mathematics: (5) _____ in 60s – sixty (6) _____ in a (7) _____, etc.
>
> Cities: divided into (8) _____ : religion, (9) _____, storage, (10) _____
>
> Royal Family: historic (11) _____ documents
>
> Early literature: Gilgamesh, story of a (12) _____

4 Discuss with your partner(s).
- Describe a historical place that you know.
- Which historical places would you like to visit around the world?
- In museums in your country, can you see things from other countries and civilisations?
- What key periods in your country's history do you know about?
- What historical heroes does your country have?
- How important is history for tourism?
- How important is history to you?

9 LESSON 2

1a Match the types of therapy to the definitions.

1 Massage   a putting people into a sleep-like state
2 Aromatherapy   b pressing and rubbing the body to reduce pain
3 Acupuncture   c putting needles into the body to reduce pain
4 Hypnotism   d using the smell of plant oils to relax

1b What do you know about the therapies in Exercise 1a? Do you use them sometimes?

2a Watch the interview with Odette Aguirre, an acupuncturist from London. In what order does she talk about the following topics?
1 How acupuncture feels
2 Acupuncture: the basic method, the theory, tools
3 Other methods, therapies and beauty
4 Problems and conditions treated

2b Compare with a partner. What can you remember about each topic?

3 There are ten mistakes in the notes below. Read the notes, watch the interview again and correct the mistakes.

> Acupuncture: needles put in points on the body – stimulates body organs
> Self-heal: reduce energy levels, increase pain and stress
> Scientific theory: acupuncture points are nerve beginnings which control the body
> Main tool: needles, single size, very thick
> Treatments for headaches, skin problems, heart problems, not sleeping, having babies
> ADULTS ONLY
> Electro-acupuncture: add electricity for stimulation
> Beauty: cosmetic acupuncture: eye treatment
> Different feelings: tingling or electric sensation
> Relaxing, but people don't fall asleep

4a Do you do any of these things when you want to relax? Put them in order of how often you do them.

Go for a walk in a park or by a river
Play some sport or do some exercise
Sit quietly and read a book
Use the internet
Watch TV/DVDs, etc.
Listen to music
Lie down and do nothing
Follow an interest (e.g. painting, horse riding, playing music)
Play a game (e.g. on a computer, chess, with friends)

4b Compare the order of your list with other students' lists. Which ways to relax seem most popular/unusual?

MEET THE EXPERT

11 LESSON 2

1 Discuss these questions.
1 What different types of building are there in your city or town?
2 Are there traditional buildings or styles?
3 Do you prefer older or modern buildings?

2a Godson Egbo is an architect. He discusses the house of the future. What do you think he says? Look at the quotes, and choose one of the words in italics.
1 I think the home of the future *will / won't* be increasingly influenced by technology.
2 I think the home of the future will also be much *more / less* energy efficient.
3 I think it *is / isn't* very important for a building to fit within its environment.
4 I believe that architecture is the most *public / private* of the arts.
5 I think we *can / can't* take lessons from the traditional architecture.
6 In the future, I'm sure our homes will be even *smarter / more expensive*.

2b Watch the interview with Godson Egbo and check your ideas.

2c Compare with a partner. What else do you remember from the interview?

3 Watch again and take notes for each of the points 1–6 in Exercise 2a. What examples does he give? These words will help.

control	heating	lighting	weather
temperature	heat	culture	tower blocks
older	waste	recycle	order

4a Do you agree or disagree with these statements? Discuss with your partner(s):

In ten years' time, I think
1 … most people in my country will live in a smart house.
2 … I will use an electric car.
3 … there will be robot cleaners in houses.
4 … I will use less energy.

4b What do you think life will be like in 30 years' time?

COMMUNICATION ACTIVITIES

LESSON 1.2 EXERCISE 7 (P. 9)
STUDENT A

Look at the table below and ask your partner questions.

Is there a river in Bangkok? (Yes, there is.)

Answer your partner's questions.

(In Amman, is there a river?) No, there isn't.

	Bangkok, Thailand	Amman, Jordan	Auckland, New Zealand	Berlin, Germany
River		✗		✓
Canals	✓		✗	
Harbour		✗		✗
Beaches	✗		✓	
Opera house	✗		✗	

LESSON 1.4 EXERCISE 4B (P. 12)
STUDENT B

Spell these words to your partner.

1. expensive
2. canal
3. university
4. cinema
5. lovely

LESSON 3.1 EXERCISE 7 (P. 23)
STUDENT B

Write four questions with these words. Then ask your partner your questions and note the answers.

1. of our bodies / What percentage / water / is / ?
   _____ percent
2. desert / of the world / What percentage / is / ?
   _____ percent
3. do / Why / fresh water, / drink / we / not sea water / ?
   _____
4. do / water / live / without / camels / How long / ?
   _____

Now choose the correct answers to your partner's questions and tell him/her.

about 95 percent   a tap   about 5 percent
only a few days

LESSON 1.3 EXERCISE 7 (P. 11)
STUDENT A

On the map below, there are six places with no name. Ask your partner questions about the places, then write the names of the places on the map.

Is there a/an … ?

car park   theatre   school   concert hall
shopping centre   fountain   university
tourist information centre

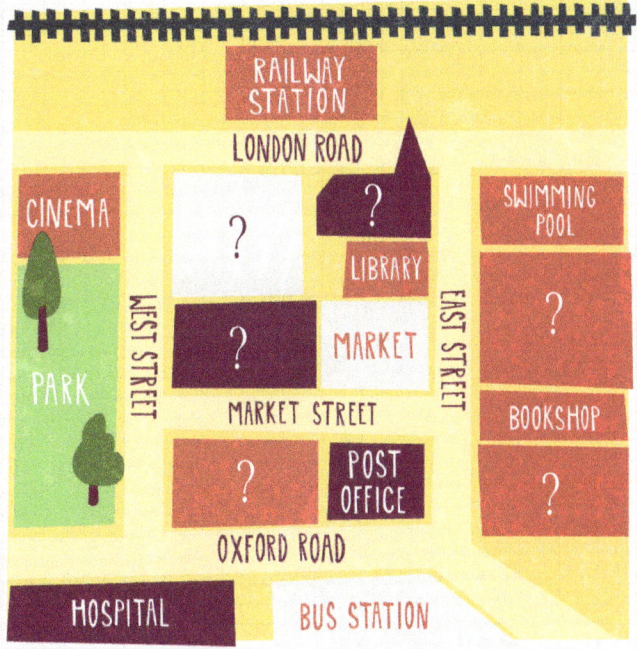

Now use the map to answer your partner's questions. Say where the places are.

Yes, there is. It's between / opposite / next to / in the …
No, there isn't.

USEFUL PHRASES

It's on the left/right of the map.
It's on the left/right of the library.
It's at the top/bottom of the map.

131

COMMUNICATION ACTIVITIES

LESSON 1.2   EXERCISE 7 (P. 9)
STUDENT B

Look at the table below and ask your partner questions.
In Amman, is there a river? (No, there isn't.)

Answer your partner's questions.
(Is there a river in Bangkok?) Yes, there is.

	Bangkok, Thailand	Amman, Jordan	Auckland, New Zealand	Berlin, Germany
River	✓		✗	
Canals		✗		✓
Harbour	✗		✓	
Beaches		✗		✗
Opera house		✗		✓

LESSON 1.4   EXERCISE 4B (P. 12)
STUDENT A

Spell these words to your partner.

1 chair
2 famous
3 market
4 mountain
5 museum

LESSON 3.1   EXERCISE 7 (P. 23)
STUDENT A

Write four questions with these words. Then ask your partner your questions and note the answers.

1 live in deserts / What percentage / world's people / of the / ?
   _____ percent
2 is in the seas and oceans / of the world's water / What percentage / ?
   _____ percent
3 How long / without / live / people / water / do / ?
   _____
4 in your house / water / Where / come from / does / ?
   _____

Now choose the correct answers to your partner's questions and tell him/her.

| because sea water has a lot of salt | about 70 percent |
| two or three weeks | about 25 percent |

LESSON 11.3   EXERCISE 7B (P. 91)
STUDENT A

You work for Flats 4 U. Look at the information below. Give your partner information when he/she asks for it, and repeat if he/she asks you.

Flat (address):	13F Church Street
Bedrooms:	2 large
Other rooms:	large kitchen, large living room, 2 small bathrooms
Floor:	4th floor, lift
Garden:	shared garden
Furniture/Equipment:	kitchen: cooker, fridge-freezer bedrooms: beds living room: sofa, 2 armchairs
Public transport:	near bus station, central location
Local facilities:	restaurants, cafés, cinemas, small supermarket
Rent:	€200 per person per week

132

LESSON 2.3   EXERCISE 8A (P. 19)

STUDENT A

Use the information below to answer your partner's questions about the project manager job.

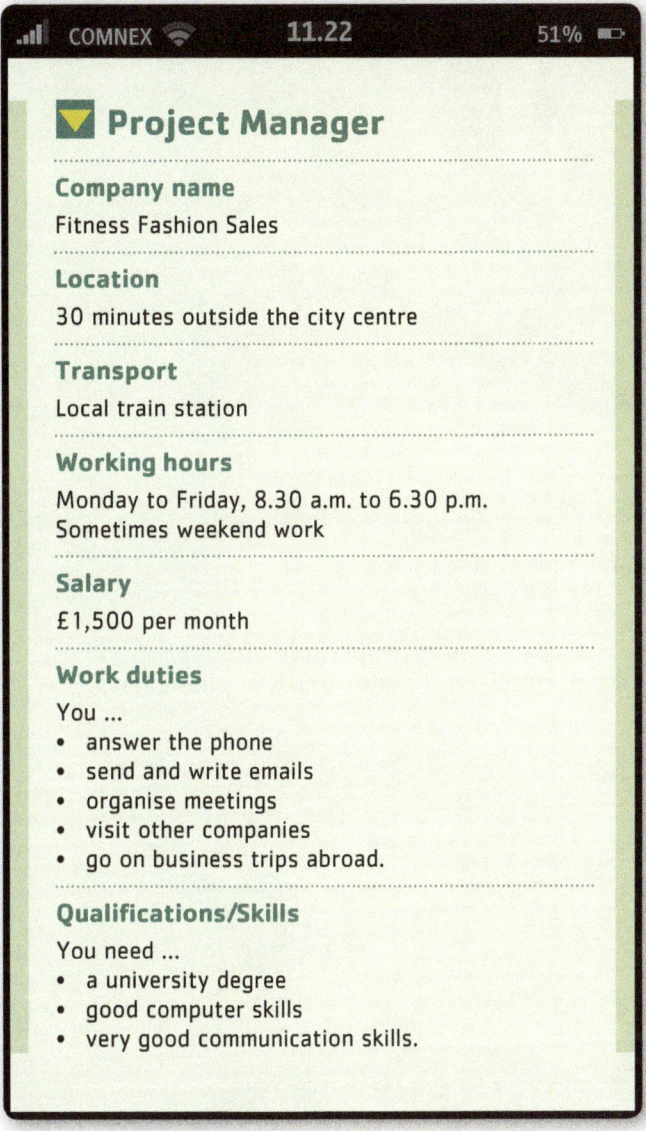

LESSON 3.4   EXERCISE 4 (P. 28)

STUDENT A

Ask your partner questions about pictures A–D. Do not show him/her the words or phonetics.

What's A in English?
How do you spell/pronounce it?

Now answer your partner's questions about pictures E–H.

It's a/an …

starfish /ˈstɑːfɪʃ/
turtle /ˈtɜːtl/
speedboat /ˈspiːdbəʊt/
lagoon /ləˈguːn/

LESSON 4.4   EXERCISE 6 (P. 36)

STUDENT A

Frequency of playing sport: EU countries 2009

	Bulgaria	Latvia	Belgium	Ireland
Never	___%	44%	28%	26%
Occasionally	28%	29%	___%	15%
Sometimes	10%	___%	34%	35%
Often	3%	8%	16%	___%

Adapted from: British Heart Foundation Physical Activity Statistics 2012

COMMUNICATION ACTIVITIES

LESSON 2.3   EXERCISE 8B (P. 19)

STUDENT B

Use the information below to answer your partner's questions about the administration officer job.

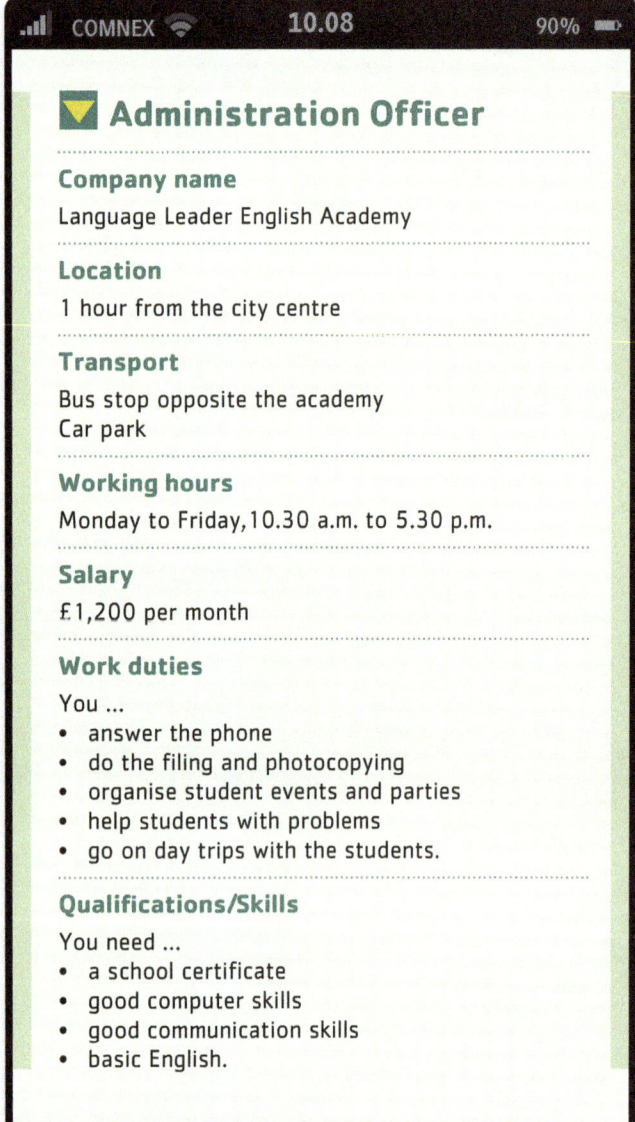

LESSON 3.4   EXERCISE 4 (P. 28)

STUDENT B

Answer your partner's questions about pictures A–D.

It's a/an …

penguin /ˈpeŋɡwɪn/
crocodile /ˈkrɒkədaɪl/
submarine /sʌbməˈriːn/
umbrella /ʌmˈbrelə/

Now ask your partner questions about pictures E–H. Do not show him/her the words or phonetics.

What's E in English?
How do you spell/pronounce it?

LESSON 4.4   EXERCISE 6 (P. 36)

STUDENT B

Frequency of playing sport: EU countries 2009

	Bulgaria	Latvia	Belgium	Ireland
Never	58%	___%	28%	26%
Occasionally	28%	29%	22%	___%
Sometimes	___%	19%	34%	35%
Often	3%	8%	___%	23%

Adapted from: British Heart Foundation Physical Activity Statistics 2012

LESSON 3.2 EXERCISES 2–4B (P. 24)

STUDENT B

Read about the park ranger in the rainforest. How many work duties does she talk about?

Answer these questions about your wildlife worker.
1. Where does she work?
2. What work with people does she do?
3. What work with animals does she do?
4. What things does she like doing?

Tell your partner about your wildlife worker. Then listen and make notes about your partner's worker. Read the other text to check the information.

A park ranger in the rainforest

I am always happy when I work in this amazing place. There is always something beautiful to see, and the work is never boring.

When the park is open, we always give guided tours. There are two tours every day. My favourite tours are the mountain walks because everyone enjoys the views over the trees.

Occasionally, there is an emergency – perhaps a visitor gets a little lost. Don't worry, we always find them!

I like checking the wildlife in the rainforests. Of course, I often see beautiful birds and unusual animals. Sadly, I never see koala bears because they don't live in the rainforest.

LESSON 4.4 EXERCISE 9A (P. 37)

Go to the cinema	54%
Go to the theatre	27%
Go to art exhibitions	17%
Go to the opera and classical-music concerts	6%
Go to museums	28%
Go to dance events and ballet	5%
Go to live pop and rock events	31%
Go to historical places	21%

LESSON 5.3 EXERCISE 9 (P. 43)

STUDENT B

You are Chris, the travel agent. Look at the timetable and information below and choose the two best flights for your customer. Then give your customer the flight details. Which flight does your customer want? Take the booking.

airline	OA	IBA	TA
dep. Sydney	Sun 8.30 p.m.	Sun 1.00 p.m.	Sun 7.30 p.m.
arr. Moscow	Mon 11.30 a.m.	Mon 1.00 p.m.	Mon 12.00 p.m.
dep. Moscow	Mon 6.30 a.m.	Mon 9.00 a.m.	Mon 11.00 a.m.
arr. Sydney	Tues 1.30 p.m.	Tues 3.00 p.m.	Tues 7.00 p.m.
flight time	22 hours	19 hours	24 hours
ticket prices			
business class	AU$1,000	Not available	AU$1,500
standard class	AU$700	AU$500	AU$900
service	**** (meals, drinks, films, snacks)	** (snacks, radio)	***** (as OA + video games and head massage)

COMMUNICATION ACTIVITIES

LESSON 4.3   EXERCISE 8 (P. 35)

STUDENT A

Look at the brochure and complete the 'Scottish Dream' column in the table.

Our resort is in the heart of the Scottish countryside.

First-class facilities
You stay in a cottage – perfect for families. You have a kitchen and a living room with satellite TV. There are five restaurants in the resort – Scottish, Chinese, Indian, Italian and American food.

Be active with us
Explore the wonderful Scottish countryside and mountains with us. You can go hiking and mountain biking. You can play tennis, and our golf course is a very popular facility.

Learn with us
There are visits to old castles and there are museum trips. We offer classes in painting and Scottish music.

Relax with us
Our Fitness Centre has two indoor swimming pools. One swimming pool is for children and teenagers. In the evening, there are music and dance shows in the two bars. There is no cinema.

Resort name	Scottish Dream Yes/No + info	Club Mexico Yes/No + info
Accommodation		
Family rooms	yes – cottage	
TV		
Internet		
Kitchen		
Sea view	no	
Sports		
Swimming		
Scuba diving	no	
Windsurfing		
Hiking	yes	
Mountain biking		
Tennis		
Golf		
Fitness centre	yes	
Activities		
Day trips		
Classes		
Kids' club	yes	
Entertainment		
Restaurants	yes – 5	
Cinemas		
Shows	yes	

Ask the travel agent questions about 'Club Mexico' and complete the column.
Then answer the customer's questions about 'Scottish Dream'.

LESSON 8.1   EXERCISE 8B (P. 63)

STUDENT B

Look at the information below. Ask your partner questions to fill the gaps.

Where was Mayan civilisation?
When was Inca civilisation important?
What were the Aztec people good at?

	Location of civilisation	Main period of civilisation	Capital city	Abilities/Skills of people	End of civilisation
Mayan	modern-day _____, _____, _____ and _____	between _____ and AD 250	_____	writing, mathematics, studying the stars and building large cities of stone	in about _____
Inca	modern-day Peru, Ecuador, Bolivia and Chile	from _____ to AD 1525	Cuzco, in Peru	building _____, building _____	in AD 1532
Aztec	modern-day Mexico	from about _____ to AD 1500	under modern-day Mexico City	_____	in _____

LESSON 6.1   EXERCISE 8 (P. 47)

STUDENT A

Look at the picture and ask and answer questions. Find differences between your picture and your partner's picture.

Is/Are there any … ?
There is/are some …
There isn't/aren't any …

LESSON 9.3   EXERCISE 9A (P. 75)

PAIR C

Mirrors

Work with your partner and prepare your talk. Follow these steps.

1 Think of an idea to use in your introduction.

You can use mirrors to bring light into your house.

2 Here are four facts about your invention. Make sentences with the verbs in the box. Choose three for your talk. Then check your sentences with your teacher.

be	use	have	invent

a   People / stone mirrors / Turkey 8,000 years ago
b   There / metal mirrors / China 4,000 years ago
c   Justus von Liebig, a German chemist, / the modern mirror / 1835
d   Modern glass mirrors / silver / the back

3 Think of four reasons to vote for your invention.

You can use mirrors to see what you look like.

4 Decide how to end your talk. Can you make a final comment about the invention?

LESSON 6.3   EXERCISE 10B (P. 51)

STUDENT B

This is your supply list. Take the conference organiser's order and say if you can supply the food.

Event Catering Company
Best food, best service

Order form	Quantity available	Quantity ordered
First course		
Tomato and cheese salad	50	
Noodle soup	50 cans	
Tomato soup	50 cans	
Main course		
Cheese salad	100	
Chicken salad (Chinese-style with noodles)	30	
Beef curry (with rice)	200	
Lamb kebab (with rice and vegetables)	60	
Vegetarian curry (with rice)	40	
Vegetarian pizza (tomato, mushroom)	100	
Burger meal (chips, onion rings)	50	
Sushi meal (fish and vegetarian)	50	
Desserts		
Chocolate ice cream	40	
Apple pie	40	
Fruit salad	40	
Drinks		
Sparkling water	100	
Still water	50	
Lemonade	100	
Orange juice	50	
Apple juice	50	

COMMUNICATION ACTIVITIES

LESSON 4.3   EXERCISE 8 (P. 35)

STUDENT B

Look at the brochure and complete the 'Club Mexico' column in the table.

Our resort is on the beautiful east coast of Mexico.

Enjoy your stay
All our hotel rooms are double rooms with sea views, TV and wi-fi.

Enjoy the sea
We have excellent water-sports facilities. You can go scuba diving, sailing and windsurfing. For beginners, we offer classes in all these sports. The sea is perfect for swimming, and there is also a swimming pool.

Enjoy the evening
There are four restaurants and two cinemas at the resort. Enjoy a meal with your friends and family – choose from Asian, American, Mediterranean and African food – and then see a film!

Enjoy your family time
We have a kids' club. There are fun activities for children all day long – the parents can come too. Every day, there is a day trip on a boat – visit wonderful beaches and local villages.

Resort name	Club Mexico Yes/No + info	Scottish Dream Yes/No + info
Accommodation		
Family rooms		
TV		
Internet		
Kitchen	no	
Sea view		
Sports		
Swimming		
Scuba diving		
Windsurfing		
Hiking		
Mountain biking		
Tennis	no	
Golf		
Fitness centre	no	
Activities		
Day trips	yes	
Classes	yes	
Kids' club		
Entertainment		
Restaurants	yes	
Cinemas		
Shows	yes	

Answer the customer's questions about 'Club Mexico'.
Then ask the travel agent questions about 'Scottish Dream' and complete the column.

LESSON 8.1   EXERCISE 8B (P. 63)

STUDENT A

Look at the information below. Ask your partner questions to fill the gaps.

Where was Inca civilisation?
When was Aztec civilisation important?
What were the Mayan people good at?

	Location of civilisation	Main period of civilisation	Capital city	Abilities/Skills of people	End of civilisation
Mayan	modern-day Mexico, Guatemala, Honduras and Belize	between 600 BC and _____	More than one – Chichén Itzá is the most famous	_____, _____, _____ and _____	in about AD 900
Inca	modern-day _____, _____, _____ and _____	from AD 1200 to _____	_____	building roads, building temples	in _____
Aztec	modern-day _____	from about AD 1200 to _____	_____	fighting	in AD 1251

138

LESSON 6.1   EXERCISE 8 (P. 47)

STUDENT B

Look at the picture and ask and answer questions. Find differences between your picture and your partner's picture.

Is/Are there any … ?
There is/are some …
There isn't/aren't any …

LESSON 9.3   EXERCISE 9A (P. 75)

PAIR D

The Post-it® note
Work with your partner and prepare your talk. Follow these steps.

1 Think of an idea to use in your introduction.

They are very important in the office.

2 Here are four facts about your invention. Make sentences with the verbs in the box. Choose three for your talk. Then check your sentences with your teacher.

be	do	invent	sell	use

a Two Americans / the Post-it® note / 1970
b The average office worker / eleven Post-it® notes / every day
c Now / 600 different Post-it® products
d In 2000 / artist / a drawing on a Post-it® note and / for $1,000

3 Think of four reasons to vote for your invention.

They're small and they save paper.

4 Decide how to end your talk. Can you make a final comment about the invention?

LESSON 6.3   EXERCISE 10C (P. 51)

STUDENT A

This is your supply list. Take the conference organiser's order and say if you can supply the food.

Event Catering Company
Best food, best service

Order form	Quantity available	Quantity ordered
First course		
Tomato and cheese salad	40	
Noodle soup	40 cans	
Tomato soup	40 cans	
Main course		
Cheese salad	75	
Chicken salad (Chinese-style with noodles)	200	
Beef curry (with rice)	30	
Lamb kebab (with rice and vegetables)	50	
Vegetarian curry (with rice)	60	
Vegetarian pizza (tomato, mushroom)	50	
Burger meal (chips, onion rings)	50	
Sushi meal (fish and vegetarian)	100	
Desserts		
Chocolate ice cream	30	
Apple pie	50	
Fruit salad	50	
Drinks		
Sparkling water	50	
Still water	100	
Lemonade	50	
Orange juice	30	
Apple juice	50	

139

COMMUNICATION ACTIVITIES

LESSON 7.3 EXERCISE 6A (P. 59)

STUDENT A

Read the information about your area and decide the advantages and disadvantages for the bookshop. Then complete the table on page 59.

The market

- The market is a tourist attraction.
- Many young people and students live in the local area.
- Parking space for 100 cars.
- Near the bus station.
- 1,000 people visit every week, number is increasing all the time.
- Low rent: small store (without air conditioning), $350 a month; open-air stall, $200 a month.
- No bookstores.
- Musical instrument store and a CD stall.
- The market closes at 10 p.m.

LESSON 10.1 EXERCISES 10B AND 11 (P. 79)

1 Compare your advice with this answer.

Dear Nadia,

I'm sorry to hear about your problems. I think that you should try to find a better job. Supermarkets usually pay more than restaurants. You shouldn't use your credit cards to buy things – they're very expensive. You should talk to your teachers at the university – they can help you.

2 Now look at these problems. What advice can you give these people?

1
I'm a student from China. I'm now living in the UK. I'm sharing a flat with three other Chinese students. We're afraid to go out after dark because we can hear a lot of police cars. We don't think that the city is safe. What should we do?

Li

2
I'm a student from Poland. I'm learning English, but I find it very difficult to remember new vocabulary. What should I do?

Veronica

3
I'm from Germany and I'm spending a year in London. I have a lot of friends and I go out a lot. I like eating in expensive restaurants and going to the theatre. The problem is, I'm an ordinary office worker and I haven't got much money. What should I do?

Klara

LESSON 4.4 EXERCISE 3 (P. 36)

STUDENT B

Listen and write your partner's numbers, then read these numbers to your partner.

13   130   8,743   34,984   8,456,00

140

LESSON 8.3 EXERCISE 10 (P. 67)

STUDENT B

1 You are a visitor at the City Museum. Ask your partner about these things.
Have five short conversations.

1. the cost of a senior citizen ticket for the 'How things began' exhibition
2. where the Egyptian mummies are
3. the museum's opening time
4. where the bookshop is and its closing time
5. what food the restaurant sells, and its opening and closing times

2 Change roles. Do the role-play again. This time, you work at the City Museum.
Use the information on this page to answer questions from a visitor.

THE CITY MUSEUM

OPENING HOURS
Open daily _____ –17.30 (Friday until 20.30)
Except for 1 January and 24, 25 and 26 December

TICKETS
Entrance to the museum is free, but there is a charge for some special exhibitions.

Life in Roman times
£15 adults and senior citizens
£12.50 students and 16–18 years
Free for children under 16

How things began
_____ adults and senior citizens
£8 students and 16–18 years
Free for children under 16

MAIN ROOMS
Europe	Upper floor (first floor)
Egyptian Mummies	_____ floor
Asia	Ground floor
Middle East	Ground floor
Greece and Rome	Ground floor
Americas	Ground floor
Africa	Lower floor

SHOPS
The bookshop is _____.
10.30– _____ (_____ on Friday)

The family shop is on the north side of the museum.
9.30–18.00

The collections shop is on the west side of the museum.
(souvenirs, postcards, guides and gifts)
9.30–17.30 (20.00 on Friday)

FOOD
The restaurant sells _____ and _____.
_____ – _____ (_____ on Friday)

The City Museum café sells sandwiches, cakes and drinks.
9.00–17.30 (Saturday to Thursday)
9.00–20.00 (Friday)

COMMUNICATION ACTIVITIES

LESSON 7.3   EXERCISE 6A (P. 59)
STUDENT B

Read the information about your area and decide the advantages and disadvantages for the bookshop. Then complete the table on page 59.

The highway shopping area

- Busiest road in Charleston – 1,000 cars drive past every hour.
- Three fast-food restaurants, a supermarket, a motel, a music CD store.
- No bookstores.
- Parking space for 50 cars + private parking for store (five cars).
- Bus stop opposite the store.
- Large stores with air conditioning.
- Low rent: $300 a month.
- Main customers: families and business people.
- Not very safe at night – high crime.

LESSON 4.4   EXERCISE 3 (P. 36)
STUDENT A

Read these numbers to your partner, then listen and write your partner's numbers.

| 19 | 190 | 3,240 | 22,587 | 4,732,000 |

LESSON 10.2   EXERCISE 8A (P. 81)
STUDENT A

Read about two people, take notes and prepare to tell your partner about them. Use full sentences.

Joelle is 27 and her business is called … She wants to …

Mobile Photo Studio
'Professional portraits without leaving your home'

Joelle Campbell, 27

Business idea
- Mobile photography studio: professional photographs (portraits) in your home
- Specialising in photographing children

Education and experience
- Photography degree from Manchester University
- Photographer's assistant in a small studio in a shop

Current state of business
- Finished market research (two months)
- Has 20 customers on her waiting list
- Has a large car and a good computer

Size of loan and need for it: £2,500
- Has to buy a new camera and portable lights
- Has to design a website

My Work of Art Gallery
'Original art: not just for the rich'

Helen McAllister, 22

Business idea
- Art gallery in fashionable East London; art that ordinary people can afford (from £20 to £2,000)
- Contemporary art by art students and young artists

Education and experience
- BA in Art Business and Management (University of the Arts London – UAL)
- Gallery assistant at Tate Modern Gallery
- Organised UAL Art Fair 2014

Current state of business
- 50 artists ready to sell their art in the gallery
- Twitter account has 5,000 followers
- A temporary gallery (one month only) sold 50 pieces (£10,000)

Size of loan and need for it: £9,500
- Has to rent gallery space for one year
- Has to buy new art to sell

LESSON 8.3 EXERCISE 10 (P. 67)

STUDENT A

1 You work at the City Museum. Use the information on this page to answer questions from a visitor.

2 Change roles. Do the role-play again. This time, you are the visitor. Ask your partner about these things. Have five short conversations.

1 the cost of a student ticket for the 'Life in Roman times' exhibition
2 where the Africa room is
3 the museum's closing time
4 where the family shop is and its closing time
5 what food the City Museum café sells, and its opening and closing times

THE CITY MUSEUM

OPENING HOURS
Open daily 10.00– _____ (Friday until _____)
Except for 1 January and 24, 25 and 26 December

TICKETS
Entrance to the museum is free, but there is a charge for some special exhibitions.

Life in Roman times
£15 adults and senior citizens
_____ students and 16–18 years
Free for children under 16

How things began
£10 adults and senior citizens
£8 students and 16–18 years
Free for children under 16

MAIN ROOMS
Europe	Upper floor (first floor)
Egyptian Mummies	Upper floor
Asia	Ground floor
Middle East	Ground floor
Greece and Rome	Ground floor
Americas	Ground floor
Africa	_____ floor

SHOPS
The bookshop is by Room 6.
10.30–19.30 (20.00 on Friday)

The family shop is on _____ side of _____ .
9.30–_____

The collections shop is on the west side of the museum. (souvenirs, postcards, guides and gifts)
9.30–17.30 (20.00 on Friday)

FOOD
The restaurant sells hot meals and afternoon teas.
12.00–17.30 (20.00 on Friday)

The City Museum café sells _____, _____ and drinks.
_____ (Saturday to Thursday)
_____ (Friday)

COMMUNICATION ACTIVITIES

LESSON 7.3   EXERCISE 6A (P. 59)
STUDENT C

Read the information about your area and decide the advantages and disadvantages for the bookshop. Then complete the table on page 59.

The shopping mall
- Car park for 1,000 cars.
- 10,000 people visit every week.
- Two department stores and 50 other stores.
- Three bookstores and two music stores.
- Large stores with air conditioning.
- High rent: $800 a month.
- Closes at 8 p.m.
- Customers: families, teenagers and professional workers.
- Very safe – private security.

LESSON 9.1   EXERCISE 10A (P. 71)

Alfred Nobel
born 1833, Sweden
(*study*) chemistry
(*write*) poetry, novels, plays
(*try*) to make safe explosive
(*kill*) brother in an experiment 1864
(*invent*) dynamite 1866
(*start*) Nobel Prize Foundation 1895

Levi Strauss
born 1829, Germany
(*travel*) New York 1846
(*move*) San Francisco 1853
(*start*) shop for gold miners
(*sell*) equipment and clothes
(*invent*) jeans 1873
(*use*) material from Nîmes, France
(*call*) material 'denim'

LESSON 9.2   EXERCISE 11 (P. 73)
ANSWERS
1. Yes, he did.
2. No, they didn't. (The Chinese made the first paper.)
3. He invented X-rays.
4. They landed on the Moon in 1969.
5. He first arrived in the Caribbean Islands.

LESSON 10.2   EXERCISE 8A (P. 81)
STUDENT B

Read about two people, take notes and prepare to tell your partner about them. Use full sentences.

Yasmin is 24 and her business is called … She wants to …

Delicious Dinner Club
'We cook, you have fun!'

Yasmin Hanif, 24

Business idea
- Hold dinner parties in unusual locations or at the customer's home
- Dinner parties have a theme, e.g. Africa, sport, a famous film
- Food, music and location connected to the theme. Diners wear fancy-dress costume.

Education and experience
- Catering college (cooking and customer service)
- Business Studies Diploma
- Worked in Liverpool Football Club's café bar

Current state of the business
- Finished market research (one month)
- Has got a business plan
- Has got a kitchen (father runs a bakery)

Size of loan and need for it: £4,000
- Has to design the website
- Has to do advertising on local radio
- Has to book the location for the first dinner party

comparegames.com
'The one-stop website for video game fans'

Mani Chavan, 20

Business idea
- A website that compares video games by finding all the information from the internet (e.g. reviews of games, best prices)
- Everything you need to know. Save time and money.

Education and experience
- School exams: computer science, maths and business studies
- Makes game apps for phones (*Peaceful Pigs, Build the Wall*)
- Ran school's student website (for three years)

Current state of business
- Finished the design of the website
- 500 friends on business Facebook page

Size of loan and need for it: £6,000
- Has to do a lot of advertising to find site users
- Has to find companies to put adverts on his website

LESSON 11.1   EXERCISE 11 (P. 87)
STUDENT A

Read these sentences. Will these things be true for you in 2037? Tick the box that best describes what you think. Then ask your partner what he/she thinks and tick the box.

	You			Your partner		
	Yes	Perhaps	No	Yes	Perhaps	No
1 I'll be in the same relationship as now.						
2 I'll own my flat/house.						
3 I'll speak four languages.						
4 I'll wear jeans a lot of the time.						
5 I won't laugh more than I do now.						
6 I'll be happy with my life.						

Discuss the statements. How many do you agree/disagree about?

LESSON 12.2   EXERCISE 7A (P. 97)
STUDENT A

Ask your partner questions and make notes in the table.

Name: _____	Yes	No	Extra information?
Visit another country?			
Climb a mountain?			
Have a winter holiday?			
Eat unusual food?			
Stay in a four- or five-star hotel?			
Go on holiday with friends?			

LESSON 9.3   EXERCISE 9A (P. 75)
PAIR B

Toy balloons
Work with your partner and prepare your talk. Follow these steps.

1 Think of an idea to use in your introduction.

Every party needs these!

2 Here are four facts about your invention. Make sentences with the verbs in the box. Choose three for your talk. Then check your sentences with your teacher.

sell   invent   be   burst
make   move

a   Professor Faraday / the first rubber balloons / 1824 for his experiments with hydrogen
b   An Englishman, Mr J. Ingram, / the first toy balloons / 1847
c   In 1912, American shops first / balloons that / not round
d   When you / a balloon, the air / faster / the speed of sound. Boom!

3 Think of four reasons to vote for your invention.

You can fill them with water and throw them at people.

4 Decide how to end your talk. Can you make a final comment about the invention?

COMMUNICATION ACTIVITIES

LESSON 10.2 EXERCISE 7A (P. 81)
STUDENT B

Read about Graeme and answer the questions.

1. What is the name of his business?
2. What does he do?
3. What training and experience did he have before he started his business?
4. What is different about his business?
5. How helpful were the banks?
6. How much did he borrow, and what is he doing with the money?
7. How many pieces of advice does he give? What are they?
8. What is his ambition?

START-UP LOANS

Graeme, 25. Evolution Music Studios

I have a music recording studio in Brighton. I offer a high-quality studio service at cheap prices for new bands and musicians. I also give music training to teenagers.

I have fifteen years of experience in the local music industry. I played in my first band when I was ten, and I was a music teacher. I know studios are very expensive, especially for young people. That's why I decided to start a studio that was cheap and helpful for young people.

The banks didn't want to lend me any money, but Start-Up Loans lent me £5,000. I am using most of the money to rent the building and to buy some equipment for my studio. Now I have to do a lot of advertising, and I am using the rest of the money to pay for that.

What advice can I give? Well, you have to have a good idea! Many young people make music, but studios are very expensive and they don't help young people. I saw a gap in the market. My studio is exactly what young musicians need – I hope! I want some of the young musicians who use my studio to become international stars one day.

LESSON 11.1 EXERCISE 11 (P. 87)
STUDENT B

Read these sentences. Will these things be true for you in 2037? Tick the box that best describes what you think. Then ask your partner what he/she thinks and tick the box.

	You			Your partner		
	Yes	Perhaps	No	Yes	Perhaps	No
1 I'll be well known in my work.						
2 I'll live with my parents.						
3 I'll travel more than now.						
4 I won't have to worry about money.						
5 I'll feel old.						
6 I'll play a lot of sport.						

Discuss the statements. How many do you agree/disagree about?

LESSON 12.2 EXERCISE 7A (P. 97)
STUDENT B

Ask your partner questions and make notes in the table.

Name: _____	Yes	No	Extra information?
Visit a famous place?			
Swim in a clear blue sea?			
Stay on a campsite?			
Have a beach party?			
Fly in business or first class?			
Go on holiday alone?			

146

LESSON 9.3   EXERCISE 9A (P. 75)
PAIR A
Tin cans
Work with your partner and prepare your talk. Follow these steps.

1 Think of an idea to use in your introduction.
You can find this invention in every kitchen in the world.

2 Here are four facts about your invention. Make sentences with the verbs in the box. Choose three for your talk. Then check your sentences with your teacher.

be	invent	make	produce

a 1796 / an Englishman, Peter Durand / first metal cans
b Forty years later / someone / the first can-opener!
c Now / square cans / for easy transport
d Britain / twenty billion cans / every year

3 Think of four reasons to vote for your invention.
Many early explorers used them.

4 Decide how to end your talk. Can you make a final comment about the invention?

LESSON 11.3   EXERCISE 7A (P. 91)
STUDENT B

You work for Flats R Us. Look at the information below. Give your partner information when he/she asks for it, and repeat if he/she asks you.

Flat (address):	14A Museum Avenue
Bedrooms:	2 small
Other rooms:	large kitchen, large living room, dining room, bathroom
Floor:	ground
Garden:	garden
Furniture/Equipment:	kitchen: fridge-freezer, cooker, microwave, dishwasher
	bedrooms: beds, desks, wardrobes
	living room: sofa, table, armchair, large cupboard dining room: table and 4 chairs
Public transport:	near bus stop (5 mins), 45 mins to city centre
Local facilities:	local shops, a park
Rent:	€100 per person per week

LESSON 3.1   EXERCISE 1B (P. 22)
ANSWERS

1 a   5 b
2 b   6 a
3 b   7 b
4 a   8 a

LESSON 1.3   EXERCISE 7 (P. 11)
STUDENT B

Use the map below to answer your partner's questions. Say where the places are.

Yes, there is. It's between / opposite / next to / in the …
No, there isn't.

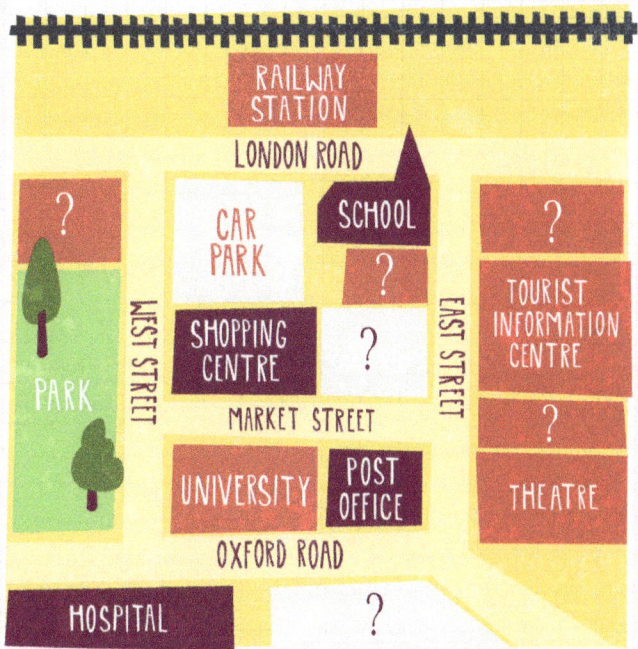

USEFUL PHRASES

It's on the left/right of the map.
It's on the left/right of the library.
It's at the top/bottom of the map.

On the map, there are six places with no name. Ask your partner questions about the places, then write the names of the places on the map.
Is there a/an … ?

bookshop   bus station   canal   cinema   harbour
library   market   swimming pool

AUDIOSCRIPTS

LESSON 1.1 RECORDING 1.1

T = Teacher, E = Edgar, A = Ayla

1
- T: Good morning. Come in. What's your name?
- E: Edgar.
- T: OK, Edgar. Have a seat. Where are you from?
- E: From Mexico City … in Mexico.
- T: Oh, OK. Tell me something about Mexico City.
- E: Well, it's a very big city. It's noisy. It's quite old. And it's the capital of Mexico.
- T: Is it a cheap city?
- E: No, it isn't. It's quite expensive. But the buses are cheap.
- T: Anything else?
- E: Well, it's famous for food, of course!
- T: OK, good, Edgar. Now why … ?

2
- T: Hello! Come in. Are you Ayla?
- A: Yes, that's right.
- T: OK. Where are you from, Ayla?
- A: Istanbul, in Turkey.
- T: OK … what's Istanbul like?
- A: Er, sorry?
- T: Tell me something about Istanbul.
- A: Oh, OK. It's a big city, very beautiful, but, um, very noisy! The mosques are very famous.
- T: I see. What about the weather?
- A: It's hot in summer and it's wet in winter, but spring and autumn are nice.
- T: Are the restaurants good?
- A: Yes, they are, very good!

LESSON 1.2 RECORDING 1.2

Y = Yukako, Pa = Pablo, S = Stefan, Pe = Peter

1
- Y: Hello! I'm Yukako and I'm from Kyoto. Kyoto's in the west of Japan. My city's old and there are a lot of old buildings. There are a lot of temples. They're very quiet. I love the old buildings.

2
- PA: Hi there! I'm Pablo. I'm from Lima, in Peru. In my city, there are hundreds of cafés. They're great. I love them.

3
- S: Hi. I'm Stefan and I'm from Chicago, in the United States. In the city, there are a lot of museums. I love the museums in Chicago.

4
- PE: Hello. I'm Peter and I'm from Cape Town in South Africa. In Cape Town, there's a beautiful mountain and there are a lot of beaches. The beaches are fantastic. I love them.

LESSON 1.3 RECORDING 1.5

SA = School Administrator,
S1 = Student 1, S2 = Student 2

SA: Good morning, everyone. Welcome to Cambridge and to the Cam English School. Right, now, please look at your maps. There are a lot of interesting places in the city centre. First of all, please find Trinity Street and King's Parade – they're on the left of your map. There are a lot of beautiful colleges on these streets. Opposite Trinity College, there's a good bookshop and a small post office. In the middle of the map, between Trinity College and the main post office, there's the main shopping area, with the market and the shopping centre. The market is nice, with food and clothes and a lot of other things. And it's cheap! The shopping centre is … well … to tell you the truth, it's ugly, but there are a lot of shops.
On the right of the map, there's the bus station, next to the park. It's quite busy in the mornings and evenings. Take the bus from there to the railway station, or to London. Any questions so far?
- S1: Yes. Is there a library?
- SA: Yes, there is. It's in the shopping centre. On your map, there's a person with a book.
- S1: Oh, yes. Thank you.
- S2: Excuse me, is there a zoo?
- SA: No, I'm afraid there isn't, not in the city. OK then, that's all for now. Don't forget – tomorrow at three o'clock, there's a guided tour of the city. Have a good time and learn a lot of English!

LESSON 1.4 RECORDING 1.8

A B C D E F G H I J K L M N O P Q R S T U V W X Y Z

LESSON 2.2 RECORDING 2.1

T = Teacher, G = Gina

- T: Gina, do you have time for me to ask a few questions?
- G: Of course. What are they about?
- T: Well, it's a survey about student life – your studies, your home life and your free time.
- G: OK, fine.
- T: Right, well, first of all, about your studies. Do you study English at the weekend?
- G: Yes, I do. On Sundays, I study for about an hour.
- T: Do you bring a dictionary to class?
- G: No, I only have a big old dictionary at home.
- T: Do you have a computer?
- G: Yes. It's our family computer.
- T: And at the school, do you use the library and study centre?
- G: No, I don't. I don't have time in the week.
- T: OK. Now, some questions about work, travel and home. You study, but do you also have a job?
- G: A job? No, I don't! But I have children! That's a job really.
- T: Yes, true. Do you travel to school by train, bus or car?
- G: By bus. It's cheap.
- T: Do you live alone, with family or with friends?
- G: You know that answer! With my family.
- T: Indeed, sorry. One or two questions now about your free time. Do you meet your classmates outside school?
- G: Yes, I do. We go to a café after class every day, for a quick coffee and a chat.
- T: Do you play sports?
- G: No, I don't. I don't like sports!
- T: OK, and finally, what other things do you do in your free time?
- G: I don't have a lot of free time – I'm a mother, you know! In the little time I have, I read books.
- T: OK. Thank you for your time, Gina.

AUDIOSCRIPTS

LESSON 2.3   RECORDING 2.2

A = Agent, P = Petra

A: Hello. How can I help you?
P: Hello. Can you tell me about the office **assistant** job, please?
A: Certainly. Let me find the information … Let me see … Right. The office assistant job … with DP Computer Export?
P: Yes, that's right.
A: OK. What information do you want?
P: Well, first of all, where is it? Is it in the city centre?
A: Yes, it is. It's a **modern** office and there's good **transport**.
P: Fine. What are the working hours and salary?
A: Well, you work from Monday to Friday, from nine o'clock to half past five. And the salary is … let me see … yes … it's £1,000 a month.
P: OK, but what does an office assistant do? Er, what are the work duties?
A: Well, in this job, you **answer** the phone, you do the **filing** and you do the **photocopying.** You also write and send **emails** and **letters.** OK?
P: Yes, thank you. What qualifications do I need?
A: Well, you need a school **certificate** and basic English. I'm sure you have those.
P: Yes, I do. And what skills do I need?
A: Um … you need good **computer** skills and good **communication** skills. OK?
P: Yes, that's fine. Thank you.
A: So, are you interested in the job?
P: Um, well … the salary isn't very good … Do you have any other jobs?

LESSON 3.1   RECORDING 3.1

P = Presenter, D = Dr Al-Shammary

P: Dr Al-Shammary, my idea of a desert is a very hot place with a lot of sand. Is this correct? I mean, what is a desert, exactly?
D: Well, there are different kinds of desert – hot deserts and cold deserts. And hot deserts aren't always hot; the temperature changes, for example, from 38 degrees to ten degrees.
P: When are deserts that cold?
D: At night. They're hot during the day but cold at night.
P: I see.
D: Also, only about 30 percent of the world's deserts are sand – a lot of deserts are just rocks and stones. But all deserts have one thing in common: they're very dry, with a maximum of 250mm of rain a year.
P: OK. So, why are deserts dry?
D: Well, for a number of reasons. Sometimes they're a long way from the sea and rain doesn't reach them. Sometimes mountains stop the rain.
P: All right, so there isn't any water – so how do animals and plants live in deserts?
D: Life in deserts isn't easy. A lot of desert animals sleep in the day and come out at night to look for food. The kangaroo rat gets all its water from its food. And desert plants have water in them. The Saguaro cactus in North America has five tonnes of water in its body and it sometimes lives for 200 years.
P: That's a long time! What about people? How do *they* live in the desert?
D: Desert people often live in groups, and move from place to place. They often live at the edges of deserts, not in the middle. In Australia, the desert people eat plants and animals and live that way, but it's a hard life!

LESSON 3.3   RECORDING 3.4

C = Chris, A = Andy, J = Jess

C: So, we have a whole weekend to plan. What kind of things shall we do? Andy, have you got any ideas?
A: Yeah, I have. Let's have a sponsored cycling event. Perhaps a ride from the town centre to the western hills. Cycling events are great fun, and people get sponsors and raise money.
J: Excellent. Let's do that all day on Sunday. What do you think, Chris?
C: Erm, I'm not sure.
J: Really? Why not?
C: I'm worried about the weather. It might rain. Cycling in the rain is not much fun.
A: I know, but the weekend is in the summer. I don't think rain's a big problem. Jess?
J: I agree with you, Andy. Chris?
C: OK. Let's just hope it doesn't rain. So, any ideas for Saturday evening?
J: No, not really. You?
C: Well, why don't we have a music event? There are many good musicians at the university.
A: Good idea!
J: Yes, it is. Music events are always popular, aren't they? We sell tickets and raise some money. Right, what about Saturday morning and afternoon?
A: Well, I'd like to have something about nature. You know, because that's what the charity is all about. What about a wildlife art and photography competition?
C: That's a nice idea. Many of the students have good photos, and the art society is very popular. We can show and sell the pictures in the afternoon.
J: OK! Let's do that. So, why don't we have a lunch break now and then look at the details?
A: OK. Let's go for a burger.
C: A burger? Er, OK.

LESSON 4.2   RECORDING 4.1

INT = Interviewer, L = Lisa, D = Dan

1

INT: Hello. We're doing a survey of our customers. Can I ask some questions?
L: Um, yes, that's OK.
INT: Thank you. First, what's your name?
L: Lisa. Lisa White.
INT: And how often do you come to the club, Lisa?
L: Three times a week, usually.
INT: Do you use the running machines?
L: Yes, I do.
INT: Right. Can you run ten kilometres in an hour?
L: Oh no, I can't. Maybe in 70 or 80 minutes.
INT: That's good. And do you work out in the gym?
L: Yes, I do, twice a week.
INT: OK, and … what weight can you lift?
L: Well, I don't usually lift a lot, but I can lift 35 kilos.

149

AUDIOSCRIPTS

INT: Mm! Do you use the swimming pool?
L: No, I don't.
INT: Really? Er, why not?
L: Well, erm, I can't swim, so I don't use it.
INT: Can't you? We offer lessons here, you know.
L: I know, I know, but I'm scared of water.
INT: Oh, I see. Well, I'm sure our trainer can help you …

2
INT: Excuse me, what's your name?
D: Dan. Dan Tobin.
INT: And how often do you come to the club, Dan?
D: Twice a week, usually.
INT: Do you use the running machines?
D: Yes, I do.
INT: Can you run ten kilometres in an hour?
D: Oh, yes, I can. Easy. I can run that in about 30 minutes.
INT: Really? That's fast! And do you work out in the gym?
D: Yes, but only once a week.
INT: OK. What weight can you lift?
D: I can lift 50 kilos.
INT: Mmm, that's good. And do you use the swimming pool?
D: Yes, I do. I usually swim two kilometres, but I can swim five kilometres.
INT: Really?
D: Oh yes, I'm super fit!
INT: Yes, clearly. Can we test your fitness today? We have a machine …
D: Oh, is that the time? I can't stay, I'm afraid, I have an important meeting. Bye.
INT: But I have … oh …

LESSON 4.2   RECORDING 4.3

1 Can I ask some questions?
2 Right. Can you run ten kilometres in an hour?
3 I can lift 35 kilos.
4 Oh, yes, I can.
5 I can run that in about 30 minutes.
6 I can swim five kilometres.

LESSON 4.2   RECORDING 4.4

1 No, I can't.
2 I can't swim.
3 Can't you?
4 I can't stay, I'm afraid.

LESSON 4.3   RECORDING 4.5

S = Sarah, TA = Travel Agent
S: Hello.
TA: Hello, can I help you?
S: Yes, please. Can you give me some information about the Sarong Holiday Resort?
TA: Yes, certainly. What would you like to know?
S: First of all, can you tell me about the accommodation, please?
TA: Yes, of course. All the rooms are double rooms. Some of the rooms have a sea view.
S: I see. Are there any family rooms?
TA: No, I'm afraid not. They can put extra beds in your room for children.
S: And what restaurants are there in the resort?
TA: There are five different restaurants – Thai, Chinese, Indian, Italian and American. You can eat breakfast, lunch and dinner in four of them. I'm afraid you can't have breakfast in the Indian restaurant.
S: The advert says that the resort offers water sports. Can I play other sports – tennis, for example?
TA: I'm sorry. I'm afraid you can't. They only have water sports at the resort.
S: I see. Finally, I've got two young children. Is there a kids' club in the day?
TA: No, I'm afraid there isn't. There's a babysitter service in the evenings. The babysitter looks after your children in your room, and you can go to the cinemas and restaurants.
S: Thank you very much for your help and the information.
TA: You're welcome, madam. Do you want to make a reservation?

LESSON 5.2   RECORDING 5.2

M = Mei, F = Fuad, S = Sandra
1
M: Hello. I'm Mei and I work in Beijing. I think the best way to get around Beijing is by electric bicycle. I've got one, and it's the quickest and cheapest way for me to travel. In Beijing, the buses are really crowded and I don't like them at all. The metro is the fastest way to travel, but there isn't a station near my home. Many people use bikes, but my electric bicycle is faster than a normal bike! It takes me 30 minutes to get to work.

2
F: Hi, my name is Fuad and I study at Cairo University. Travelling around my city is not very easy because the roads are very small and very busy. The metro here is quite small and my college isn't on a metro line. That's a pity, because the metro is the most comfortable way to travel in Cairo. I travel by bus to college. It's the cheapest way to travel, but it's also the most popular, so the buses are very crowded. I never get a seat and it takes about an hour to get to my college!

3
S: I'm Sandra, and I live in Amsterdam. Every day, I cycle to university. It only takes me about 20 minutes. A bike is the cheapest way to travel, of course, and it's also very popular here, because the city is very flat. In the city centre, trams are the best way to get around – I always use them when I go shopping. Many tourists travel on the canal boats, but I don't because they're the most expensive way to travel.

LESSON 5.3   RECORDING 5.4

TA = Travel Agent, K = Kasia Kaplinska
TA: Hello.
K: Hello, it's Kasia Kaplinska here.
TA: Hello, Kasia, I've got your email about New York.
K: Great! I'd like to book the trip now. Have you got some details for me?
TA: Well, I've got two flights for you: one is with Oz Air, the other one is with Top Air.
K: Can you tell me about the Oz Air flight first? When does it leave?
TA: OK. Well, the flight leaves at eight in the morning and it arrives at seven in the morning, their time.
K: OK. How long does that flight take?
TA: It takes 14 hours.
K: Fourteen, that's not bad. And how much does it cost?
TA: Um, it costs 300 Australian dollars.
K: That's a good price. Is it a good airline?
TA: Oh yes. The in-flight service is very good.
K: Fine. And what about the second flight?

AUDIOSCRIPTS

TA: The second one is with Top Air. This is a very good airline. Their in-flight service is excellent – it's better than Oz Air's. You can have a head massage, and the food is great.
K: Sounds good. When does it leave? And when does it arrive?
TA: Well, it leaves at six in the evening and gets there at 5 p.m., their time.
K: How much does it cost?
TA: This one costs 600 Australian dollars.
K: I see. How long does it take?
TA: It also takes 14 hours.
K: Mmm, that's good, but it's expensive.
TA: Do you want to make a booking now?
K: Um, I think so. Yes.

LESSON 5.3   RECORDING 5.5

TA = Travel Agent, K = Kasia Kaplinska

TA: Do you want to make a booking now?
K: Um, I think so. Yes.
TA: Which airline would you like to travel with?
K: I'd like to book the Oz Air flight, please.
TA: OK. When do you want to travel?
K: Next Tuesday.
TA: Next Tuesday – that's the first of October – and what about the return flight?
K: One week later, please.
TA: OK, on the eighth, that's no problem. So, would you like business or standard class?
K: Oh, standard class. The company doesn't want to spend a lot of money.
TA: Fine. And finally, would you like a window or an aisle seat?
K: Can I have a window seat, please?
TA: Certainly. OK, that's all. How would you like to pay?
K: Oh, by credit card, please – the company credit card.
TA: OK, can I have the card number, please?

LESSON 6.2   RECORDING 6.1

M = Miranda, C = Conrad

M: Hi, Conrad, thank you for helping me with my blog. My first question is: What is traditional food in South Africa?
C: That's a hard question to answer. There are many different cultures in my country. There's a lot of food from different African cultures, from Portugal, from Holland, from India and from Asia. The African dishes have a lot of vegetables, like beans and green leaves. And dried meat, called *biltong*, is very popular. Peri Peri chicken comes from the Portuguese culture. It's a spicy chicken dish. It's really tasty. And of course, from India we have many curries.
M: Ah yes, we have a lot of curry restaurants in Britain, too. Are there any traditional drinks?
C: Well, we have a red tea, called *rooibos*. This is a very healthy drink and it's popular. In fact, in some cafés, they use it to make latte and cappuccino drinks.
M: That's interesting, a cappuccino made from red tea. So, is food important in people's social lives?
C: Oh, it's very important. Every weekend, we have big barbecue parties with friends and family. We cook a lot of meat at these barbecues: chicken, lamb, sausages and kebabs. Usually, the men cook the meat and the women prepare salads and desserts.
M: That sounds fun. In Britain, we have barbecues, but perhaps only two or three a year, because there is a lot of rain! Anyway, is food important at festivals and ceremonies?
C: Oh yes, certainly. In the countryside, they have a ceremony when the first fruit of the year is ready to eat. The local people eat meat at this ceremony. Also, in some places, people eat rice cakes at baby-naming ceremonies. What else? Oh yes, on September the 24th, we have a national barbecue day – that's great fun!

LESSON 6.3   RECORDING 6.2

J = Jane, T = Tariq

J: Good morning, Event Catering Services. How can I help?
T: Hi, it's Tariq here, from the university.
J: Ah, hi, Tariq. This is Jane. How are you?
T: Fine, thanks. And you?
J: Great. So, how can I help you this time?
T: Well, there's a conference at the university next week, and I'd like to order some food for the conference lunch.
J: OK, so, what would you like for the first course?
T: Well, have you got any tomato soup?
J: Yes, we have. How much would you like?
T: We'd like 50 cans, please.
J: That's fine. And for the main course?
T: Could we have 50 chicken salads, please, 50 vegetarian pizzas and 40 lamb kebabs?
J: Oh Tariq, I'm sorry. I'm afraid we haven't got any chicken salads at the moment. We can provide cheese salads.
T: OK, can we have 50 cheese salads then?
J: Sure, no problem.
T: Thanks. For dessert, we'd like 100 ice creams and 50 apple pies.
J: That's no problem. Would you like some water or fruit juice?
T: Yes, please. Could we have 50 large bottles of still water and some small bottles of apple juice?
J: How many bottles of juice would you like?
T: Oh, 100, please.
J: Fine. Uh, anything else? Would you like some coffee?
T: No, thank you.
J: Some tea?
T: No, thanks. That's everything.
J: OK. And when do you want the delivery?
T: Ah yes, well the conference is …

LESSON 7.1   RECORDING 7.2

SA = Shop Assistant, C = Customer

1
SA: Do they fit?
C: Yes, they feel fine.
SA: Walk around the shop and check they're OK. There's a mirror over there. How do they feel?
C: OK, but perhaps the left one is a little small.
SA: Right, well, try a bigger size.

2
SA: Can I help you?
C: Yes, I'm looking for *Birds Without Wings*.

151

AUDIOSCRIPTS

SA: I'm afraid we don't have that one in the shop.
C: Oh, I see. That's a pity. I really want to read it.
SA: We can order it for you.
C: Really? Great! Thanks very much.
SA: That's fine. Can I have your name?

3
SA: OK, so that's £15. How would you like to pay?
C: By credit card, please.
SA: Fine.
C: Here you are.
SA: Thank you. Can you enter your number, please?
C: Of course.
SA: Great. Here's your receipt, and here's your shirt. I've only got a large bag, I'm afraid.
C: That's fine. Thank you very much. Bye.

4
SA: Hello, madam, what would you like?
C: I'd like a cappuccino, please.
SA: Certainly. Small, medium or large?
C: Just a small one, please.
SA: OK. To have here or takeaway?
C: To have here, please. It's very cold outside today.

5
C: Hi, are there still tickets for *The Hobbit* at eight tonight?
SA: For the 3D screening?
C: Uh-huh.
SA: Oh, I'm afraid not. That's all sold out. We've got some for the ten o'clock screening.
C: Oh, that's bit late really. How about for tomorrow at eight?

LESSON 7.2   RECORDING 7.4

S = Stephen Chen, M = Monica Patel
S: Good morning. I'm Stephen Chen, from the Consumer News website.
M: Oh, yes. Come in. Have a seat. Would you like a coffee?
S: Yes, please.
M: Here you are.
S: Thanks a lot. That's very kind of you.
M: Now, you have some questions about shopping trends, I believe?
S: Yes, that's right, especially about online shopping.
M: OK. Fire away! I'm quite busy this morning.
S: Of course, I can see that … well, here's my first question – what are people buying on the internet now?

M: Well, it's really the same as before – books, travel – they're the most popular things.
S: And is online shopping growing quickly these days?
M: Yes, it is, but consumers are still buying most of their things in-store. For example, if we take clothes – people are still buying nearly 80 percent of their clothes in-store.
S: So, how are they using the internet, then?
M: Well, here's one way – people are reading about other customers' experiences before they buy anything. So, for example, if they're looking at a hotel, they read other people's comments about it. If they don't like the comments, they look at another hotel. Also, these days, we're seeing something new – in-store shopping and online shopping are coming together. Actually, it has a name. Some people call it 'in-line shopping'. It's a mixture of *in*-store and on*line*.
S: Can you explain how it works?
M: It works in different ways. For instance, people are researching a product online and then they're going to a store to buy the product. It works the other way round, too. People are using stores to look at products and compare them, and then they're buying those products online – perhaps from other companies.
S: Are they doing that because it's cheaper?
M: Exactly.
S: What about mobile devices? Are people using them more for shopping?
M: Yes, they are. They're using smartphones and tablets to buy goods from home, from their offices, from trains – anywhere, really. But – and this is interesting – they're also using their mobiles in-store – to get more information about a product, or check prices or to look for discounts. It's another example of in-line shopping.
S: Well, Monica, that's fantastic. I've got some really good points. Thanks a lot.
M: My pleasure.

LESSON 7.3   RECORDING 7.5

B = Brad, Z = Zara
B: So, what advantages does downtown have?
Z: Well, first of all, I think it's a nice place for people to visit, and there are some interesting local shops.
B: Oh yeah? What are they?
Z: Well, there are some cafés and there's a music shop, and also an art shop. This means that people are interested in the books we sell.
B: OK. Are there any more advantages?
Z: Yes, another advantage is that the area is safe – crime is low. And, of course, there's a bus station.
B: Right. What about the disadvantages?
Z: I think there are two main disadvantages. One disadvantage is that the rent is high, and the other is that a lot of people go to the shopping mall outside the town. This means that sometimes there aren't very many customers downtown.
B: I see. So, the area is a nice one, but the rent is expensive and most people go to the mall.
Z: Yes.
B: Mmm. What do you know about the shopping mall?
Z: Well, it's …

LESSON 8.1   RECORDING 8.2

1 The city was lovely.
2 There were gardens everywhere.
3 It was very safe, too.
4 The people were kind.
5 The women were beautiful.
6 The streets were busy.
7 There was an interesting market.

LESSON 8.2   RECORDING 8.3

T = Tutor, P = Pedro, M = Marjorie
T: OK, everyone! Today's presentation is by Pedro and Marjorie. Start when you're ready, Pedro.
P: OK. Hello, everyone. Our presentation is called *A Smaller World* and it's about technology and cultural change. The talk focuses on technology that makes the world smaller, for example the internet.

AUDIOSCRIPTS

M: First of all, can you imagine life without cars and planes? Before the invention of these means of transport, people could only travel by train or boat, and they couldn't travel very fast. Now, with cars and planes, we can travel further and faster. Some people even live in one country and work in another because they can fly to work. Fifty years ago, people certainly couldn't do that. And of course, many people fly thousands of miles to go on holiday, and while their grandparents could only read about distant places, they see them. Before we move onto the next type of technology, it is important to remember that planes and cars do have their negative points. They can be dangerous and they cause a lot of pollution, and this also changes the way we live.

P: OK. Second, communications technology, like the internet and smartphones, certainly makes the world smaller. We stay in our house or office, but we can see news and blogs from all around the world. With the internet, we can write and chat to people all over the world. This is an incredible invention. We can find anything we want in seconds. It makes the world smaller, and it makes it faster! And with smartphones, we can do this anywhere at anytime. But do these things have any negative points? Well, yes, they do. Nowadays, people spend more time using the technology than they do meeting other people. We're spending more and more of our time on computers or phones, talking to strangers in other countries, than we are with our friends and neighbours. My grandmother could name all the people in her street, but I don't even know the names of my neighbours!

M: So, you can see that technology changes our way of life and culture, in both positive and negative ways. A lot of technology makes the world a smaller place, but does it make it a better place?

T: OK. Thank you, Pedro and Marjorie, that was great. Are there any questions?

LESSON 8.3   RECORDING 8.6

H = Harshil, J = Jessica, V1–6 = Visitors

1
V1: Excuse me.
H: Yes, madam. How can I help you?
V1: Could you tell me where the cloakroom is, please?
H: Certainly, madam. You see the main entrance over there?
V1: Yes.
H: Well, the cloakroom is just on the right.
V1: Oh yes. I see it. Thank you.
H: You're welcome.

2
V2: Excuse me, could you help me, please?
J: Yes, of course. What would you like?
V2: Well, I'm interested in the multimedia guides. What do they do exactly?
J: Right. Well, they give you information about a lot of the objects in the museum – 200 objects, actually. They're in ten languages.
V2: Could you tell me how much they cost?
J: Certainly, sir. They're £5 each, £4.50 for students, and £3.50 for children under 12.
V2: I'm afraid my student days were a long time ago! Could you give me one for myself, please, and one for my daughter, too. She's 11.
J: OK. So that's £8.50, please.
V2: I'm afraid I've only got this £50 note.
J: That's no problem, sir. There's your change.
V2: Thanks very much.

3
V3: Excuse me.
H: Yes, madam, how can I help?
V3: Well, I'd like to see the film about life and death in Pompeii. Could you tell me when it starts?
H: Of course. Let me just check … Um, yes, it starts at 6.30.
V3: At 6.30?
H: Yes, madam. That's right.
V3: OK. Isn't there one before that?
H: I'm afraid not, madam. We only show the film in the evening.
V3: OK, thank you.
H: You're welcome.

4
V4: Excuse me.
J: Yes, sir, how can I help?
V4: I'm really interested in this statue. Could you tell me how old it is?
J: Mmm, let me see … Yes, this is a Roman statue. It's about 2,000 years old. It's a statue of Venus, the goddess of love.
V4: I see; it really is lovely. Thank you.
J: Not at all.

5
V5: Excuse me.
H: Yes, madam?
V5: We're visitors. Could you give us a map of the museum, please?
H: Of course, madam. Where do you come from?
V5: Italy. Why?
H: Well, would you like the map in Italian or in English?
V5: Oh, could you give us both, please, so we can practise our English?
H: Certainly. There you are.
V5: Thank you very much.
H: Not at all. Enjoy your visit.

6
V6: Excuse me.
J: Yes?
V6: Could you take a photo of us with this statue, please?
J: Er … All right … Where do I press? Here?
V6: That's right.
J: OK, everyone … Are you ready?
V6 AND FRIENDS: Yeeees!
J: Sorry. Could you move a little to the left, please? I can't see the statue. That's it. OK, smile. Say cheese!
V6 AND FRIENDS: Cheese!
J: I hope it's a nice photo.
V6: Oh yes, very nice. Thank you very much.
J: Enjoy the rest of your visit.
V6: Thank you.

LESSON 8.3   RECORDING 8.7

1 Could you help me, please?
2 Could you tell me when the film starts?
3 Could you give us a map of the museum, please?

AUDIOSCRIPTS

LESSON 9.1   RECORDING 9.3

Alfred Nobel was born in 1833 in Sweden. He studied chemistry but he also wrote poetry, novels and plays. He tried to make a safe explosive, but, unfortunately, he killed his brother in an experiment in 1864. He invented dynamite in 1866. In 1895 he started the Nobel Prize Foundation.
Levi Strauss was born in Germany in 1829. He travelled to New York in 1846 and moved to San Francisco in 1853. He started a shop for gold miners: he sold equipment and clothes. In 1873, he invented jeans – he used a material from Nîmes in France and called it 'denim'.

LESSON 9.2   RECORDING 9.4

P = Presenter, S = Stephen Bayley

P: Welcome to this week's edition of *Understanding Science*. With me in the studio is Professor Stephen Bayley of Nottingham University. Professor Bayley, I'd like to start by asking you this question: what is the most important medical invention of the last 30 years?
S: Well, that's a difficult question because there are a lot of important inventions. Certainly, one of the most important is the MRI scanner.
P: The scanner? Can you tell us something about it?
S: Yes, well, basically it's a big box with a hole in the middle …

LESSON 9.2   RECORDING 9.5

P = Presenter, S = Stephen Bayley

P: … And how does it work?
S: Well, you lie in the hole and the scanner takes pictures of you. Like an X-ray machine, the MRI scanner can look into our bodies, but normal X-ray machines can only show the hard parts of our bodies – the bones and teeth for example – while the MRI scanner can show both the hard and soft parts of the body, so it's more useful. It can take a picture of the whole body, and you get the pictures very quickly. It's not dangerous, either, like X-ray machines.
P: That's good. When did scientists invent it?
S: Well, it didn't happen overnight. In 1945, scientists discovered NMR – Nuclear Magnetic Resonance. In the 1950s, an American scientist named Felix Bloch did some experiments in the lab and understood the importance of NMR for looking inside the human body.
P: So did Felix Bloch invent the MRI scanner?
S: No, he didn't. Another American, Raymond Damadian, and his team built the first full-body MRI scanner.
P: When did they do that?
S: In 1977.
P: And when did doctors start to use this new machine?
S: A few years later. In 1984, hospitals around the world bought their first MRI scanners.
P: It all sounds fantastic. Are there any problems with the scanner?
S: Well, it isn't good for people who don't like small spaces!

LESSON 9.3   RECORDING 9.6

Hello and welcome to *The Nation's Favourite Everyday Invention*, the show that tells you the story behind the everyday objects that we use in our daily lives. Each week, we tell you some key facts about the inventions and I tell you why I think they are wonderful or important. At the end of each programme, you can vote for your favourite invention. Simply send a text message to 0810 40 50 60, giving the name of your personal choice. So, vote for an invention and let's find our national favourite.

LESSON 9.3   RECORDING 9.7

The first of today's everyday inventions is that classic symbol of the English businessman – the umbrella. Nowadays, everyone has got one, but before 1750, men never carried umbrellas. So, what's the story of the umbrella, or brolly?
Here are today's four facts.
First, many hundreds of years ago, rich and important people in hot countries, such as China, India and Egypt, used umbrellas. These rich people didn't use their umbrellas in the rain, they used them in the sun. Of course, poor people worked in the sun, but they didn't have umbrellas.
Secondly, the Chinese invented the first umbrellas for use in the rain. They put oil and wax on their paper umbrellas.
Thirdly, umbrellas reached Britain about 400 years ago, but at first, only women had umbrellas: men didn't like them. In 1750, Jonas Hanway, a British traveller, was the first man to use an umbrella on the streets of England. Other men followed his example and the umbrella at last became very popular in Britain.
And finally, the first umbrella shop, James Smith and Sons, opened in London in 1830, and it's still open today.
And did you know that over 7,000 people lose an umbrella on London Transport every year, and all these umbrellas go to the Lost Property office. That's a lot of umbrellas!

LESSON 9.3   RECORDING 9.8

So, why vote for the umbrella? Well, the most important reason is that it's one of the oldest inventions in the world. People found it very useful thousands of years ago, and we still find it useful today.
Secondly, the umbrella is a great invention because it's got several different uses. We can use it in the rain, we can use it in the sun and we can use it as a walking stick.
Thirdly, vote for the umbrella because umbrellas bring colour to our grey, rainy streets.
My final reason is that umbrellas are very cheap to make and cheap to buy. So, that's the wonderful umbrella. When it rains, the rich and the poor can all stay dry. It's an invention for everyone. If you think this is the greatest everyday invention, vote now by sending a text message to …

LESSON 9.4   RECORDING 9.11

Ada Byron was born in Picadilly, London. Her parents (the poet Lord Byron and Anne Milbanke) separated immediately after her birth. Four months later, Lord Byron left England forever. In 1828, at the age of 13, Ada produced a design for a flying machine. This was very unusual for a young girl at that time. Then, in 1833, she met the mathematician and inventor Charles Babbage for the first time. Two years after that, she married

AUDIOSCRIPTS

William King (later Lord Lovelace) and they had two children. After the birth of her third child, she began work with Charles Babbage. During their work together, she developed the idea of using binary numbers (zero, one) and understood many ideas that we use in computer programming today. She died in 1852.

LESSON 10.1   RECORDING 10.1

SC = Sue Cutler

SC: Good afternoon, everyone. How are you today? My talk this afternoon is about how to stay safe in the city.
First of all, let me tell you that the city of Sheffield is actually one of the safest cities in the UK. Most other big cities are much more dangerous than here. So don't be scared! But we should always be careful and look after ourselves and our possessions. We can talk about our personal safety later, but let's start by saying something about looking after our money. Here are a few things you should and shouldn't do. A lot of this is common sense, of course, and I'm sure you already do most of these things in your own countries.

LESSON 10.1   RECORDING 10.2

SC = Sue Cutler, S1 = Student 1, S2 = Student 2, S3 = Student 3

SC: Anyway, here goes, starting with things you *should* do. Number one – you should be careful in crowded places. By this, I mean on trams, on buses, in busy markets and shopping streets. Pickpockets – that's people who steal your wallets, purses, cameras and so on – pickpockets love crowded places. So take care. The next thing is about cards – credit cards and debit cards. You should keep your PIN safe and secret – only you should know it. Cashpoints are usually outside banks. When you use them, have a look at who is behind you. Are they too close? Are they interested in what you're doing? Don't let anyone see you put in your PIN. Another important point. If you carry a bag, carry your bag carefully. Make it difficult for someone to take it off you. And if you carry just a wallet, you should keep it in your jacket, in an inside pocket, not in the back pocket of your trousers.
Now, that brings us to some things you *shouldn't* do. You shouldn't carry a lot of cash about with you. By that, I mean lots of big notes, and coins. You can replace traveller's cheques and credit cards. But you can't replace lost cash. Next, you should never take your money out of your wallet or purse in busy public places. This one is obvious, isn't it? Don't attract the attention of thieves by counting your money on a busy street! OK. Any questions so far?

S1: Should I wear a money belt when I go out?
SC: Well, most people here don't wear money belts. Also, money belts are often uncomfortable, so I don't think that it's necessary, but it's up to you, I suppose.
S2: Last night, some of us went out to a café. One of the girls had her mobile phone on the table all the time. Is that OK?
SC: Well, no, she shouldn't do that. That's really not a good idea. She should keep it in her bag.
S3: Should I leave money in my university room?
SC: The rooms are generally very safe, but, no, you shouldn't really have a lot of cash in your room, just in case. Any other questions? OK, now let's move on to talk about personal safety …

LESSON 10.3   RECORDING 10..3

R = Researcher, K = Katie, D = David

R: Excuse me, I'm working for a bank and we're doing a survey about money. Can I interview you?
K: Well, actually, we're rather busy.
D: Yes, we're doing the shopping and we have to be back at the car park in ten minutes.
R: I understand, but it's only a short interview, and you can win a holiday to Thailand.
K: Really? Oh. I don't see any problems.
D: But darling, we should finish the shopping.
K: Five minutes isn't a problem, is it, David? So, what's the first question?
R: Right, well, if you're sure. Erm, what's your opinion about having credit cards?
D: Well, personally, I think that they are a bad idea. It's very easy to spend more than you can afford.
R: And you, madam, what's your opinion?
K: Well, in my opinion, they're great. They give you a chance to buy expensive things when you want them. You don't have to wait for them.
R: OK, madam, and do you think that saving money is important?
K: Erm, yes, I suppose it is, but to be honest, I don't save very much each month. I prefer to spend my money now.
R: And sir, do you think that saving money is important?
D: Oh yes, definitely. When you're old, you can't live without money, so I save something every month, for my pension.
R: Right. Do you think that borrowing money from friends is a good idea?
D: Oh, no, not at all. I think that it's a terrible idea, because if you forget to pay them back, well, things can get very difficult, can't they?
R: Mmm, I guess so. And you, madam, do you think that it's a good idea?
K: Well, I'm not sure. It's cheaper than borrowing from banks. But you have to be careful, you shouldn't borrow a lot or often, and of course, you have to remember to pay your friend back!
R: OK. Finally, do you agree that people should give money to charity every month?
K: No, not at all. I believe that the government should look after everyone. My money is my money.
R: And you, sir? Do you agree that we should give money to charity?
D: Well, yes, I do. We should give some money, but we aren't very rich, so I can't always give something, but I do try, when I can.
R: Well, thank you very much …

AUDIOSCRIPTS

LESSON 10.4   RECORDING 10.2

Let's say something first about our online banking service. There are some great reasons why you should start online banking today. You can manage your money when it suits you – 24 hours a day, seven days a week. For instance, you can move money from one of your accounts to another. Also, you can pay your bills without leaving your accommodation, even while you watch TV! In addition, you can send money to people – family and friends. If you want to make a payment to a non-UK bank account, you can do it online – but there are charges for this service. As well as all this, our great service is very safe. It's very difficult for anyone to steal from your account. So, online banking is the answer – 96 percent of our customers recommend our service. It's quick, easy and safe. OK, Kathy, what about mobile banking?

LESSON 11.2   RECORDING 11.2

R = Rachel, F = Friend

R: So, would you like to see the plans for my new house?
F: Oh yes. It's so exciting that you're going to build a new house. Are you going to have lots of exciting modern features?
R: Definitely. Here, have a look at the picture. Basically, we're going to have a standard house with three bedrooms, but with lots of modern features. It's going to be a truly smart home.
F: What kind of things are you going to have?
R: Well, first of all, we're going to use technology to save energy. For example, we're going to put in a smart meter because we want to know how much electricity we use. To go with that, we're going to put a wind turbine on the roof. That means we can cut our energy costs and help save the environment.
F: What about having automatic lighting? That helps save money.
R: I know, but we're not going to have that. We think it doesn't save much money and we're not that lazy! We can turn the lights on and off ourselves!
F: I guess so. Are you going to have anything more fun? How about a swimming pool?
R: No, we're not going to spend money on a pool. They're really expensive and they use a lot of energy! But we are going to have a multi-room entertainment system. If we do that, we can watch TV, DVDs and use the internet in every room. It's great. I'm going to have a big screen in the kitchen!
F: That sounds cool.
R: Let me tell you something cooler. We're going to have fingerprint door locks.
F: What! Why?
R: Well, to be honest, mainly because I often lose my keys. But they're also good for security.
F: And what's this thing outside the house? Is that something for security, too?
R: Oh no, that's an electric car-charging point. That's Simon's idea. We need one because he's going to buy an electric car soon.
F: Really? You really are thinking green, aren't you? Talking of green, why is the roof green? It's not grass, is it?
R: Yes, it is. We're going to have a living roof.
F: A living roof? What on earth is that?
R: Well, it means you …

LESSON 11.2   RECORDING 11.3

1 I'm not going to buy a car.
2 You're going to buy a car.
3 He's going to buy a car.
4 She isn't going to buy a car.
5 We're going to buy a car.
6 They aren't going to buy a car.
7 You're not going to buy a car.

LESSON 11.3   RECORDING 11.4

EA = Estate Agent, C = Colleen

EA: Hello, Find-a-Flat-Fast. How can I help?
C: Oh, hello. I'm looking for a flat to share with a friend. Hello, can you hear me?
EA: Yes, I can. How many bedrooms do you want?
C: Two bedrooms.
EA: OK, let's see. I've got one here, it looks lovely – two bedrooms, kitchen, living room, two bathrooms … ground floor with a garden … but there's no furniture, just a cooker and fridge-freezer in the kitchen.
C: That's OK. Is it near the city centre?
EA: No, it's not. But it's only a ten-minute walk from a metro station, and the metro takes about 20 minutes to get to the city centre.
C: Right. What about the local area?
EA: Oh, it's got everything you need. There's a big supermarket, and some cafés and other shops.
C: Well, it sounds really good. How much is the rent?
EA: It's 150 euros a week per person.
C: Sorry? Was that 115 or 150?
EA: A hundred and fifty. One–five–zero.
C: Oh, that's very expensive. We're students; we don't have a lot of money.
EA: I see. Well, here's another one. It's got two bedrooms, and both are large. There's a small kitchen, a dining room and a living room. There's also a large bathroom.
C: Right. What floor is the flat on?
EA: It's on the fourth floor, and I'm afraid there isn't a lift.
C: I'm sorry, could you repeat that, please?
EA: Sure. It's on the fourth floor.
C: And there isn't a lift?
EA: That's right.
C: OK, um … what furniture is there?
EA: Well, in each bedroom, there's a bed, a desk and a wardrobe. In the kitchen, there's a cooker, a fridge-freezer and a washing machine. There's a table with chairs in the dining room, and a sofa in the living room.
C: Er, just a moment. So, there is a cooker, a fridge-freezer and a washing machine. Is that right?
EA: Yes, it is.
C: What about the local area? Is it near public transport?
EA: Well, there's a bus stop about 15 minutes away.
C: I'm sorry, could you say that again?
EA: Sure. There's a bus stop about 15 minutes away.
C: A bus stop. OK. And, was that 15 or 50 minutes?

AUDIOSCRIPTS

EA: Fifteen, one–five. And the bus takes about 45 minutes to get to the city centre.
C: What about trains? Is there a metro station?
EA: No, I'm afraid there isn't a local station. The local area is nice and quiet, with good local shops.
C: Mmm, and how much is it?
EA: It's 90 euros a week, per person.
C: I'm sorry, did you say 19 or 90 euros?
EA: No! It isn't that cheap! It's 90, nine–zero. Would you like to see the flat?
C: Well, we really want a flat nearer the city centre, so I don't think that we will. But thanks for your help. Goodbye.
EA: Goodbye.

LESSON 12.1   RECORDING 12.1

P = Peter Knight, K = Kirsty Andrews
P: G'day.
K: Hi there!
P: My name is Peter Knight. I'm doing research into people who grow up in different countries and I'm talking to people here at the university today. Is it OK if I ask you a few questions?
K: Sure, go ahead.
P: Well, first, tell me, have you ever lived abroad?
K: Yes, I have.
P: Oh, that's lucky for me! What's your name?
K: Kirsty Andrews.
P: OK, Kirsty. Which countries have you lived in?
K: Erm … England, Oman and Japan. That's it, I think.
P: Why have you lived in so many places?
K: Because of my dad's job.
P: I see. And … erm … what's your favourite country?
K: Australia! No, seriously, I really like Japan. It's amazing! It's so different.
P: Can you speak Japanese?
K: A little bit, yeah.
P: Have you ever worked in any of these countries?
K: No, I haven't.
P: OK. Next question. Has your experience changed you in any way?
K: OK. Let me see … well … I know a lot more about the differences between cultures … and I don't think that my way is the best way or the only way.
P: What about friends? I mean, do you see your old friends from the different countries?
K: Yeah, that's a problem. My best friend is in Japan. She's visited me once or twice here and we send emails all the time, but I still miss her a lot.
P: I can understand that. Right … final question … are there any other countries you'd like to live in?
K: Well, I've never lived in a poor country. I think it could be an important experience. Maybe an African country, or something like that. And I haven't lived in South America. I'd like to spend some time there. Maybe I'll do these things after graduation.
P: Right … I'll let you get on with your lunch. Thanks a lot for your time, Kirsty.

LESSON 12.3   RECORDING 12.4

I = Interviewer, W = Woman
I: What's the tallest building you've ever seen?
W: The tallest building? Well, let me see … um … I haven't seen many really tall buildings, but last year, I went to New York and I visited the Empire State Building, and I really liked it. Um … I first saw the building from the plane. That was fantastic; it made me think of the film *King Kong*. Then I visited the building the next day. It's very tall and it's also beautiful, I think. It's different from most tall buildings because … um, it's made of bricks and has a lot of windows. Other tall buildings are all glass, so it's very different, and that's why I think that it looks beautiful. Anyway, I went to the top of the building in the lift, and the view from the top is wonderful. You can see all of Manhattan in every direction – the yellow taxis look so small, like tiny insects! Well, what else? Oh yes, I also went up the building at night. That was great – you can see all the lights of New York City below your feet. That was a very special moment for me. So, that's the tallest building I've seen.

LESSON 12.4   RECORDING 12.1

OK, now I'm going to talk about technology and learning. First of all, the internet. Over 50 percent of all websites are in English – so there's a lot of useful material out there. There are many ways you can use the internet to improve your English, and it can help you to develop all your skills – listening, speaking, reading and writing.

Writing practice is also excellent for your learning; it's almost as important as speaking. One of the easiest things you can do on the internet is to create your own blog – don't try to write too much. Just a few lines each day is enough. You can put up some of your photos and write a short description of them. You can also write in a live chat room. Live chat rooms are great for improving your fluency because you have to write quickly. It's like a conversation.

Now, the internet is a good place to practise your listening. There are thousands of videos on sites like YouTube. It's easy to find a topic you're interested in. As well as this, you can download apps, for example, a grammar practice app, to continue the work from the classroom, or a pronunciation app, to help you recognise different sounds in English. You should also visit a good news site such as the BBC or CNN and watch the short video clips.

Before you watch, you can read about the story and then you can watch the clip as many times as you want. In order to improve your listening, you have to be an active listener: make notes, try to write down the main points, try to write down new vocabulary.

Finally, on the internet there are many sites for English language learning, with extra practice exercises and reading materials. The BBC World Service also has an excellent site for learning English. You can ask questions about English and they'll give you an answer.

The best thing about the internet is that it gives you the chance to do things with the language, and that's very important. All right? Good, now I'm going to talk about …

IRREGULAR VERB LIST

Infinitive	2nd form (past simple)	3rd form (past participle)
be	was/were	been
become	became	become
begin	began	begun
break	broke	broken
bring	brought	brought
build	built	built
buy	bought	bought
can	could	been able
catch	caught	caught
choose	chose	chosen
come	came	come
cost	cost	cost
dig	dug	dug
do	did	done
draw	drew	drawn
drink	drank	drunk
drive	drove	driven
eat	ate	eaten
fall	fell	fallen
feed	fed	fed
feel	felt	felt
find	found	found
fly	flew	flown
forget	forgot	forgotten
get	got	got
give	gave	given
go	went	gone/been
grow	grew	grown
have	had	had
hear	heard	heard
hold	held	held
hurt	hurt	hurt
keep	kept	kept
know	knew	known
learn	learned/learnt	learned/learnt

Infinitive	2nd form (past simple)	3rd form (past participle)
leave	left	left
let	let	let
lose	lost	lost
make	made	made
mean	meant	meant
meet	met	met
pay	paid	paid
put	put	put
read /ri:d/	read /red/	read /red/
ride	rode	ridden
ring	rang	rung
run	ran	run
say	said	said
see	saw	seen
sell	sold	sold
send	sent	sent
shine	shone	shone
show	showed	shown
sing	sang	sung
sit	sat	sat
sleep	slept	slept
speak	spoke	spoken
spend	spent	spent
stand	stood	stood
steal	stole	stolen
swim	swam	swum
take	took	taken
teach	taught	taught
tell	told	told
think	thought	thought
throw	threw	thrown
understand	understood	understood
wear	wore	worn
win	won	won
write	wrote	written

PHONETIC CHARTS

SOUND–SPELLING CORRESPONDENCES

In English, we can spell the same sound in different ways, for example, the sound /iː/ can be 'ee', as in *green*, 'ea' as in *read* or 'ey' as in *key*. Students of English sometimes find English spelling difficult, but there are rules, and knowing the rules can help you. The chart below gives you the more common spellings of the English sounds you have studied in this book.

ENGLISH PHONEMES

CONSONANTS

Symbol	Example	Symbol	Example
p	park	s	sell
b	bath	z	zoo
t	tie	ʃ	fresh
d	die	ʒ	measure
k	cat	h	hot
g	give	m	mine
tʃ	church	n	not
dʒ	judge	ŋ	sing
f	few	l	lot
v	view	r	road
θ	throw	j	yellow
ð	they	w	warm

VOWELS

Symbol	Example	Symbol	Example
iː	feet	əʊ	gold
ɪ	fit	aɪ	by
e	bed	aʊ	brown
æ	bad	ɔɪ	boy
ɑː	bath	ɪə	here
ɒ	bottle	eə	hair
ɔː	bought	ʊə	sure
ʊ	book	eɪə	player
uː	boot	əʊə	lower
ʌ	but	aɪə	tired
ɜː	bird	aʊə	flower
ə	brother	ɔɪə	employer
eɪ	grey	i	happy

Sound	Spelling	Examples
/ɪ/	i y ui e	this listen gym typical build guitar pretty
/iː/	ee ie ea e ey ei i	green sleep niece believe read teacher these complete key money receipt receive police
/æ/	a	can man pasta land
/ɑː/	a ar al au ea	can't dance* scarf bargain half aunt laugh heart
/ʌ/	u o ou	fun sunny husband some mother month cousin double young
/ɒ/	o a	hot pocket top watch what want
/ɔː/	or ou au al aw ar oo	short sport store your course bought daughter taught bald small always draw jigsaw warden warm floor indoor
/aɪ/	i y ie igh ei ey uy	like time island dry shy cycle fries die tie light high right height eyes buy
/eɪ/	a ai ay ey ei ea	lake hate shave wait train straight play say stay they grey obey eight weight break
/əʊ/	o ow oa	home cold open show throw own coat road coast

* In American English the sound in words like *can't* and *dance* is the /æ/ sound, like *can* and *man*.

ABOUT THE AUTHORS

Far left: Simon Kent
Centre left: David Falvey
Centre: Gareth Rees
Centre right: Ian Lebeau
Far right: David Cotton

Elementary, Pre-intermediate and Advanced levels

Gareth Rees studied Natural Sciences at the University of Cambridge. Having taught in Spain and China, he currently teaches at the University of the Arts, London. As well as teaching English, he is an academic English course leader, and unit leader on courses in cross-cultural communication for the London College of Fashion. He has also developed English language materials for the BBC World Service Learning English section, and he makes films which appear in festivals and on British television.

Ian Lebeau studied Modern Languages at the University of Cambridge and did his MA in Applied Linguistics at the University of Reading. He has thirty-five years' experience in ELT – mainly in higher education – and has taught in Spain, Italy and Japan. He is currently Senior Lecturer in English as a Foreign Language at London Metropolitan University.

Intermediate, Upper Intermediate and Advanced levels

David Cotton studied Economics at the University of Reading and did an MA in French Language and Literature at the University of Toronto. He has over forty-four years teaching and training experience, and is co-author of the successful *Market Leader* and *Business Class* course books. He has taught in Canada, France and England, and has been visiting lecturer in many universities overseas. Previously, he was Senior Lecturer at London Metropolitan University. He frequently gives talks at EFL conferences.

David Falvey studied Politics, Philosophy and Economics at the University of Oxford and did his MA in TEFL at the University of Birmingham. He has lived in Africa and the Middle East and has teaching, training and managerial experience in the UK and Asia, including working as a teacher trainer at the British Council in Tokyo. He was previously Head of the English Language Centre at London Metropolitan University. David is co-author of the successful business English course *Market Leader*.

Simon Kent studied History at the University of Sheffield, and also has an M.A in History and Cultural Studies. He has over twenty-five years' teaching experience including three years in Berlin at the time of German reunification. Simon is co-author of the successful business English course *Market Leader*. He is currently Senior Lecturer in English as a Foreign Language at London Metropolitan University.

SHEFFIELD UNIVERSITY RESOURCES

ONLINE LEARNING RESOURCES

why not have a look at these useful websites to help you improve your English?

ELTC's favourite sites https://sites.google.com/a/sheffield.ac.uk/eltc-favourite-sites/	The University of Sheffield Self-access Centre's list of useful websites to practise General and Academic English.	
BBC Learning English http://www.bbc.co.uk/learningenglish/	BBC Learning English has been teaching global audiences since 1943, offering free audio, video and text materials	
Using English for Academic Purposes http://www.uefap.com/	Produced by University of Hertfordshire – general information about Academic English + exercises	
British Council - Learn English http://www.learnenglish.org.uk/	A website with lots of different English learning activities	
Dave's ESL Cafe http://www.eslcafe.com/	"The Internet's Meeting Place for ESL/EFL Students and Teachers from Around the World!"	

DICTIONARIES AND REFERENCE MATERIALS

Longman Dictionaries http://www.pearsonlongman.com/dictionaries	A variety of Longman dictionaries including Active Study, American English, Phrasal verbs	
Longman Dictionary of Contemporary English http://www.ldoceonline.com	A useful resource	
Academic PhraseBank http://www.phrasebank.manchester.ac.uk/	Produced by the University of Manchester, this site gives a wide range of commonly used phrases and their usage.	